WORLD SERIES

AN OPINIONATED CHRONICLE

WORLD SERIES

AN OPINIONATED CHRONICLE

100 YEARS

JOSEPH WALLACE

IN MEMORY OF PAUL GOTTLIEB

Editor: Sharon AvRutick
Designer: Eric Janssen Strohl, Eric Baker Design Associates
Production Manager: Jane Searle

Library of Congress Cataloging-in-Publication Data

Wallace, Joseph E.
  World Series : an opinionated chronicle of the fall classic : 100
years / Joseph Wallace.
    p. cm.
Includes bibliographical references and index.
  ISBN 0-8109-4639-4 (hard)
  1. World Series (Baseball)—History. I. Title.

  GV878.4.W35 2003
  796.357'646—dc21

                            2003005116

Printed and bound in China

10 9 8 7 6 5 4 3 2 1

Harry N. Abrams, Inc.
100 Fifth Avenue
New York, N.Y. 10011
www.abramsbooks.com

Abrams is a subsidiary of

Endsheets: A sheaf of dreams.

CONTENTS

JOIN THE CONVERSATION!

WORLD SERIES MEMORIES LAST FOREVER, AND YOU DON'T HAVE TO BE A PLAYER, MANAGER, OR SPORTSWRITER TO HAVE A GREAT STORY TO TELL. WHETHER YOU'RE A LIFELONG FAN OF THE YANKEES, CUBS, RED SOX, OR ST. LOUIS BROWNS, I WANT TO HEAR YOUR FAVORITE SERIES MOMENT. FUNNY, BITTER, BIZARRE—SHARE THEM ALL.

I'LL POST AS MANY AS I CAN ON MY WEBSITE (WWW.JOSEPHWALLACE.COM)
—AND HOPE TO INCLUDE THE BEST IN A FUTURE EDITION OF THIS BOOK.

EMAIL ME AT
MEMORIES@JOSEPHWALLACE.COM
OR SEND YOUR TALE THE OLD-FASHIONED WAY TO:
JOSEPH WALLACE, SUITE 208, 980 BROADWAY, THORNWOOD, NY 10594.

AND BE SURE TO CHECK THE WEBSITE OFTEN FOR UPDATES!

Giants' Manager John McGraw (left) schmoozes
with sportswriters including Damon Runyon
and Francis Richter (with moustache) in the Polo
Grounds press box during the 1911 Series.

My first World Series memory dates back to 1966.

I was nine years old, and I'd already been a New York Mets fan for a couple of years. Of course, being a Mets fan back then meant having no reason to pay attention to the Series...until I turned on Game One and saw Moe Drabowsky saunter onto the field. From that moment, I was hooked.

Moe Drabowsky sounded like someone I'd see in Midwood, my Brooklyn neighborhood. ("Hey, Moe! You! Drabowsky!") White and kind of lumpy-looking, he could have been one of the guys slinging pizzas or working at the deli around the corner. I felt comfortable watching him.

The other thing about Moe Drabowsky: He was cool under pressure, the way I dreamed I'd be someday. He came into a game that was filled with tension. His Baltimore Orioles had taken a 4–0 lead,

but now the Los Angeles Dodgers had cut the lead in half, and were threatening more. The O's brought Drabowsky in to hold the lead.

As I watched, riveted, on the old RCA black-and-white in my parents' bedroom, Moe mowed down the Dodgers. Strikeout after strikeout—six in a row!—without even seeming to break a sweat. I'd always imagined myself as one of the Mets, maybe Ron Hunt, making a great play in the field or hitting a single (we Mets fans had modest dreams), but now I wanted to be Moe, standing in front of tens of thousands of fans, waiting patiently to get the ball back as another disappointed Dodger walked back to the plate. A World Series hero.

Since then, the World Series has helped me count off the important moments of my life. I don't recall much of what I learned in seventh grade, but I sure can remember where I was during the Amazin' Mets' 1969 Series victory. (Playing basketball, a scratchy radio giving the bad news as the Mets lost Game One; screaming in front of the television set a kindly history teacher had brought into class as Game Five drew to a close.)

And sitting in a small TV lounge at my New England college in the fall of 1975, surrounded by Red Sox fans, feeling their joy sweep over me as Carlton Fisk hit his immortal Game Six home run.

And being a grown-up (finally), a writer, back in New York in 1986, visiting my ailing father in his Brooklyn Heights brownstone, sharing quiet happiness as Gary Carter cranked two home runs out of Fenway Park and we began to believe that the Mets might after all come back and win that messy, controversial, enthralling World Series.

And carrying my fussy newborn daughter back and forth across an Ottawa hotel room as Joe Carter cavorted around the bases after his game-winning home run in the 1993 Series—and, a moment later, hearing the shouts and honking horns on the streets outside as all Canada began to celebrate.

And watching my daughter and son become Yankee fans as the Bombers won Series after Series in the late 1990s...and not being able to do a thing about it.

And, of course, I can remember the surprising 2002 Series between the two California Cinderella teams, San Francisco and Anaheim...Barry Bonds' magnificent home runs and the Angels' thrilling Game Six win on their way to their first-ever championship.

All of these Series will always stay vivid in my memory. But so will many that took place before I was born. In my mind's eye I can see Christy Mathewson, tall and regal, tossing three shutouts in 1905; old Pete Alexander trudging in from the bullpen to face the powerful Yankees with the bases loaded in 1926; Babe Ruth pointing—or not—at the outfield fence before blasting a famous home run in 1932; Jackie Robinson swiping a base and letting everyone know he was here to stay in 1947; Ty Cobb and Honus Wagner and Hank Greenberg and Mickey Mantle and Bob Gibson on the biggest stage of all, thrilling me just as Moe Drabowsky did in 1966.

I can almost see these classic moments, simply because so many others did—and then took the time to describe the great events they witnessed. These players, fans, and sportswriters made the moments immortal through their words. They're the ones who can tell us what the Series sounded like, looked like, smelled like, *felt* like.

For example, when the Yankees captured their first-ever championship with a 6–4 win in Game Six of the 1923 Series, sportswriter Grantland Rice saw so much more than the box score. "The Yankees rode through the storm at last to reach the shining haven where the gold dust for the winter's end lies ankle-deep in the streets," Rice wrote, in a game that "massed and concentrated the fall of Rome, the destruction of Carthage, the feast of Belshazzar, the rout of Cyprus, the march of Attila, the wreck of the Hesperus and the Chicago fire."

And every baseball fan knows about Pete Alexander's bases-loaded strikeout of Tony Lazzeri to help the St. Louis Cardinals defeat the powerful Yankees in 1926. But the moment becomes so much more vivid when Alexander himself weighs in, with a line so stalwart that even stoical Gary Cooper or Clint Eastwood would envy it. "Bases filled, eh?" Alexander told manager Rogers Hornsby as he walked to the mound to face Lazzeri. "Well, don't worry about me. I'm all right. And I guess there's nothing much to do except give Tony a lot of hell."

And we've all seen the grainy black-and-white photos of Willie Mays' spectacular catch and throw of Vic Wertz's blast in the 1954 Series. But how much less impressive they are, how much less alive, than in the description by writer Arnold Hano, who was sitting that day in the bleachers of New York's Polo Grounds. "Mays caught the ball, and then whirled and threw, like some olden statue of a Greek javelin hurler," Hano wrote. "What an astonishing throw…the throw of a giant, the throw of a howitzer made human."

Grantland Rice and Pete Alexander and Arnold Hano, Heywood Broun and Joe Williams, Christy Mathewson and Leo Durocher, Roger Angell and Jack Sher and Peter Gammons and Tom Seaver and Joe Morgan. Stephen King on the 1956 and 1986 Series, Pete Hamill on the Brooklyn Dodgers, Bill James on what it is like to root for a team as it wins its first Series. These and so many more are here, all working to reanimate the Series, to put flesh and blood on the bare bones of statistics and the historical record.

Most of the following people get thanked in book acknowledgments all the time, so they may be getting a bit jaded by now. But they deserve the accolades, for dealing with squadrons of pushy writers every year, and for putting up with me in particular.

Jim Gates, Tim Wiles, Pat Kelly, Greg Harris, Bill Burdick, Rachael Crossman-Kepner, Claudette Burke, and many others at the National Baseball Hall of Fame Library and Archive provided, as always, an unbeatable mix of skill and warmth as I worked my way through a million player and photo files. I couldn't write a baseball book without them. Mary Bellew and photographer Milo Hamilton helped immeasurably with illustrations.

The staff of the New York Public Library Reading and Microfilm Rooms was always competent, managing a smile even when faced with a line of twenty-seven New Yorkers who all needed to be helped *now.*

Mark Rucker of The Rucker Archives/Transcendental Graphics, Jorge Jaramillo at AP/Wide World, and Paul Cunningham at Major League Baseball Photos all provided invaluable help as I gathered the images for this book.

Leslie Dutcher handled permissions as if born for the job.

At Abrams, editor-in-chief Eric Himmel liked my original ideas and understood when I needed to change course. His thoughtful suggestions helped make this a better, sharper book. Harriet Whelchel shepherded the manuscript through its early months, and Sharon AvRutick, the brilliant editor of my three Abrams baseball books, did her usual superb job. Eric Baker and Eric Strohl gave the book its eye-catching design.

My deepest gratitude goes to the late Paul Gottlieb, former editor-in-chief of Abrams. It was Paul who, in his characteristically warm and utterly self-confident way, gave me the chance to take on *The Baseball Anthology,* my first baseball book, and then let me run free with my second, *The Autobiography of Baseball.* To me, Paul was the ideal editor-in-chief: sharp and funny and amazingly vibrant, possessed always of vision and a sharp sense of what would make a book work. Knowing him, I was glad to be an author.

The first year of the "true" World Series, the annual postseason matchup between the American and National Leagues, took place when the Pittsburgh Pirates played the Boston Pilgrims in 1903. But for two decades before that, teams had sporadically challenged each other to lucrative head-to-head battles, some lasting as many as fifteen games. Though often billed as "World Series," none of these tournaments came close to satisfying the fans' desire for a titanic clash between powerful teams.

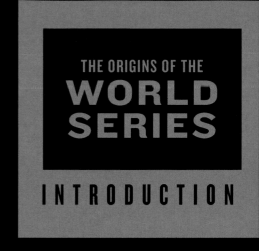

The best remembered of these series, which ran from 1884 to 1890, pitted the champions of the National League and the American Association, at the time also a major league. Some of the team names are at least semifamiliar—the New York Giants, Chicago White Stockings, St. Louis Browns, and Brooklyn Bridegrooms—but this early championship was no success. As Bill James puts it in his *Historical Baseball Abstract*, "The games, to be honest, weren't great, and there is no clear evidence of enormous intent on the part of either side; the games, though in retrospect viewed as an early World Series, seem to have been treated as an exhibition."

With the demise of the American Association in 1892, the first "World Series" came to an unlamented end. But team owners, always on the lookout for revenue enhancers, tried something new right away. In 1892, they instituted a split season in the N.L., with the first-half winner playing the champion of the second half. This method worked about as well as it did during the split 1981 season—that is, it was a fiasco, and wasn't repeated.

"AS OWNERS FINALLY LEARNED FROM THEIR REPEATED FAILURES, A MEMORABLE WORLD SERIES REQUIRES TWO HIGHLY COMPETITIVE LEAGUES, PRIZE MONEY THAT ACTUALLY FAVORS THE WINNER, AND A SET OF RIGOROUS, HONEST RULES GOVERNING THE GAMES."

Starting in 1894, the N.L. tried again, this time pitting the first- against the second-place finisher for possession of the Temple Cup, a silver trophy given by a wealthy Pittsburgh businessman. The players were supposedly motivated by the larger share of receipts going to the winners, but it was common knowledge that the competing teams worked out a fifty-fifty split beforehand, and then played the games for fun. After four years, the Temple Cup was retired for good.

As owners finally learned from their repeated failures, a memorable World Series requires two highly competitive leagues, prize money that actually favors the winner, and a set of rigorous, honest rules governing the games. The first requirement was met when the American League arrived in 1901, placing teams in formerly N.L.–dominated cities, grabbing players and managers from the established league, and loudly promoting a cleaner, less rowdy version of baseball. In 1903, when the owners of the Boston Pilgrims and Pittsburgh Pirates set forth the regulations for a post-season set of games to determine which league was superior, a firm, lasting basis for a true World Series had finally been established.

In the century since the setting of these ground rules, only twice has the World Series failed to take place: in 1904, when the N.L. New York Giants refused to play, and in 1994, when a players' strike wiped out the entire postseason. Once, in 1919, a Series was played but the results were later called into question. And a few times teams have followed rules that have now been abandoned: in 1903 and 1919–21, when the Series was best of eight, and in 1907, 1912, and 1922, when lack of ballpark lights forced games to end in ties. Still, for an event that has thus far lasted a hundred years, the World Series has followed the original outline amazingly faithfully.

10 BEST SERIES

NO. -1
"TENTH INNING, GAME SEVEN, 0-0, JACK MORRIS STILL ON THE MOUND..."
1991

NO. -2
GAME SIX AND SO MUCH MORE
1975

NO. -3
THE BIG TRAIN WINS ONE AT LAST
1924

NO. -4
THE YANKEE DYNASTY FINALLY CRUMBLES
2001

NO. -5
MATTY VS. SMOKY JOE
1912

NO. -6
"PESKY HOLDS THE BALL!"
1946

NO. -7
ROBERTO CLEMENTE'S PRIDE
1971

NO. -8
THE YANKEE-DODGER RIVALRY BEGINS
1947

NO. -9
ONE FOR THE BUMS!
1955

NO. -10
"IF ONLY..."
1962

10 WORST SERIES

NO. 1
THE REASONS ARE OBVIOUS
1919

NO. 2
EVERYTHING THAT'S WRONG WITH
MODERN-DAY BASEBALL IN
ONE MESSY PACKAGE
1997

NO. 3
BASEBALL IN THE MIDST OF DISASTER
1989

NO. 4
A SEASON TO FORGET, FROM
START TO FINISH
198

NO. 5
IS THIS NEWFANGLED WORLD SERIES
REALLY SUCH A GOOD IDEA?
1907

NO. 6
THE BIG RED MACHINE ROLLS ON
1976

NO. 7
A QUICK JOB AGAINST
A "MIRACLE" TEAM
1961

NO. 8
A TENSION-FREE FALL "CLASSIC"
1928

NO. 9
YANKEES SWEEP, BUT THERE'S
SOMETHING WRONG WITH LOU GEHRIG...
1938

NO. 10
CAN'T ANYONE BEAT THIS TEAM?
1939

Long before the 1903 season came to an end, it was clear that the Pittsburgh Pirates were the class of the long-established National League and the Boston Pilgrims the best team in the upstart American League. But which team was stronger? No one knew—there was no guarantee that they'd ever play each other, no provision for a championship series between two leagues that treated each other with suspicion, if not derision.

As the season went on, pressure for some sort of ultimate contest grew. Fans wanted to see the two teams battle it out, and in particular wanted to see one of the greatest hitters of all time face off against one of the greatest pitchers: Honus Wagner (he of the lifetime .327 batting average and 3,415 career hits) and Cy Young (who would go 28–9 in 1903 on his way to 511 wins). Seeing the two of them on the same field was irresistible—just as a postseason Barry Bonds–Pedro Martinez duel would be today.

Irresistible…but no sure thing, as the season drew to a close. In fact, the Series might not have taken place if not for Pittsburgh owner Barney Dreyfuss. One of the most clearheaded and financially savvy team owners ever, Dreyfuss made the first overture, writing to Boston owner Henry Killea in August.

"The time has come for the National League and American League to organize a World Series," he announced. "It is my belief that if our clubs played a series…we would create great interest in baseball, in our leagues, and in our players. I also believe it would be a financial success."

When Boston agreed, though, Dreyfuss and Pittsburgh Manager Fred Clarke got cold feet. As the headline said in the September 19 issue of *Sporting Life*: "The National League Champion Team in Such a Crippled Condition That it May be Compelled to Decline to Enter an Unequal Contest."

Years later, Fred Clarke discussed this with Bill Bryson, Sr., sportswriter for the *Des Moines Register*. "Up until late in the season," he explained, "I had three crackerjack pitchers. But then Ed Doheny went—well, I guess you'd say he had a nervous breakdown…. That was tragic. But what happened to Sam Leever was just plain ridiculous. The day after the season ended, Sam went out and shot two hundred clay pigeons. It made his shoulder so sore, he could hardly throw."

Still, injuries or no, the Pittsburgh owner and manager decided to go ahead with the Series. The result was a contract between Boston and Pittsburgh, pecked out on a typewriter with a faded ribbon, which set the stage for a century's Fall Classics to come. This initial contest was to be the best of nine games, with a minimum admission price of fifty cents, the teams splitting the proceeds.

With the logical theory of "trust, but verify," a handwritten addition to the contract (Item 4 $\frac{1}{2}$) prevented either team from packing the roster with ringers by stating that no player could participate who hadn't been a regular member of his team as of September 1, 1903. In effect, the same rule still applies today.

The Series itself, played at Pittsburgh's rickety Exposition Park

1903

LET'S GIVE IT A TRY

When the Pirates found themselves short of pitching as the Series began, Deacon Phillippe stepped into the breach, pitching an astounding five complete games.

1903

BOSTON
PILGRIMS

5

PITTSBURGH
PIRATES

3

and Boston's only slightly fancier Huntington Avenue Grounds, was (in the words of Pirate Tommy Leach), "probably the wildest World Series ever." As he told Lawrence Ritter in *The Glory of Their Times*, "Arguing all the time between the teams, between the players and the umpires, and especially between the players and the fans. That's the truth, the fans were part of the game in those days. They'd pour right out onto the field and argue with the players and the umpires."

It could be hard to keep the game going at times. Overflow crowds in the small parks meant that hundreds of fans stood in the outfield, sometimes not even very deep in the outfield. They got a great view—and a chance to interfere with play, whether they wanted to or not. (Balls hit into the crowd were considered ground-rule triples, leading to a record-setting twenty-five triples in the eight games played.)

"Our baseball grounds are too small" to show off the game to its best advantage, groused *Sporting Life*—but the crowds at Boston's Huntington Avenue Grounds demonstrated the enthusiasm fans felt about the new invention called the World Series.

Setting a precedent that would endure, the biggest names didn't play starring roles in the Series. Cy Young pitched well, starting four games and going 2–1, but he was overshadowed by Boston teammate Big Bill Dineen, who pitched four complete games with a 2.06 ERA. It was Dineen, not Young, who pitched a shutout in Game Eight to best the Pirates' Deacon Philippe (who, manfully taking on the burden of Pittsburgh's shortage of pitchers, threw *five* complete games) and give the Pilgrims the World Series championship, five games to three.

The 1903 Series provided nothing but frustration for the great Honus Wagner, who batted just .222.

And Pittsburgh's Honus Wagner? He had a forgettable Series, with just six hits (five of them singles) in the eight games for a .222 average. The usually sure-handed shortstop also committed six errors.

Legend has it that Wagner was bedeviled by the yelling and singing of the noisy Boston rooters, but it's more likely that the injuries reported in *Sporting Life* in September finally caught up with him. Wagner's leg, his throwing arm, even his usual high spirits went out on him as the Series progressed, leading the great shortstop to threaten to quit the game for good. Boston fans were not sympathetic: One sent him a copy of *American Undertaker*, a mortician's journal, to celebrate the imminent interment of Wagner and his mighty team.

The impact at the time of Boston's victory over the long-established Pirates—and of the upstart A.L.'s victory over the N.L.—can't be underestimated. The closest equivalent might be the New York Jets' Super Bowl III victory over the mighty Baltimore Colts in 1969, a Super Bowl that proved at last that the AFL could compete and win against the NFL.

It would be two years before the National League would have the chance for revenge.

"THE TIME HAS COME FOR THE NATIONAL LEAGUE AND AMERICAN LEAGUE TO ORGANIZE A WORLD SERIES."

Sometimes a baseball star's image and reputation only seem to grow after he leaves the game. All the warts, all the rough edges, seem to get sanded away as fans make the effort to create a perfect hero in retrospect. Joe DiMaggio, Sandy Koufax, Mickey Mantle, Ted Williams—all of these superstars were booed during their careers and idolized after they retired.

Every once in a while, however, there appears on the scene a player of such physical strength, dignity, and inherent marquee quality that his reputation never changes. He is looked upon with awe from beginning to end, by fans and fellow players alike. The Giants' Christy Mathewson was one such star.

"I had admired him so much," said Mathewson's teammate, second baseman Larry Doyle, describing their first meeting. "That first sight of him was something. He was standing by his locker and he looked as big as a house. There was no mistaking him. That was Matty. And my heart stopped for a moment."

1905
MATTY'S MOMENT

1905

NEW YORK GIANTS

4

PHILADELPHIA ATHLETICS

1

Mathewson's skills matched his physical size. In 1905, he posted his third successive season with thirty or more wins. His Giants, with a record of 105–48, dominated the National League, just as they had in 1904, when they refused to play Boston in a World Series. This time, though they agreed to play the A.L. champions: the Philadelphia Athletics, who had barely edged out the Chicago White Sox in a tight pennant race.

The scrappy Giants were led by stocky, aggressive Manager John ("The object of the game is to win") McGraw. Meanwhile, the Athletics were managed by sepulchral, teetotaling Connie ("There is room for gentlemen in any profession") Mack. In a wonderful baseball puzzle, McGraw's most valuable player was the handsome, reserved Matty, while Mack had hitched his wagon to pitcher Rube Waddell, perhaps the wildest of all the wildmen who populated baseball early in the century.

The irrepressible Waddell, famous for chasing after fire engines, diving off ferryboats, and disappearing unexpectedly in the course of the season, won twenty-seven games in 1905 and should have been the Athletics' leading pitcher in the Series. But before the start

A distant view of the goings-on at New York's Polo Grounds, with Philadelphia's Chief Bender facing the Giants.

of the 1905 Series, he mysteriously injured his arm and was unable to pitch. (The reason given at the time—that he got hurt punching a hole in a teammate's straw boater—seems a bit unlikely.)

The Athletics still had two other star pitchers, Chief Bender and Eddie Plank, as well as a strong lineup that included such fine hitters as Lave Cross and Harry Davis. Even with the loss of Waddell, many pundits gave the edge in the Series to Philadelphia over the Giants. The comments of *The Sporting News'* Joseph Vila were typical: "Mathewson," he wrote before the Series started, "has been the team's mainstay all the year, but look at what a lot of weak-hitting teams he has been opposed to." The A's, he concluded, "will outbat the Giants."

Mathewson put the lie to such predictions in the very first game, a four-hit shutout in the Giants' 3–0 win. After Bender led the Athletics to a 3–0 victory in Game Two, it was Matty's turn again: a four-hitter in an easy 9–0 win. Game Four was much the same: a five-hit, 1–0 shutout by the Giants' Joe McGinnity that gave the Giants a 3–1 Series lead.

"The game of ball is only fun for me when I'm out in front and winning," said Giants' Manager John McGraw (left, with Joe McGinnity). In 1905, he had fun.

By the time Game Five was a few innings old, the overflow crowd of 24,000 at New York's Polo Grounds knew they were witnessing one of the great performances in baseball's history. Mathewson was on the mound again, for the third time in five days—and for the third time he threw a shutout, this time a six-hitter in the Giants' tense 2–0 victory.

Three shutouts in five days! Even so, in *The Sporting News,* Joseph Vila was grudging in acknowledging Mathewson and the rowdy Giants' superiority. "We must call them world champions!," he wrote. "It is a pill, without a sugar coating, but down it goes with a grimace."

Vila might have been the only person on earth who begrudged Mathewson his magnificent World Series.

"WE MUST CALL THEM WORLD CHAMPIONS! IT IS A PILL, WITHOUT A SUGAR COATING, BUT DOWN IT GOES WITH A GRIMACE."

What was the greatest team of all time? The Philadelphia Athletics of the late 1920s and early 1930s? The Oakland Athletics of 1972–74? The Giants of 1921–23? The Yankees of the mid 1920s? The Yankees of the late 1930s? The Yankees of 1949–53? The Yankees of 1956–62? The Yankees of 1976–78? The Yankees of 1996–2001?

The Chicago Cubs' Joe Tinker and Johnny Evers, two-thirds of the most famous double-play combination of all time—and bitter enemies. "Tinker and myself hated each other, but we loved the Cubs," said Evers.

1906 1907 1908

THE DYNASTY THAT HATED ITSELF

But there's another candidate, largely forgotten today: the 1906–08 Chicago Cubs, who were perhaps even greater than the Athletics, Athletics, Giants, Yankees, Yankees, Yankees, Yankees, Yankees, *or* Yankees.

Led by the famed double-play combination of fiery second baseman Johnny Evers, gloomy shortstop Joe Tinker, and stoical first baseman–manager Frank Chance ("These are the saddest of possible words/Tinker to Evers to Chance," immortalized Franklin Pierce), the Cubs also boasted a spectacularly talented pitching staff that included Mordecai "Three Finger" Brown, Orval Overall, Ed Reulbach, and Jack Pfiester.

Most remarkable about the Cub dynasty was how many of the players couldn't stand each other. It's been known for decades that Johnny Evers and Joe Tinker loathed being on the same diamond, but the ferocity of their mutual hatred remains startling. "Every time something went wrong on the field, we would be at each other and there would be a fight in the clubhouse after the game," Evers told sportswriter Frank Graham in *Baseball Extra*. "Joe weighed 175 pounds and I weighed about 135, but that didn't make any difference to either of us. He'd rush at me and get me by the throat and I'd punch him in the belly and try to cut him with my spikes and then Chance or one of the other big guys would come to my rescue."

According to Evers, how the Cub teammates felt about each other simply didn't matter. "What a guy thinks about the team as a whole is something else. Tinker and myself hated each other, but we loved the Cubs. We wouldn't fight for each other, but we'd come close to killing people for our team. That's one of the answers for the Cubs' success."

After winning 116 games and destroying the closest competition by twenty games during the 1906 season, the Cubs marched confidently into the World Series against their crosstown rivals, the Chicago White Sox. The Sox, though boasting a bonafide superstar pitcher in the spitballer Ed Walsh, had no one anywhere near the leaders in any batting category. In fact, the team as a whole batted just .230, causing them to be dubbed the "Hitless Wonders."

1906

CHICAGO WHITE SOX
4

CHICAGO CUBS
2

This was to be a blowout, said the pundits. And they were right. They just got the team wrong.

It was the Cubs who were the Hitless Wonders in this Series, batting just .196. Meanwhile, led by Ed Walsh's two victories and the unlikely heroics of reserve third baseman George Rohe (who stroked seven hits, including two crucial triples), the Sox hitters erupted to pound Reulbach in Game Five and Brown in Game Six to take the Series, four games to two.

The Hitless Wonders won the 1906 Series on the back of Ed Walsh, who went 2–0 with an ERA of 1.20.

Not everyone loves seeing Cinderella fitted for a new glass slipper. As *The Sporting News* complained, "No use trying to dope out the World Series any more. Who would have thought the Sox would show up the Cubs the way they did? We had been shouting that it was merely luck that had carried the White Sox to the front and that when they struck the Cubs they would not know that they had been to the series."

"Then," the grumpy correspondent said, "we woke up."

A rare action shot from Game Three of the 1906 World Series, at the West Side Grounds in Chicago. The three White Sox on base would soon score on George Rohe's triple, giving the "Hitless Wonders" a 3–0 win on their way to their shocking Series defeat of the powerful Cubs.

10 WORST SERIES

NO. 5

1907

1907

CHICAGO CUBS

4

DETROIT TIGERS

0

In 1907 the Cubs coasted to another runaway victory in the National League, while the Detroit Tigers captured their first A.L. flag. Led by bonafide superstars Ty Cobb and Sam Crawford, and with a pitching staff headed by Wild Bill Donovan (who'd gone 25–4 during the regular season), the Tigers seemed likely to give the Cubs a battle in the Series.

But it was not to be. Cobb batted a measly .200, with no RBI and no stolen bases, and Crawford was little better. Donovan pitched brilliantly (including all twelve innings in Game One—but the game didn't count, since it ended in a 3–3 tie when the sun went down). The fact is, the Cubs were just too much. The Tigers managed only five hits in the next four games, losing meekly to Pfiester, Reulbach, Overall, and Brown. It was one of the least competitive World Series on record—and a testament to the mightiness of the Cubs.

The next Series wasn't much better. The Cubs barely repeated as N.L. champions, besting the Pirates and the Giants in one of the most famous pennant races of all time (it was the Year of Merkle's Boner) and then facing off against Cobb and the Tigers once again.

This time Detroit improved upon its meek 1907 showing. In fact, Game Three ended with them on the long end of an 8–3 score. Unfortunately, the Cubs won the other four games played, including easy shutouts hurled by Brown and Overall in the final two games. Cobb in his second of three successive Series appearances (the only three of his long career), managed a .368 batting average, but it wasn't nearly enough.

"IT'S ALL OVER

AND THOSE CUBS HAVE ACCOMPLISHED

WHAT SEEMED WELL-NIGH

IMPOSSIBLE."

The unique and wonderful Mordecai "Three Finger" Brown. A childhood accident with a corn chopper deprived him of parts of three digits—but gave him the stuff that led to the Hall of Fame.

William Phelon in *Sporting Life* paid fitting tribute to Chicago's dynasty. "Well, it's all over and those Cubs have accomplished what seemed well-nigh impossible," he wrote. "They have, in the space of a few days, done more than any other ball club ever did before, and, perhaps, more than any club will ever do again. Wonder if the fans fully realize all that those Cubs achieved?!"

If they didn't realize it then, Cubs' fans have certainly had a chance to let it sink in since: The 1908 World Series title was the last for the Cubs in the twentieth century.

Above: Bears everywhere: the scorebook for the great 1907 champions.

Opposite: "The great American game should be an unrelenting war of nerves," said Ty Cobb. Perhaps it was Cobb's nerves that led him to subpar performances in the Tigers' three straight World Series defeats.

In 1909, the Pittsburgh Pirates finally knocked the Cubs off their perch atop the National League. Meanwhile, the Detroit Tigers, punching-bag losers to the Cubs in 1907–08, returned as A.L. champions.

The Pirate-Tiger Series was a dream matchup for fans and writers, because it brought together the most dominant hitters in each league: Honus Wagner and Ty Cobb. Wagner was coming off his fourth straight batting title, while all Cobb did in 1909 was hit .377 and steal seventy-six bases. It looked like a classic confrontation, and a chance for the two superstars (neither of whom had ever dominated a World Series) to show their stuff at last.

It didn't happen. Wagner had a fine Series, hitting .333 with 6 RBI and six stolen bases, but was not the deciding factor in any game. Meanwhile, the fearsome Cobb, in his last postseason appearance, managed to hit just .231. The mantle of World Series star, as it does so often, settled instead on perhaps the least likely candidate: Charles "Babe" Adams, a twenty-seven-year-old rookie pitcher.

Even on his own pitching staff, Adams was overshadowed. An astonishing six Pirate pitchers—Vic Willis, Howie Camnitz, Deacon Philippe, Nick Maddox, Sam Leever, and Lefty Leifeld—had won twenty or more games at some point in their careers.

Still, Pirates Manager Fred Clarke chose to cross up the Tigers by going with Adams in Game One. Adams couldn't believe it when, just before warm-ups, Clarke approached him and said, "You're it."

Years later, in a conversation with sportswriter Bill Bryson, Sr., Clarke recalled the moment vividly. "I handed him a new ball and his hands started to shake so much, he almost dropped it. I gave him a look of contempt and said, 'What's the matter, kid, you yellow?'"

For the first few innings, Clarke kept it up, riding the rookie pitcher from the bench. Then, as the game went on, he switched tactics, praising Adams. The result: a six-hitter for Adams, and a 4–1 win for the Pirates. "When it was over," Clarke said, "I shook his hand and I said, 'Tell me, Babe, what were you thinking about when you went out there to pitch?' And he said, 'I was thinkin' you were the meanest so-and-so I ever saw and, as soon as I won that game, I was coming in and punch you right in the nose.'"

With the Pirates' more vaunted starters struggling and the Series knotted 2–2, Adams returned to pitch another complete game in the Pirates' 8–4 victory in Game Five. But Detroit came back by winning Game Six—a vicious game, filled with fistfights and spikings. The Pirates were back on their heels, "wrought-up and shaky," as Clarke described it to Bryson.

So the canny manager filled his hotel room with beer and soft drinks, hired a singing quartet, and invited in a couple of local storytellers. Then he let his players know that they were expected to show up in his room that night for a meeting. "They came in expecting a lecture," he said. "You never saw such surprised looks as when I began handing out beer and pop and the quartet started to sing. Well, we sat around two or three hours, talking and laughing and listening to the singing, never mentioning the next day's game. Finally, I told 'em: 'All right, boys, let's go to bed now. We've got a ballgame tomorrow. If we win, all right. If we don't, well that's all right, too. We've already had a good season.'"

Honus Wagner reached baseball immortality after leading the Pirates to the 1909 World Championship.

Opposite: No one knew who Babe Adams was until he tamed Ty Cobb and the Tigers three times in the 1909 Series.

1909

**PITTSBURGH
PIRATES**

4

**DETROIT
TIGERS**

3

Tough guys Babe Adams, Fred Clarke, George Gibson, and Honus Wagner helped lead the Pirates to their World Series triumph over the Tigers.

Again, his moves worked like a charm. The Pirates showed up loose and confident, Cobb and the Tigers were tight as a drum, and Babe Adams was at the top of his game. With Wagner and Tommy Leach leading an offense that put eight runs on the board, Adams pitched a six-hit shutout for his third win of the Series. In their second try, the Pirates had their first World Series championship.

"I HANDED HIM A NEW BALL AND HIS HANDS STARTED TO SHAKE SO MUCH, HE ALMOST DROPPED IT. I GAVE HIM A LOOK OF CONTEMPT AND SAID, 'WHAT'S THE MATTER, KID, YOU YELLOW?'"

SERIES SPOTLIGHT
PSYCHED OUT!

Sometimes teams lose the World Series not only because they have less talent than their opponents, but also because they enter the games thinking, knowing, they're going to lose. ("Oh, my. Do they do that often?" members of the N. L. champion Pittsburgh Pirates supposedly said while watching Babe Ruth, Lou Gehrig, and other members of the Yankees' Murderer's Row slug batting-practice home runs before the 1927 Series—which the Yankees swept.)

In at least one case, a great team's instability prevented it from becoming a dynasty. At least, that was the great pitcher Christy Mathewson's take on his New York Giants, who went down to defeat in three straight World Series between 1911 and 1913. In 1911 and 1913, the Giants' tormentors were the Philadelphia Athletics, a stoical team headed by the unflappable Connie Mack, who provided a stark contrast to the emotional Giants, led by the Napoleonic John McGraw.

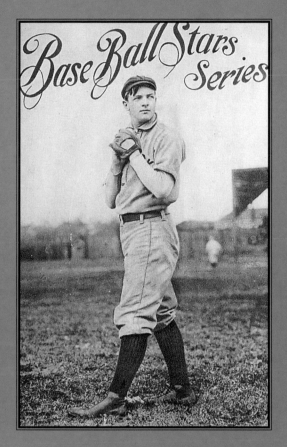

In a scathing 1914 article in *Everybody's Magazine*, Mathewson got to the heart of how team psychology can mean the difference between winning and losing a tight Series. "The Athletics are what baseball men call 'money players,'" he wrote. "They played that [1911] series with the zest of college boys. They seemed to enjoy every minute, while the Giants made labor of it."

Matty's examples of the Giants' struggles are revealing and convincing. Here's one, describing a crucial matchup between Giants pitcher Red Ames and the Athletics' Jack Barry—and the moment when the 1911 World Series was lost:

> The last game of that 1911 series showed us at our worst. Growing more and more nervous and self-conscious under the tension, we snapped in a way that made us look ridiculous. I was sitting on the bench feeling that we still had a chance if the men would only pull together. Ames was pitching, and with two men on base Barry bunted. Hurrying his throw, Ames was way off his aim, for the ball hit Barry in the head and all the Philly baserunners scampered home.
>
> "Nice head work!" yelled one of those megaphone voices from the depths of the grand stand.
>
> For the first time during the series I laughed. So did all the other men on the bench. With that laugh it was all over.

The Athletics went on to romp, 13–2, and capture the Series against Matty's favored, but psyched-out Giants, four games to two.

"**B**y his looks he might be a retired manufacturer and former Sunday School Superintendent," wrote John R. Tunis, "one of the thousands each winter in those havens of refuge along the West Coast of Florida."

"A tower of sobriety in a landscape of joyous tippling," was how Joseph Durso described him.

They were both talking about Connie Mack, perhaps the most remarkable figure in baseball during the first half of the twentieth century. At a time when the game was filled with rough-hewn, scrappy players and managers—people like Ty Cobb and John McGraw, who were always yapping and nipping at your ankles—Mack presented a unique and wonderful contrast.

He was a tall, skinny, reserved older man with the demeanor and careful speech of a country parson. And he never changed. In 1901,

1910 1911 1913 1914

THE OLD MAN'S GLORY YEARS

he became the Philadelphia Athletics' first manager. When he retired fifty years later, at the age of eighty-seven, he was gaunter, grayer, but otherwise exactly the same polite, cautious gentleman he'd always been.

During his epochal fifty-year reign, Mack endured plenty of losing seasons—but he also managed two of the greatest dynasties in major-league history. The first came between 1910 and 1914, when the upstart A's confronted and defeated two of the most feared National League teams of all time: the Cubs and the Giants.

In 1910 it was the Cubs' turn. Johnny Evers missed the Series with an injury, but Joe Tinker, Frank Chance, "Three Finger" Brown, and others from the Cubs' great years of 1906–08 were still around. It was obvious, though, that the Cubs' run was about over, and no one was much surprised when the Mackmen pounded Brown, Orval Overall, and Ed Reulbach and ran over the Cubs with little problem,

The Giants' Fred Snodgrass steals third in an action shot from the 1911 World Series. The Athletics' Frank Baker applies the late tag.

winning four games to one. Frank Baker hit .409, Eddie Collins .429 with four stolen bases, Danny Murphy drove in nine runs, and Jack Coombs won three games, including the fifth and final one.

Not every year brings a great World Series, but the 1911 *Reach Guide* complained at the lack of entertainment value provided by the 1910 contest. After doling out praise to the Athletics ("a team of surpassing power and skill"), it went on to gripe that the games were "the poorest series yet played…due to poor pitching on both sides, and the complete collapse of the Cubs' once invincible pitching staff."

1910

PHILADELPHIA ATHLETICS
4

CHICAGO CUBS
1

In 1911 the A's swept to another A.L. championship, while John McGraw's Giants captured the N.L. flag. The rematch between McGraw and Mack (after the Giants' one-sided victory in 1905) promised a World Series of unsurpassed strategy and controversy.

Again, it was not to be. All drama and momentum was dissipated when the Series was delayed for a week by a monsoon, and even after it resumed in windswept cold, the quality of play just wasn't up to snuff.

The Giants, overwhelmed by Bender, Coombs, and Eddie Plank, hit just .175 in the Series. They didn't field any better, committing sixteen errors, and though Christy Mathewson pitched well, he lost twice. The only controversy found Matty and fellow Giant pitcher Rube Marquard sniping at each other in the press over the home runs they gave up to Frank "Home Run" Baker. Game Six, the final game, was a perfect summing-up of the Series: a 13–2 Athletics laugher in which the two teams combined for eight errors. The A's won, four games to two, but no observer thought the Series was even that close.

1911

PHILADELPHIA ATHLETICS

4

NEW YORK GIANTS

2

Connie Mack lets it all hang out beside his equally flamboyant star pitcher, Albert "Chief" Bender. "If I had all the men I'd ever handled and they were in their prime and there was one game I wanted to win above all others, Albert would be my man," said Connie.

The A's gave way to the Boston Red Sox in 1912, but were back atop the A.L. in 1913. Once again their opponents were McGraw's Giants, who were still reeling from their heartbreaking loss to the Red Sox the year before.

Again the Giants were no competition for the well-managed A's, who won in five games. Again the Giants didn't hit or field. Again Mathewson pitched beautifully (including a shutout in Game Two, for a record four career World Series shutouts) but came up short, losing the fifth and final game to Eddie Plank, 3–1. Again fans were left hungry for more.

And not just fans. In October 1914, in what must be the most brutally honest writing by a still-active ballplayer, Christy Mathewson put his name on a remarkable article in *Everybody's Magazine*. Titled "Why We Lost Three World Championships," the article was likely put down on paper by longtime ghostwriter John Wheeler, but it is clear that the words and the unchecked emotions are Mathewson's own.

"It is a chapter in the 'psychology' of baseball," Matty fumed. "Almost without exception every man on our team fell below his standard. Self-consciousness, overanxiety, and nervousness weighed on our shoulders like the Old Man of the Sea."

Manager John McGraw and the Giants, he went on, compared unfavorably to the unflappable Mackmen and

1913

PHILADELPHIA ATHLETICS

4

NEW YORK GIANTS

1

"I KNEW HE HAD ME FEELING THAT ALL THE OTHER CATCHERS IN BASEBALL WERE GRADE A DOPES COMPARED TO ME AND I ACTUALLY BELIEVE THAT'S WHY I HIT SO WELL IN THE SERIES. THE FELLOW HAD ME MESMERIZED OR SOMETHING."

their leader. "The Athletics are a calm, stoical crew, while the Giants happen to be composed of a number of very highly strung, nervous, almost temperamental players," he explained. "It is impossible to exaggerate McGraw's part. From the bench he absolutely directs the game. The men absolutely rely on him. With the exception of a very few veterans, they cannot stand on their own two feet. They have never had to…. Unlike McGraw, Connie Mack had not been forced to build a team of puppets worked from the bench by a string."

It is not recorded how the Giants and McGraw responded to Mathewson's plain speaking. Perhaps they understood that their great pitcher was nearing the end of his career, with still just the one championship (way back in 1905) to his name. Most likely they forgave his outburst. Maybe they agreed with him.

1914
BOSTON BRAVES
4
PHILADELPHIA ATHLETICS
0

After two years of watching the Giants self-destruct, National League fans must have breathed a sigh of relief in 1914, when the unlikely Boston Braves won sixty of their last seventy-six games to capture the N.L. pennant. But not one pundit thought the Braves had a chance to dethrone the Athletics, who were seeking their fourth championship in five years.

The Mackmen, however, weren't what they'd been a year or two earlier. "Home Run" Baker, Chief Bender, Eddie Collins, and the rest of the A's were finally nearing the end of the line. And the Braves, led by ace pitcher Dick Rudolph and Series-tested veteran Johnny Evers, were as hungry as only a miracle team could be.

The Braves also had the perfect manager for a miracle: George Stallings, often bitter and scornful but also a master tactician. "He'd go all the way down the line, taking one player after another, and make him admit before anybody in the clubhouse that he was the best damned player at his position in the league," said Braves catcher Hank Gowdy of

Stallings. "I knew he had me feeling that all the other catchers in baseball were Grade A dopes compared to me and I actually believe that's why I hit so well in the Series. The fellow had me mesmerized or something."

How mesmerized was Gowdy, who had hit only .243 during the regular season? All he did was slug a home run, a triple, and three doubles among his six hits in eleven at bats in the brief series—which the Braves won in a four-game sweep. He was also behind the plate as Braves' pitcher Dick Rudolph stopped the A's , 7–1; Bill James outpitched Eddie Plank in a 1–0 thriller; Lefty Tyler and James combined to stop the A's at crucial moments in the Braves' 5–4, twelve-inning victory; and Rudolph returned to win, 3–1, for the sweep.

Gowdy's unexpected exploits made at least one observer burst into song—or into poetry, at least. "What do you know of Hero Hank?/Hank Gowdy is his name!/He'll surely take the highest rank/In Baseball's Hall of Fame!" wrote a transported Leonard B. James.

Writing in the *New York Journal*, Sam Crane was calmer, but no less decisive. "It was dramatically pathetic to see the World's Champions go down to defeat," he said, "but youth and verve must prevail in baseball, and the seasoned veterans of Connie Mack, loaded with the honors of a heroic past, had to give way to the fiery activity of the young and more energetic and ambitious rivals."

In his fifty-year career as A's manager, Mack suffered many disappointments, but none worse than the 1914 loss to Boston, which still stung decades later. "Those Braves, they really hurt us," he said. "Nobody expected what they did, and it took a long time for us to get over it. Our pride had been shattered."

1912 1915 1916 1918

WHEN THE RED SOX
RULED

It's hard to believe now, after so many decades of frustration, but from 1912 through 1918 the Boston Red Sox were the best team in baseball. They didn't win the pennant every year—the Philadelphia Athletics were strong competition early, and the Chicago White Sox later on—but they were consistently at or near the top of the league for seven straight years.

Even more importantly: When they made it to the World Series, they won every time.

In 1912, the Sox interrupted Philadelphia's mini-dynasty by riding Tris Speaker's spectacular offense and Joe Wood's thirty-four wins to a 105–47 record and an easy American League flag. Their opponents in the Series were the powerful but star-crossed New York Giants, who boasted a battle-tested line-up and pitchers Christy Mathewson and Rube Marquard at their peak.

At first it looked like Boston would march to an easy victory, though, as Joe Wood's two wins gave the Sox a 3–1 Series lead, with one additional game declared a tie when darkness fell. But then the Giants made a valiant comeback, earning two easy wins to knot the Series, 3–3.

Then came Game Eight, a magnificent contest pitting Mathewson against Boston's brilliant Hugh Bedient. After seven innings, the score was knotted at 1–1. Wood came on in relief, and he and Mathewson matched zeroes until the tenth, when the Giants scored a run on a single by Fred Merkle. Only three outs to go, and the Giants would be World Champions for the first time since 1905.

But Mathewson never got his second championship. Giant centerfielder Fred Snodgrass dropped an easy fly ball hit by pinch hitter Clyde Engel (perhaps the most famous "muff" in baseball history); Tris Speaker got a second chance after the Giant infielders mishandled a routine pop-up and singled in a run; and the winning run scored on a sacrifice fly. The Red Sox, so close to extinction, were champions of the world.

Today, 1912 is considered one of the best World Series of all time, and even back then John B. Foster in the *Spalding Guide* said it was "crammed with thrills and gulps, cheers and gasps, pity and hysteria, dejection and wild exultation, recrimination and adoration, excuse and condemnation."

But the Sox didn't get as much credit as they deserved. Most observers focused on the Giants' error-strewn play in the last inning. Snodgrass came in for blistering treatment, despite making a spectacular catch on a Harry Hooper fly ball right after his notorious muff. In a front-page story, the *New York Times* provided a typically intemperate opinion. "Sox Champions on Muffed Fly," blared the above-the-fold headline. "Write in the pages of world's series baseball history the name of Snodgrass," the article thundered. "Write it large and black. Not as a hero, truly not. Put it in rather with Merkle, who was in such a hurry that he gave away a National League championship. Snodgrass was in such a hurry that he gave away a world championship."

Start spreading the news: Telegraphers follow the action at the Polo Grounds during the 1912 World Series.

1912

BOSTON
RED SOX
4

NEW YORK
GIANTS
3

1915

BOSTON
RED SOX
4

PHILADELPHIA
PHILLIES
1

While the Giants crumbled under the weight of such disappointments, the Red Sox came back bigger and stronger in 1915— a dynasty at the peak of its powers.

The Sox, featuring superb pitching from Ernie Shore, Rube Foster, Dutch Leonard, and (later) Babe Ruth; great defense; and terrific hitting from Tris Speaker and Harry Hooper, were so strong that a succession of National League champions barely had a chance against them. In 1915 the victims were the Philadelphia Phillies, who rode an extraordinary year from Grover Cleveland Alexander (thirty-one wins, including twelve shutouts) to their first N. L. flag. But though they kept the games close, they were no match for the Sox.

Alexander pitched beautifully, winning one of his starts 3–1 and losing the other 2–1. Every other game was decided by a single run, but the Sox won them all, including the decisive Game Five, 5–4, on a pair of home runs by Harry Hooper. Despite the close scores, said F. C. Lane in *Baseball Magazine*, "to those who have watched the Red Sox through the summer there wasn't anything very close about the series. The Red Sox are the greatest defensive team that has been gathered together in years. Their whole policy is to win games by close scores."

"WRITE IN THE PAGES OF WORLD'S SERIES BASEBALL HISTORY THE NAME OF SNODGRASS. WRITE IT LARGE AND BLACK."

Young gun versus old pro: Boston's Ernie Shore and Philadelphia's Grover Cleveland Alexander before Game One of the 1915 Series.

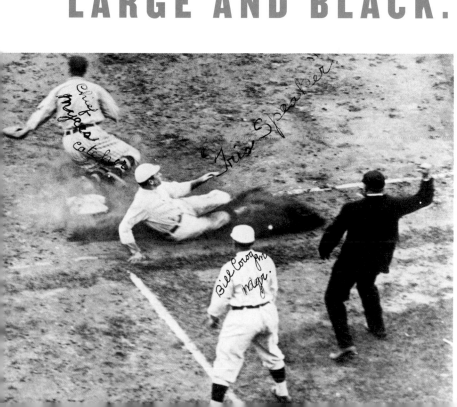

He's out! Boston's Tris Speaker nipped at first by Giants catcher Chief Myers during 1912 Series action.

1916

**BOSTON
RED SOX
4**

**BROOKLYN
ROBINS
1**

A year later the Red Sox were back for more. Their 1916 opponents were the Brooklyn Robins, claiming their first N.L. flag. Despite a strong pitching staff featuring such old-timers as Jack Coombs and Rube Marquard, the Robins managed just one win (by Coombs), going down meekly in five games. Highlights were few and far between for the Robins: a home run by Hy Myers, four hits in the Series by a young outfielder named Casey Stengel, thirteen superb innings pitched in Game Two by Sherry Smith—in a game the Robins lost in fourteen, 2–1.

The Boston pitcher who defeated Smith in the marathon Game Two duel was a second-year man named Babe Ruth. Ruth held the Robins scoreless for the final thirteen innings of the match, which he called "the greatest game I ever pitched."

When the series was over, F. C. Lane, who had followed the Sox all year, gleefully sang their praises. "It was a spectacular finish to a glorious season," he said of the brief Series. "To be sure some might call it an anti-climax, but they were glum National League rooters who thought or professed to think that the raw strength of the Brooklyn club would be a match for the well-oiled mechanism of that powerful baseball engine, the Red Sox."

After a disappointing 1917 (they finished nine games behind the Chicago White Sox), the Sox were back on top in 1918. This was the year that the United States entered World War I, and per presidential orders, the baseball season came to an end at Labor Day, when teams had played about 130 games. As a result, the World Series—pitting the Sox against the Chicago Cubs—started on September 5, just when fans would normally have been settling in to watch the pennant races.

The odd timing, the loss of some prominent players who signed up for the military and headed overseas, and a mid-Series strike threat by players unhappy about the size of their shares, didn't affect the quality of the play. Every game was a tight one, with the two teams combining for a mere eighteen runs over six games.

Babe Ruth was spectacular in this World Series. Beginning the transition from pitcher to slugger, he had started just twenty games as a pitcher (going 13–7) during the regular season, while playing seventy-two games in the outfield and at first base. Still, Boston Manager Ed Barrow knew a big-game pitcher when he saw one—and the Babe, in his own inimitable way, was ready and willing.

When I told Ruth he was going to pitch the opener [Barrow wrote in *My Fifty Years in Baseball*], I also went over the hitters in the Chicago lineup with him. I particularly stressed Leslie Mann, the Cub left fielder, a stocky right-handed hitter who didn't have a big average, but who was particularly rough on left-handed pitching.

"Don't let up on him at any time," I warned Ruth. "And don't let him dig in at the plate. Bear down on him."

"Don't worry," Babe said. "I'll take care of him."

When the game started, Max Flack, who was roughly Mann's size, though not so stocky, but a left-handed hitter, led off for the Cubs. Ruth threw one close to Flack's head and Max reared back from the plate. Then the Babe breezed three fast ones past him for a strike-out.

When Ruth came back to the bench after the inning he sat down next to me and said, "Well, I guess I took care of that Mann all right, eh?"

Good old Babe! He never could remember names or faces.

1918

**BOSTON
RED SOX
4**

**CHICAGO
CUBS
2**

Ruth, pitcher

Neither Flack nor Mann nor any of the other Cubs bothered Ruth much in Game One, a stifling six-hit shutout for the Babe in the Sox' tense 1–0 win. While Lefty Tyler shut down the Sox in Game Two, Carl Mays came back to pitch Boston to a 2–1 Game Three win.

Then, in Game Four, it was the Babe's turn again. This time all he did was add another seven innings of shutout ball before the Cubs scored twice in the eighth—for a World Series record 29 $^2/_3$ consecutive scoreless innings (including his thirteen in 1916). Ruth also blasted a triple to drive in two runs in the Sox' 3–2 win…a harbinger of countless Series slugging escapades to come.

When Boston's Carl Mays won Game Six, 2–1, the Sox had their third world championship in four years. They were no longer a young team, but with Ruth in the center of their line-up, it looked as though their reign might last forever.

It didn't, of course. The 1918 triumph was the Red Sox' last World Series title to date. And Ruth? He was destined to win a passel more World Series games—but as a hitter, not a pitcher.

And for another team, of course.

ATTACK OF THE MIGHTY MITES

AGAIN AND AGAIN, WORLD SERIES ARE DOMINATED NOT BY THE SUPERSTARS—THE COBBS, WILLIAMS, DIMAGGIOS, MCGWIRES—BUT BY LITTLE-KNOWN PLAYERS WHO MAKE THE MOST OF THEIR MOMENT OF GLORY.

HERE'S A SAMPLING:

"Here's a ballplayer who can't hit or field, can't run or throw, but he's one of the best I ever saw."
— Chicago White Sox Manager Fielder Jones on little-known Frank Isbell, whose four doubles in Game Five helped lead the "Hitless Wonders" to a surprise 1906 Series win over the powerful Chicago Cubs.

"Kneeling in the on-deck circle before my first time up, it just flashed through my mind: Here I am playing in a World Series in Cincinnati, about a hundred miles from my hometown, with about twenty family and friends in the park along with 53,000 others and millions more watching on television. I kind of lost the game situation. But then this other stuff just left my head, and I walked to the plate so totally relaxed."
— Gene Tenace, who hit just .225 with five home runs during the regular season—but then hit .348 with four homers and 9 RBI to lead the Oakland A's to an upset victory over the Cincinnati Reds in the 1972 World Series.

"My regret is that I didn't walk him oftener."
— Philadelphia A's Manager Connie Mack, after unsung catcher Hank Gowdy batted .545 to carry the Miracle Boston Braves to a shocking sweep of the A's in 1914.

"I swung as hard as I could and figured it might get between the outfielders and roll to the wall, so I put my head down and ran like hell. By the time I turned first base, the crowd was going crazy and I looked up. That's when I saw the umpire giving me the signal, the overhead wave of the hand to tell me I had hit a home run. But I still ran around the bases as fast as I could, as though someone might take it back if I didn't get to home plate soon enough."
— Al Weis (career average: .219), whose Game Five home run helped the Mets overthrow the powerful Baltimore Orioles in the 1969 Series.

"All I know is that I'm not going to sell clothes this winter like I did last year."
— Brian Doyle, whose professional career included just thirty-two hits—but who went seven for sixteen to lead the Yankees in the 1978 Series.

"Years from now when they're sitting around some tavern, or on a park bench, and some fellows ask John Rikard Dempsey what he used to do for a living, he can say, 'I was the Most Valuable Player in the World Series in 1983.' Then they can laugh heartily and say, 'Yeah, and I was a nuclear scientist and Charlie here is a brain surgeon.'"
— Columnist Furman Bisher in *The Sporting News*, after Baltimore catcher Rick Dempsey (lifetime average .233) hit .385 and slugged .923 as the Orioles defeated Philadelphia in the 1983 Series.

Unlikely postseason superstar Gene Tenace slamming one during the 1972 Series. "Somehow it's always a guy like that who beats you in a World Series," said Cincinnati pitcher Gary Nolan. "An underdog."

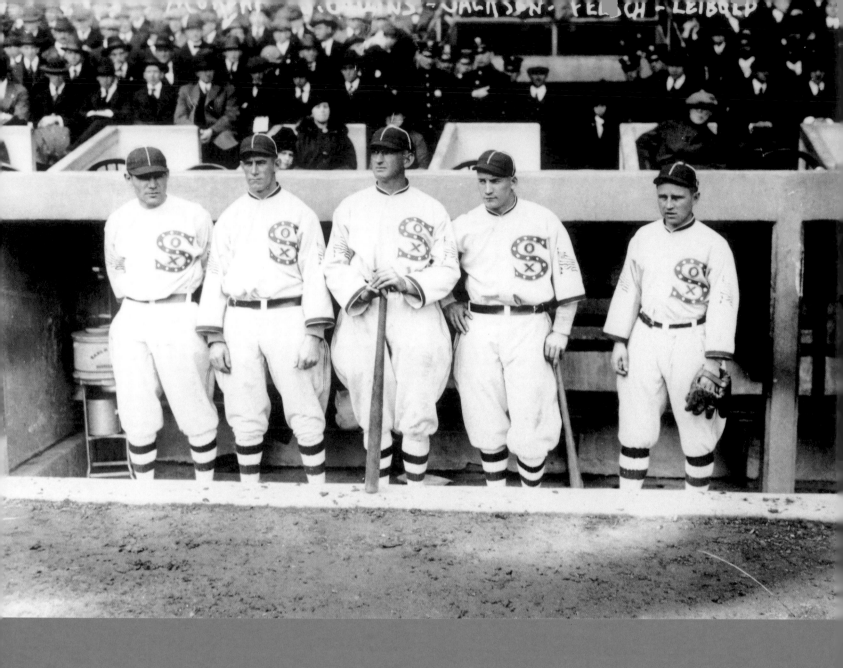

WE ALL KNOW THE (FICTIONAL) STORY OF THE YOUNG BOY WHO FIXED JOE JACKSON WITH A LOOK OF MISERY AND SAID, "SAY IT AIN'T SO," BUT WHAT ABOUT THE REAL IMPACT ON REAL CHILDREN?

In 1917, the Chicago White Sox fired a shot across the Boston Red Sox' bow, capturing the American League flag seemingly owned by their Boston rivals. The White Sox' opponents were John McGraw's New York Giants, making their first appearance in the Series since their heartbreaking losses in 1911, 1912, and 1913.

For Sox fans, the wait for a pennant had stretched eleven years…a lifetime for children with no memory of the "Hitless Wonders" of '06. One such was the renowned novelist James T. Farrell, who was thirteen in 1917, and wildly excited to see his team in the Series.

His memoir of the first game (published in 1957's *My Baseball Diary*) remains fresh today, revealing all the sense of adventure that children get from the sport they love. There is something about being a small person surrounded by grown-ups acting like kids, the game's two or three hours stretching ahead, that makes being a child at the ballpark such a thrilling experience.

Farrell tells of the early journey he and his friend Earl made to ensure that they'd get bleacher seats for the opening Series game at Comiskey Park:

1917

CHICAGO
WHITE SOX
4
NEW YORK
GIANTS
2

1917
1919

THE
BETRAYAL

Finally, and well before 5 A.M., we were off, leaving by the back door, going down the back stairs, and along the alley to Fifty-Eighth Street in the chilly pre-dawn. We took the elevated train to Thirty-Fifth Street, the Thirty-Fifth Street trolley to Wentworth Avenue and found the line-up of men waiting before the bleacher ticket office. It was still dark when we took our places in this line. There were about three hundred men ahead of us in one of the waiting lines. My anxiety disappeared. I had feared that there might be thousands waiting when arrived. I had attributed to others, and to grown men, my own feelings about baseball. I was a boy still in short pants. The men about us in line greeted our coming with friendliness. They liked seeing such a young and devoted fan waiting as they were.

It was a bit raw, and here and there, men had built fires. Venders were out with hot coffee and we bought and drank quite a quantity of it. About every hour, we ate. I felt important and I was very happy. All the cares I had in my mind were those of my own impatience for time to pass, so that it would be time for the game to begin. And, of course, there was the greater care or worry—would the White Sox win?

As it turned out, the young Farrell didn't have to worry. The Sox, behind star pitcher Eddie Cicotte, held on for a 2–1 Game One victory. "I went home thrilled and happy," he said.

The rest of the Series must have thrilled him as well. Led by Cicotte, Joe Jackson, Happy Felsch, and other stars, the White Sox cruised to a six-game triumph, capped by Red Faber's 4–2 victory over Rube Benton in the final game. The White Sox, a young, talented, and aggressive team, looked to be set to compete for the crown for years to come.

After a disappointing season in 1918, the White Sox survived a tense pennant race to capture the A.L. flag again in 1919. The team was at its peak, a fearsome combination of great hitting (Joe Jackson, Eddie Collins, Buck Weaver, and others) and superb pitching (twenty-nine-game–winner Eddie Cicotte, twenty-three-game–winner Lefty Williams). Chicago's opponents were the upstart Cincinnati Reds, who boasted strong pitching from Hod Eller and Slim Sallee and some potent hitting of their own from Edd Roush and Heinie Groh. Still, going into the Series, no one gave the Reds much of a chance.

Joe Jackson (center) and Happy Felsch (second from right) during the 1917 World Series. Just two years later, they and six other players would be banned from the major leagues for life.

Joe Jackson. "Oh, he was great," said Smokey Joe Wood. "Poor fellow."

What happened next is a story told a thousand times: How rumors began churning that the fix was in, that some of the Chicago stars had accepted payment to throw the Series. How Cicotte and Williams pitched uncharacteristically poorly, Jackson failed to hit at important moments, and Happy Felsch and Swede Risberg looked overmatched. How the Reds went on to win the best-of-eight Series, five games to three, with Williams lasting just one-third of an inning in the climactic eighth game. How the full story didn't come out till near the end of the next season, when one player after another confessed to being paid to throw the Series. How those accused (Cicotte, Williams, Jackson, Risberg, Felsch, Chick Gandil, Fred McMullin, and Buck Weaver) were acquitted in court, but were banned from baseball forever by new baseball czar Kenesaw Mountain Landis. How baseball suffered for years from this betrayal.

The facts are known, but what about the human impact? In particular, what about the effect on young fans, the children who, in growing up, pass their love of the game on to their own children? We all know the (fictional) story of the young boy who fixed Joe Jackson with a look of misery and said, "Say it ain't so," but what about the real impact on real children?

In 1950, *The New Yorker* published an essay by James Maxwell, a Cincinnati native who was seven years old in 1919. Titled "Shine Ball," it provides a harrowing look at what happens when crooked players plunge a dagger into a young child's faith.

About the middle of September, after weeks of constant nervous strain for all Cincinnatians, the Reds clinched the National League pennant. The city erupted into celebration, but once the first outburst had passed, everyone began to worry about the Reds' opponents in the forthcoming World Series, the Chicago White Sox. Fearsome stories of Shoeless Joe Jackson's power, of the impenetrability of the Chicago infield, of the pitching of Ed Cicotte circulated freely among the faithful. I heard my father and grandfather discuss the relative merits of the two teams again and again, and they always agreed that a Chicago victory was almost certain. This adult opinion made me somewhat uneasy but did not entirely obliterate my hope.

The Series began at last, and on the first two afternoons a half dozen of my friends and I went A.W.O.L. from school, stationed ourselves on the street just outside the ballpark long before game time. There was no way for us to get inside for those games, of course, but I don't recall that any of us felt especially envious of the fortunate people who went past us through the gates. I know that I, at least, was completely happy just to be near the action. The excitement and noise of the crowd, the bellowed commands of policemen, the honking horns of taxis, the impatient clanging of streetcar bells, the cries of the hawkers selling peanuts, soft drinks, and scorecards, the pervading sense of drama were sufficient reward for being there, and even just for being alive.

Once the game started, we reveled in the flat, revolverlike crack of the bats, the explosive bursts of hoarse voices, and the moments of tense quiet, when we could hear only the shouts of the venders. Inside the stadium, some men stood with their backs against a grating high above us, and from time to time we got the attention of one of them and learned the score.

The Reds won the first two games, making me forget that I had ever doubted their invincibility. Then the teams went to Chicago for the next three games. My friends and I attended school on those afternoons, though to little purpose, and as soon as classes were dismissed, we raced to Ahler's Café [a neighborhood saloon that had a sports ticker which communicated scores cross-country in the age before radio broadcasts]. The Reds lost the first game in Chicago and won the two others. (In 1919, it took five games to win the championship.)

On the evening of the day the Reds won their fourth game, my father, who had been reading the paper, lowered it and stared at the wall for a moment. "This doesn't make sense," he said. "The Reds aren't that good and Chicago isn't that bad. I can't figure it out."

I looked up from the homework I was doing on the floor beside his chair. "It's the shine ball," I said. "They can't hit the shine ball." I had no clear idea what a shine ball was, but it was the specialty of my favorite pitcher, Hod Eller, and to me the name suggested that he did something mysterious to the ball that caused it to reflect light, like a mirror, thus temporarily blinding the opposing batter.

Cincinnati's Hod Eller. His shine ball—and the fix— helped him win two games in the 1919 Series.

"THE REDS AREN'T THAT GOOD AND CHICAGO ISN'T THAT BAD. I CAN'T FIGURE IT OUT."

"It just couldn't happen this way," Father said to himself, ignoring me.

The teams came back to Cincinnati. Those of us who had stayed out of school for the first two games had been punished with extra homework assignments, but our number had been so great that our principal dismissed school an hour early for the Reds' sixth Series game, and, after Chicago won that, for the seventh, too.

My companions and I returned to our posts by the ballpark, and when the Reds lost the sixth game, we consoled ourselves with the thought that their lead was too great to be overcome. When they were defeated again the following afternoon, however, Chicago was within one game of tying the Series. Doubt invaded all of us, and we walked away from the park with scarcely a word to say to one another.

"The percentages are beginning to pay off," my father said at dinner that evening. He spoke in the unhappy, yet satisfied, tone of a man who has correctly predicted a disaster. "That Chicago team has everything—pitching, hitting, fielding—and they were bound to get their stride. With the last two games on their home field, it doesn't look good for the Reds," he concluded, and for the first time in my life I was unable to eat dessert.

The next day was Thursday, and our group skipped school again and gathered outside Ahler's Café a few minutes before game time. My spirits were somewhat higher than they had been the night before. Hod Eller was to pitch for the Reds, and I had an almost mystic faith in his shine ball. The game began, and we waited what seemed an interminable while for the ticker to give the score. I knew the batting order by heart, of course, and I visualized the scene in Chicago, recalling the idiosyncrasies of the various players—how this one tugged at the peak of his cap before each pitch, how that one always swung four bats before going to the plate, how another never failed to knock the dirt from his spikes. Finally, we heard the faint, staccato clicking of the ticker and saw the men in the saloon gather around the machine. After a few moments, there was a

"BUT MOST OF THE PLAYERS HAD GONE," HE RECALLED. "IT WAS GETTING DARK. A BALL PARK SEEMS VERY LONELY AFTER THE CROWD HAS CLEARED AWAY. NEVER WAS A BALLPARK LONELIER OR MORE DESERTED FOR ME THAN ON THAT SEPTEMBER SUNDAY AFTERNOON."

great roar, and some of the men pounded one another on the back while three or four danced a jig. My friends and I almost broke Mr. Ahler's front window trying to hurry him to the scoreboard, and, for once, he didn't glower at us as he went toward it with a strip of yellow ticker paper in his hand. He waved to us gaily, then picked up the chalk and marked four runs for the Reds. We shouted until we were breathless.

There was never any doubt about the outcome after that first inning, and the game ended with the Reds the winners by the score of 10–5. As soon as it was over, we ran up and down the street screeching the news at the tops of our high, pre-adolescent voices. Heads popped out of windows, and before long many adults had joined us.

I talked and played little but baseball that year until snow and Christmas provided new interests. Christmas was especially thrilling in 1919 because my Uncle Dave, who lived in Chicago, came to Cincinnati for the holidays. He had been gassed during the war, had spent several months in a government hospital, and had recently become the operator of a racing handbook in

Chicago. He was by far the most romantic figure in our family, and my affection for him was great.

He arrived the day before Christmas, still looking pale and considerably underweight, but he was full of vivacity. According to family custom, we gathered at my grandparents' home that evening and exchanged presents. I must have received many gifts that night, but all I recall is opening a large white box from Uncle Dave and finding in it a blue-gray baseball uniform with the word "Reds" spelled out in crimson felt across the shirt front. I walked toward Uncle Dave with the shirt in one hand and a blue-and-white striped stocking dangling from the other, but when I tried to thank him, my voice quavered, and all the adults laughed.

A ticket to Game Three of the only World Series ever lost on purpose.

On the Sunday evening between Christmas and New Year's, Uncle Dave and my father sat in the living room after dinner, smoking their pipes and talking, while I lay on the floor next to the sofa and read the comic sheet from the morning paper. I paid no attention to their conversation until I heard my father say, "What did you think of the World Series?"

"Not much," Uncle Dave said. I looked up with interest.

Father laughed. "We thought the Reds did pretty well," he said. "They weren't exactly the favorites, you know."

"They should have done pretty well," Uncle Dave said. "They had a lot more than nine men playing for them."

Father looked puzzled. "What are you talking about, Dave?" he asked.

"I mean the Series was fixed," Uncle Dave said. "The White Sox threw those games."

I looked at the two men to see if they were enjoying some joke I didn't understand, but neither of them was smiling. Father was staring blankly at my uncle. For a while neither of them spoke. "You're kidding," my father said, at last.

"Kidding, hell!" Uncle Dave said. "Shoeless Joe Jackson, Cicotte—damn near the whole Chicago team was trying to lose that Series."

A cold, wet band seemed to wrap itself around my chest, chilling my body and making breathing difficult.

"My God!" Father said softly.

"Every gambler in Chicago knew that the Series was in the bag for Cincinnati," Uncle Dave said. His voice sounded tired. "Why do you think the odds on the Reds went to hell before the first game? The Sox seemed a cinch to win, but there wasn't a dime's worth of smart money on them." I didn't understand much of what he said from then on, but I knew it was all bad.

"Of course," Father said. "Of course. It had to be something like that. It's the only explanation that makes sense."

"The Reds didn't win the Series," Uncle Dave said. "The Sox gave it to them."

I found myself suddenly on my feet. "That's a lie!" I shouted. "That's a dirty lie!"

The two men looked at me in astonishment. They had probably forgotten I was in the room. "Jim!" my father said to me sternly.

"You're just mad because Chicago lost!" I said. "You're a dirty loser! A dirty loser!"

"Jim, stop that!" my father said, getting up from his chair.

"Dirty loser!" I cried once more, and then I turned, ran upstairs to my room, and slammed the door. I stood there in the dark for what seemed a long time, with my face and body pressed against the wall, my hands and arms rigid at my sides, trying to control my trembling. My eyes were tightly closed, and I remember that the plaster was cool against my forehead. My stomach tightened and I fought against being sick. My breath came out with a harsh, rasping sound, but I didn't, or couldn't, cry.

Finally the door opened and Uncle Dave came quietly into the room. He didn't turn on the light, but the lamp in the hall lightened the darkness somewhat. Uncle Dave stood directly behind me. "I'm sorry, Jim," he said gently. "I know how you feel." He didn't touch me, but I pushed myself harder against the wall. "I know how you feel," he repeated sadly, and then he left, closing the door behind him.

It was in the fall of 1920, almost a year later, that the newspapers began to print the story of what came to be known as the Black Sox Scandal. Uncle Dave's correspondence with my family usually consisted of infrequent brief notes, but in November of that year—just a few weeks after the Chicago players admitted before a grand jury that bribes had been accepted—I received a long, carefully documented letter that, I realize now, must have taken him hours of research to prepare. He had gone through the complete records of the 1919 World Series. By making his own deductions from figures I didn't wholly understand, he contrived to demonstrate to me that, as far as statistics went, nobody could say the White Sox hadn't tried their best to win, despite having been paid by the gamblers to lose. He pointed out, among other things, that Joe Jackson had tied the batting record for a World Series with twelve hits and had averaged .375, and that Chicago had made no more fielding errors than Cincinnati had. "The Reds would have won anyway," he concluded. "Remember that. The Reds would have won anyway."

My Uncle Dave was an able man with percentages, and I have never seen any reason to question his interpretation of those he sent me. As a result, I suppose I am one of the few baseball fans in the country who are still convinced that the Reds were the real champions in 1919.

Nice try, Uncle Dave. But the pure, raw emotion, the sense of personal betrayal, felt by the young Jim Maxwell before he grabbed the lifeline thrown to him by his kind uncle was repeated among countless children in the months that followed the 1919 World Series.

In his *Baseball Diary*, James T. Farrell, ardent White Sox fan, told of his reaction to the news, late in the 1920 season, that the rumors were true. Farrell, sixteen years old, went to see a game at Comiskey Park after the news broke, and recalled that "a subtle gloom hung over the fans. The atmosphere at the park was like the muggy weather."

After the game (which Eddie Cicotte won for the Sox), Farrell went down to the clubhouse door. Among a crowd of fans, he watched first Lefty Williams and then Joe Jackson and Happy Felsch leave the clubhouse, for nearly the last time, as it turned out. The players didn't seem to hear when fans called out, "It ain't true. It ain't true," just got into their cars and drove away.

Farrell turned back to the clubhouse. "But most of the players had gone," he recalled. "It was getting dark. A ball park seems very lonely after the crowd has cleared away. Never was a ballpark lonelier or more deserted for me than on that September Sunday afternoon."

The 1920 World Series was played under as dark a shadow as has ever obscured major-league baseball. Just a few days before the end of the season, the Black Sox scandal broke wide open in the press. Joe Jackson, Eddie Cicotte, Lefty Williams, and five other players confessed to accepting bribes (or knowing of the fix) and were suspended by White Sox owner Charles Comiskey.

At the time, the White Sox were in close contention for the A.L. flag. The 1920 Series would surely have been memorable—in a grisly way—if the suddenly undermanned Sox had managed to eke out the pennant. But instead they fell just short of player-manager Tris Speaker's Cleveland Indians, who claimed their first-ever A.L. pennant.

Cleveland had labored under its own shadows for much of the season. On August 16, the team's popular shortstop Ray Chapman was hit by a pitch thrown by Yankee Carl Mays. Players didn't wear batting helmets then (and wouldn't until the 1950s), and Chapman had seemed to freeze as the ball streaked toward his head. He died the next day of a fractured skull.

Fans looked to the best-of-nine World Series pitting the Indians against the Brooklyn Robins to provide some distraction. The Indians were led by Tris Speaker (.388) and pitchers Jim Bagby, spitballer Stan Coveleski (the spitball was legal back then), and Ray Caldwell, who "conquered both the other teams and Demon Rum to win twenty games" in the words of sportswriter Franklin Lewis.

The aging Robins featured such familiar faces as onetime batting champ Zack Wheat, slugger Hy Myers, and pitcher Rube Marquard, veteran of several heartbreaking Series losses with the Giants. But their most vivid player was the take-no-prisoners spitballer Burleigh Grimes, notorious for knocking down opposing batters. "I didn't mind decking guys. I didn't mind anything," he said after his career was over. "You think I'm going to pitch in somebody's alley? And have them knock the hell out of me?"

After Stan Coveleski held the Robins to one run in Game One, a 3–1 Indians' victory, Grimes pitched a 3–0 shutout in Game Two to even the Series. After that, though, Cleveland seemed to solve Grimes' intimidating deliveries, pounding him for seven runs in an 8–1 Game Five thrashing and beating him again, 3–0, behind Stan Coveleski, in the final game of the Series. The Indians' Joe Sewell revealed Cleveland's secret years later:

> The Dodgers had a little second baseman named Pete Kilduff. And Burleigh was throwing that spitter so good it looked like the batters were swatting flies. But every time Burleigh was going to throw the spitter, Pete Kilduff would reach down and get himself some sand to make sure that his throwing hand was dry.
>
> We picked that up and just watched Kilduff. If he didn't pick up the sand we knew it was a fastball or a curveball and we could jump on it. And that's the way we beat him.

Stan Coveleski was Cleveland's biggest star in the Series, pitching three complete-game victories and giving up just fifteen hits and two runs in the twenty-seven innings. But, as so often happens, it was the smaller names that made the biggest splash.

In particular, Game Five, a critical game in a Series that was then tied 2–2, was as packed full of treats as a piñata. The game, an 8–1 Indians win, featured the first-ever Series homer by a pitcher (the Indians' Jim Bagby) and the first Series grand slam, smacked by journeyman out-fielder Elmer Smith.

But it was a third first-ever event that gave the 1920 Series its immortality. The man in the spotlight was Cleveland's second baseman Bill Wambsganss, also known as Bill Wamby. ("It was a real relief to me when people commenced to call me Wamby," he said. "That's a rather queer name itself, but at least they could pronounce it without choking and getting black in the face.")

1920

CLEVELAND
INDIANS

5

BROOKLYN
ROBINS

2

"IT WAS A REAL RELIEF TO ME WHEN PEOPLE COMMENCED TO CALL ME WAMBY," HE SAID. "THAT'S A RATHER QUEER NAME ITSELF, BUT AT LEAST THEY COULD PRONOUNCE IT WITHOUT CHOKING AND GETTING BLACK IN THE FACE."

Above: A grin and three glowers: Bill Wambsganss with his triple-play victims, Pete Kilduff, Otto Miller, and Clarence Mitchell.

Right: Cleveland's Stan Coveleski, winner of three games in the 1920 World Series.

In the fifth inning of Game Five, with the Indians leading 7–1, Wamby became famous for something other than his name. Brooklyn pitcher Clarence Mitchell, who'd replaced Burleigh Grimes, came to the plate with Otto Miller on first base and Pete Kilduff on second, and immediately smoked a line drive toward center field. It looked like a hit, and perhaps the start of a big Brooklyn rally.

"I took a step to my right and jumped," Wambsganss said. "The ball stuck in my glove and my momentum carried me toward second base. Well, Kilduff, who took off for third when the ball was hit, was easy. All I had to do was touch second with my toe. Miller apparently didn't see what happened because I looked at first base and saw him within five feet of me. He stopped running and stood there, so I just tagged him."

It was an unassisted triple play. Kilduff, Miller, and all 26,884 spectators at Cleveland's Dunn Field were stunned into silence as they figured out what had happened. Then the crowd erupted, sailing straw hats and scorecards onto the field and letting loose a roar "that must have echoed on the shores of Lake Erie," as F. C. Lane put it.

Wambsganss, who continued to be a productive player for several more years, enjoyed his fame—but he also discovered its less-appealing side. "The only thing anybody seems to remember about me is that once I made an unassisted triple play in the World Series," he told Lawrence Ritter forty years later. "Many didn't even remember the team I was on, or the position I played, or anything. Just Wambsganss—unassisted triple play…. You'd think I was born the day before and died the day after."

Bill Wambsganss tags a stunned Otto Miller to complete the only unassisted triple play in World Series history. "It's almost as if my career began and ended with that one play," Wamby said.

When John McGraw's New York Giants edged the Pittsburgh Pirates to win the National League flag in 1921, it marked the fifth time in eleven seasons that the team represented the N.L. in the World Series. In 1911, 1912, 1913, and 1917, however, they had lost heartbreaking Series, leaving their intense manager seething.

When the Giants won the pennant again in 1921, McGraw was in his nineteenth season managing the team. The Giants had a strong pitching staff led by twenty-game–winner Art Nehf, airtight infield defense, and an opportunistic offense featuring third baseman Frank Frisch ("The Fordham Flash"), who had hit .341 with 211 hits during the season.

McGraw and the Giants were facing a new opponent this time: the New York Yankees, making their first World Series appearance after a series of close calls. ("Loyal rooters, who have watched the Yankee skid into the slough of blasted hopes season after season…gave vent to all the feelings that had been smothered in failure in other years," proclaimed sportswriter Jack Lawrence when the Yanks clinched.)

The Yankees, who had played the 1921 season at the home of the Giants, the Polo Grounds, had a strong line-up—but you'd never know it from reading the papers. It sometimes seemed as if they had won the pennant due to just one player: Babe Ruth. In 1921 Ruth had what was probably the best season of his career: 44 doubles, 16 triples, 59 home runs, 171 RBI, and an astonishing .378 batting average. Fortunately, given that the rules do require eight other men to participate, some of Ruth's teammates weren't half-bad either, especially pitchers Carl Mays and Waite Hoyt, who had combined for forty-eight wins during the season.

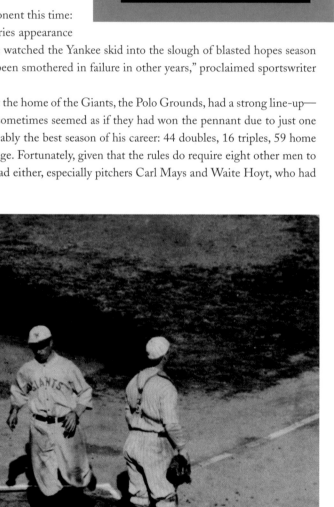

Dave Bancroft scoring the only run of Game Eight—the run that gave the Giants the 1921 championship.

**1921
1922**

GIANTS
ONCE MORE

1921

NEW YORK GIANTS 5

NEW YORK YANKEES 3

The first World Series between New York teams got emotions simmering. Challenges were flung about like confetti before the best-of-nine contest even started. "They say the Giants will show us up on the bases," Ruth was quoted as saying. "Well, we don't have to be good base runners. We knock the ball out of the park and simply jog around."

Meanwhile, McGraw, who had bristled at the extraordinary attention lavished on the Babe since his arrival in New York two years earlier, exploded when asked by a reporter how he would pitch to the mighty slugger. "Why all the excitement about Ruth?" he said. "We've been pitching all along to a better hitter than Ruth will ever be."

The better hitter, McGraw explained, was Rogers Hornsby, legitimately a great but nowhere near Ruth's all-around class in 1921. And the Giant manager knew that. He was just trying to get under the Babe's skin.

As it turned out, the Babe and no one else did much slugging in the first two games, won by the Yankees' Carl Mays and Waite Hoyt by identical 3–0 scores. The only Giant who seemed awake was Frisch, who went 4–4 in Game One, even though (as he told sportswriter Bob Broeg later), "I don't know whether I was numbly nervous or nervously numb, but I don't remember a blasted thing I saw or hit that day."

It looked a lot like the Giants were going to suffer another awful World Series defeat, especially when the Yankees jumped out to a 4–0 lead in Game Three. But then the Giant offense finally awoke, pounding four Yankee pitchers for twenty hits in a 13–5 rout. Seven strong relief innings by Jesse Barnes in relief of Fred Toney gave the Giants time to come back.

"WELL, WE DON'T HAVE TO BE GOOD BASE RUNNERS. WE KNOCK THE BALL OUT OF THE PARK AND SIMPLY JOG AROUND."

The Giants then added another win, 4–2, as Phil Douglas bested Carl Mays in Game Four. Babe Ruth, kept mostly in check by the Giant pitchers thus far, hit his only home run of the Series in this losing effort.

Game Five, a 3–1 Yankee victory behind the overpowering Waite Hoyt, was pivotal—but not in the way the Yankees would have hoped. Ruth, who had been struggling with a wrenched knee, surprised everyone by bunting for a hit with the game tied 1–1 in the fourth. Bob Meusel then hammered a long double to left center.

As Grantland Rice wrote in the *New York Tribune* the next day, the entire crowd at the Polo Grounds held its breath as it watched the injured Babe lumber around the bases:

> His arms and legs were only hanging by a thread as he worked his way through the contest. At any moment it looked as if he might break into eight or ten pieces and clutter up the ballfield with his scattered remains….
>
> With his right leg ready to fall off few expected to see the Bambino ever reach third with his system intact. But in place of weakening he put on a new burst of speed as he rounded the bag and tore for the plate, a pachyderm running on greyhound legs….
>
> A doctor had to be called in to collect the pieces and put them together again as one builds up a picture puzzle from a hundred intricate segments.

Jesse Barnes relieved Fred Toney twice in the 1921 Series—and all he did was pitch 15 ⅓ brilliant innings to help lead the Giants to their first World Series title in sixteen years.

The Babe's run broke the tie, and the Yanks grabbed a 3–2 lead in the Series. But Ruth never recovered from his mad dash and was restricted in the remaining games to a single pinch-hitting appearance.

The Giants, overjoyed to be playing the Ruthless Yanks, still proceeded to fall behind, 5–3, in Game Six. Again Fred Toney couldn't get the Yankees out. Again Jesse Barnes came to the rescue, this time pitching brilliantly for the last 8 ⅔ innings as the Giants roared back for an 8–5 victory.

"Have you ever seen a Kansas cyclone in midseason form with a hop to its fast one?" Grantland Rice said of Barnes. "Just as the ambitious Yanks were in the act of reaching for their fourth victory one of those funnel-shaped cyclones from Circleville, Kan., came bellowing out of an azure autumn sky and blew the red tin roof from above their aching heads, leaving them to the mercy of the pitiless elements that raged without."

The Giants then won Game Seven, 2–1, behind Phil Douglas, and Game Eight, 1–0, as Art Nehf bested Waite Hoyt. The Giants scored their lone run in the final game on an error by Yankee shortstop Roger Peckinpaugh, and then put the game away as second baseman Johnny Rawlings grabbed Frank Baker's ninth-inning smash and turned it into the double play. After so much disappointment, the Giants were Series champions for the first time since 1905.

Let Grantland Rice speak of the victory in his inimitable fashion: "The wanderer in far countries is home again with the spoils of war. The dust is on his knapsack and the rust is on his canteen, but the booty follows in his victorious wake. For the Giants have made port at last, to dock in triumph at the Harbor of Dreams-Come-True. After riding the storm in vain for nearly two decades they are once more champions of the world."

The Giants docked in the Harbor of Dreams-Come-True again in 1922, and again the team that sank in the Sea of Nightmares was the Yankees.

It was as lousy a year for the Yankees as any pennant winner ever had. Babe Ruth and Bob Meusel were both suspended for the first six weeks of the season (for defying a ban on barnstorming tours after the 1921 Series), and the Babe never really got on track, hitting just .315 with thirty-five home runs. Carl Mays and others had indifferent years.

McGraw's men took full advantage of the Yanks' vulnerabilities. It was a low-scoring, tightly played Series, but in every game but one (declared a 3–3 tie), the Giant pitchers were superior. One by one, Art Nehf, Jesse Barnes, Jack Scott, and Hugh McQuillan mowed down the Yankee sluggers, holding Ruth to a miserable .118 batting average. The Giants, behind the hitting of Frank Frisch (.471) and Heinie Groh (.474) took the Series 4–0, with the one tie.

In their wonderfully purple way, the sportswriters were royally displeased by the lack of entertainment value provided by the 1922 Series. "The Yankee corpse got its final pat in the physiognomy yesterday," complained John Kieran in the *New York Tribune* after the final game. "Thousands of mourners attended the interment, which was public."

1922

NEW YORK GIANTS

4

NEW YORK YANKEES

0

Opposite: No love was lost between John McGraw (left) and Babe Ruth, seen here during the 1922 Series. Luckily, Ruth's ghostwriter, Christy Walsh, was there as a buffer.

WORLD SERIES 1922
GIANTS - YANKEES

Yours truly
John J. McGraw

"Babe" Ruth

Periodically throughout the history of the World Series, a manager plays a hunch and chooses a starting pitcher whose very name stuns the crowds and sends the pundits into conniptions. Remarkably, the choice often proves brilliant, as when unheralded twenty-seven-year-old rookie Babe Adams won three games in the 1909 Series, thirty-five-year-old journeyman Howard Ehmke defeated the Chicago Cubs in Game One in 1929, and rookie Spec Shea starred for the Yankees in their classic seven-game defeat of the Brooklyn Dodgers in 1947.

But few managerial hunches can match Giants' manager John McGraw's choice of Jack Scott to start Game Three of the 1922 Series against the Babe Ruth-led Yankees.

Though just thirty years old, Scott was like a million other former big league players en route to nowhere as the 1922 season began. The big, strapping right-hander had a sore arm that left him unable to pitch for his team, the Cincinnati Reds.

Desperate, Scott consulted an endless line of expensive medical specialists:

Dr. Eastland	$58.00
Hotel Claridge, St. Louis	6.95
Mineral Wells (Nurse)	72.15
Dr. Singleton	17.00
Mineral Wells doctor	3.00
Bonesetter Reese	38.95
Dr. John C. Schmidt	54.00
Langdon-Meyer Laboratories	32.50
Dr. V. B. Dalton	15.00
Dr. Sidney Lange	10.00
Dr. H. H. Hines	50.00

A total of $357.55 in search for a cure for a sore arm, but nothing seemed to work. The Reds released him in May, and suddenly Scott found himself back at his North Carolina tobacco farm, wondering if the time had come to say a final goodbye to baseball.

But then, unaccountably, his arm began to feel better. Looking to hook on with a new team, Scott immediately thought of Giants' manager John McGraw. "I didn't know him to speak of, but I knew that, of all the managers, he was the one who would be most likely to give me a chance," Scott told writer Frank Graham later.

The pitcher asked McGraw if he could work out at the Polo Grounds. McGraw's response: "You're on." The manager's only requirement was that Scott not sign with the Yankees, who were currently sharing the Giants' ballpark. "I may want you to pitch against them when we get to the series," McGraw said.

"I won't sign with anybody but you," Scott replied.

McGraw was thrilled with what he saw in Scott. He signed the pitcher for the stretch run, using him as a spot-starter/reliever (Scott went 8–2), and then brought him along as the Giants prepared to play the Yankees in the World Series.

Still, no one expected Scott to get a start. No one, that is, but McGraw. He announced that the right-hander, who a few months before had been without a job in baseball, would start Game Three. Reporters and fans were stunned. "Scott?" wrote Graham. "The cast-off? The fellow who couldn't pitch up an alley when the Reds let him go?"

Scott. And all he did was shut Babe Ruth and the Yankees out on four hits, helping propel the Giants to their easy Series victory. After the game it was hard to tell who was more excited, the grateful Scott, back from purgatory, or his emotional manager. Wrote Frank Graham: "[McGraw] had picked a pitcher off the scrap heap and given him another chance—had staked him…and watched over him and been patient with him…and had started him in a World Series game and seen him hang a shut-out against the Yankees."

It's almost beyond the realm of believability today, but it's true: Going into the 1923 season, the Yankees were looked upon as chronic underachievers. They were thought to be good enough to ride Babe Ruth's broad shoulders to the American League pennant, but no further.

And in 1923, they were facing the New York Giants, the N.L. champion who'd whupped them in 1921 and '22. The pundits expected more of the same in 1923, and who could blame them?

But some things had changed since the two teams had met the previous fall. The Yankees had finally ended their years as second-class citizens playing in the Giants' home, the Polo Grounds, and had moved into Yankee Stadium, the most magnificent ballpark yet built. More importantly, Babe Ruth had recovered from his mediocre 1922 season to hit an astonishing .393, with 41 home runs and 131 RBI.

A revived Ruth in the spectacular House that Ruth Built was big news as the 1923 Series began. Unsurprisingly, this drove John McGraw absolutely crazy. "McGraw always hated all American Leaguers and especially the Yankees, but his hatred was at a peak as we prepared for the Series," said Giants star Frank Frisch. "He was so annoyed with the enemy that he wouldn't let us dress at the Stadium in the visitors' clubhouse. He insisted that we suit-up at the Polo Grounds and make the trip to and from the Stadium in taxicabs."

"WHEN LAST SEEN THE BALL WAS CROSSING THE ROOF OF THE STAND AT AN ALTITUDE OF 315 FEET. WE WONDER WHETHER NEW BASEBALLS CONVERSING TOGETHER IN THE ORIGINAL PACKAGE EVER REMARK: 'JOIN RUTH AND SEE THE WORLD.'"

Game One, at Yankee Stadium, followed a familiar pattern. The Yankees jumped out to an early 3–0 lead, but then watched helplessly as the Giants came back to win 5–4 in the ninth on an inside-the-park home run by a creaky, aging journeyman outfielder named Casey Stengel.

Heywood Broun, writing in the New York World, called it "the best baseball game ever played in a World Series," and gave due credit to the Giants' uniquely charismatic Stengel, whose shoe started to fall off as he dashed around the bases. "Stengel proceeded furiously in all directions at the same time," Broun wrote. "The dust flew as Casey tossed one loose foot after another, identified each one and picked it up again…. It would have been a thrilling sight to see him meet an apple cart or a drug store window."

Before Game Two, John McGraw, allowing his hatred of Ruth and the Yankees to outweigh his better judgment, repeated his claim of two years before. "Why shouldn't we pitch to Ruth?" he asked. "I've said it before, and I'll say it again, we pitch to better hitters than Ruth in the National League."

It's never a good idea to yank a tiger's (or a Yankee's) tail twice. In Game Two, Ruth the regular-season slugger finally transformed himself into Ruth the World Series colossus, slamming two monstrous home runs as the Yankees beat the Giants, 4–2, to knot the Series at a game apiece.

To Heywood Broun, seeing John McGraw get his comeuppance was a joy. Ruth's first clout, which left the Polo Grounds entirely, "was a pop fly with a brand new gland," Broun wrote. "When last seen the ball was crossing the roof of the stand at an altitude of 315 feet. We wonder whether new baseballs conversing together in the original package ever remark: 'Join Ruth and see the world.'"

The Giants went on to win Game Three (the first World Series game ever played at Yankee Stadium), 1–0, on another home run by Casey Stengel. This one was out of the park, which gave Casey a chance to taunt the catcalling Yankees. "I made like a bee or a fly was bothering me," he said later, "so I kept rubbing the end of my nose, with my fingers pointing toward the Yankee dugout."

1923

NEW YORK
YANKEES

4

NEW YORK
GIANTS

2

"It was Casey at the Bat all over again," said the *New York Times*. But this time Casey didn't strike out: He hit an inside-the-park homer to give the Giants a 5–4 Game One victory.

Commissioner Kenesaw Mountain Landis immediately issued a stern warning to Stengel and fined him $50 for his unsportsmanlike behavior. But he refused to inflict a greater punishment, with the single wise sentence: "Well, Casey Stengel just can't help being Casey Stengel."

As it turned out, Stengel's Game Three shenanigans were about the last highlights of the Series for the Giants. The Yankees pounded Jack Scott to win Game Four, routed Jack Bentley to take Game Five, and scored five runs off Art Nehf in the eighth inning of the decisive Game Six to erase a three-run deficit and win the game, 6–4.

The underachievers had captured their first championship. Or, as Grantland Rice put it, "The Yankees rode through the storm at last, to reach the shining haven where the gold dust for the winter's end lies ankle-deep in the streets."

What pressure? Before the deciding seventh game of the Series, Babe clowned around during the Girl Scouts' "Million Cookie" fund-raising drive. Then he blasted a home run in the Yanks' 6–4 Series-clinching win. "The Ruth is mighty and shall prevail," wrote Heywood Broun.

Irish and Bob Meusel, brothers who faced off in three Series in a row. In 1923, it was finally Bob's turn to gain a World Series ring.

Everyone liked Walter Johnson. And everyone felt sorry for him. The Big Train was, by all accounts, one of the gentlest and most thoughtful of all baseball stars, loved by fans, writers, and even opposing players. Yet Johnson had every reason to be bitter and frustrated. Possessed of the most blinding speed in either league ("I had a dread amounting almost to positive fear of his fastball," said Ty Cobb), Johnson was cursed to play for the American League's perennial doormat, the Washington Senators.

While piling up twenty-five or more wins every year, Johnson watched his team post records like 47–102, 42–110, 64–90, and 56–84. Even when the Senators would briefly improve, they were never able to get over the hump and capture the American League flag.

By the time 1924 rolled around, Johnson was thirty-six, in his seventeenth season, and nearing the end of the string. After a series of indifferent seasons, he went 23–7, leading the league with six shutouts and carrying the Senators to their first pennant ever. Their opponents: the New York Giants, making their fourth World Series appearance in a row.

"We were all kind of glad that Washington got into the Series on account of Walter Johnson," said Giant star shortstop Travis Jackson. Not that the Giants wanted to lose: John McGraw and his men were still smarting over their loss to the upstart Yankees the previous year, and were eager to take revenge.

From the start, the 1924 Series was a classic, seesaw battle. Art Nehf, the Giants ace, outpitched Johnson in Game One, a thrilling twelve-inning contest that saw the Giants score twice in the top of the twelfth and hold on when the Senators scored once in the bottom of the inning. The Senators, with a run in the bottom of the ninth, won the equally nail-biting second game, 4–3. The Giants took Game Three, 6–4, and the Senators Game Four, 7–4, to tie the Series at two games apiece.

Game Five, at the Polo Grounds, pitted Johnson against the Giants' Jack Bentley. But on this day the Big Train simply didn't have his best stuff. In eight innings, he gave up thirteen hits and six runs, as the Giants cruised to a 6–2 win that left them one game away from the championship.

Johnson knew he'd had his last start in the Series, perhaps his last start ever in a World Series, and he'd failed. As he boarded the train after this loss, he said later, "There were tears in my eyes. I was carrying my youngest boy on my shoulder and trying not to speak to people when [Washington owner] Clark Griffith put a hand on my arm. 'Don't think about it anymore, Walter,' he said. 'You're a great pitcher. We all know it.'"

Johnson watched as the Senators staved off defeat in Game Six, winning yet another thrilling game, 2–1, as Tom Zachary bested Art Nehf. Then came Game Seven, to be played at Washington's Griffith Stadium, home to years of pent-up hopes and dreams.

The game was one of the unquestioned classics of postseason play, featuring extraordinary strategic moves by both managers, clutch hitting by Washington player-manager Bucky Harris and the Giants' indefatigable Frank Frisch, and nerve-racking pitching by what seemed like both teams' entire staffs. It seemed inevitable when Senators scored two runs in the eighth inning to tie the game, 3–3—inevitable that this great game, this great Series, should come down to the very end undecided.

But few could have guessed who'd they see walking to the mound in the ninth inning: the Big Train, Walter Johnson.

1924 1925
ONE FOR THE GOOD GUY

Goose Goslin rounding third base after his three-run homer that led Washington to a 7–4 Game Four win in 1924.

1924

WASHINGTON SENATORS
4

NEW YORK GIANTS
3

10 BEST SERIES
NO. 3

1924

Muddy Ruel and the great Walter Johnson peer into the future—and see the Senators' first-ever World Series championship.

The wunderkind: the Senators' youthful player-manager, Bucky Harris.

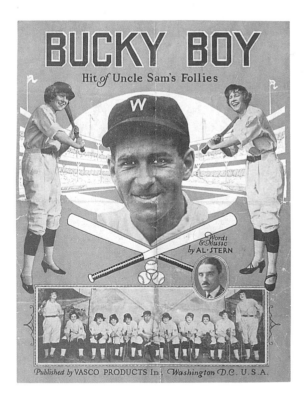

"THERE WERE TEARS IN MY EYES. I WAS CARRYING MY YOUNGEST BOY ON MY SHOULDER AND TRYING NOT TO SPEAK TO PEOPLE WHEN CLARK GRIFFITH PUT A HAND ON MY ARM. 'DON'T THINK ABOUT IT ANYMORE, WALTER,' HE SAID. 'YOU'RE A GREAT PITCHER. WE ALL KNOW IT.'"

"I'll always believe that Harris gambled on me because of sentiment, but he said no," Johnson recalled. "He just told me: 'You're the best we got, Walter...we've got to win or lose with you.'"

Johnson didn't have much, but his fastball still had some zing to it. And he was aided by the fact that this took place at a time when ballparks weren't equipped with lights. "One thing everyone should remember about that last game is that it was getting dark in the late innings," said Giants shortstop Travis Jackson, "and with Walter Johnson out there, even if he had lost some of his speed, the way he whipped that ball in from the side you couldn't pick it up until it was right on you."

Still, Johnson was in trouble in the ninth, in the tenth, in the eleventh, and in the twelfth, but each time he wriggled out of it. ("I'd settled down to believe, by then, that maybe this was my day," he said.) He'd almost won the game himself in the tenth, missing a home run by only a few feet, but in the bottom of the twelfth the game was still knotted at 3–3.

The inning, filled with freak events, remains famous three-quarters of a century later. With one out and the bases empty, the Senators' Muddy Ruel hit an easy pop foul...but Hank Gowdy, the Giant catcher, stepped on his mask and was unable to make the play. Ruel, reprieved, stroked a double.

Walter Johnson then hit an easy grounder to Travis Jackson, which Jackson booted. With runners on first and second, still just one man out, lead-off man Earl McNeely came to the plate.

McNeely hit a sharp but playable grounder down to Fred Lindstrom at third. But before Lindstrom could field the ball, it took a bad hop and bounded high over his head and toward left fielder Irish Meusel.

Allow Bill Corum, the *New York Times* correspondent who was covering the game to describe what happened next: "As the ball rolled into left, Ruel, running as he had never run before, rounded third and charged toward the plate. Meusel, galloping from deep left, picked up the ball, but didn't even throw.... Irish knew, as did the joy-mad crowd, that the game was over. He kept running on in toward the plate with the ball in his hands. The rest of the Giants stood motionless and stunned and in the next instant the crowd swirled over the field and blotted out the quiet men in gray and the leaping ones in white."

"I could feel tears smarting in my eyes as Ruel came home with the winning run," said Walter Johnson. "I'd won. We'd won. I felt so happy that it didn't seem real."

Firpo Marberry, the Senators' unflappable ace reliever. "I have confidence in myself," he said, "and I don't worry."

Today, Walter Johnson's 1924 feats remain among the most vivid in baseball history. Blessedly, his experiences in 1925 have dimmed, leaving the Big Train perched atop the mountain, where he belongs.

A season after winning their first Series, the Senators found themselves back for another go-round. Their opponents this time were not the Giants, but the Pittsburgh Pirates, making their first Series appearance since 1909. The Pirates, who had batted an astonishing .324 as a team during the season, were led by such hitting stars as Max Carey, Pie Traynor, and Kiki Cuyler, helping support a less stellar pitching staff.

The thirty-seven-year-old Walter Johnson pitched brilliantly his first two Series starts: a five hitter for a 4–1 victory in Game One, and a six-hit, 4–0 shutout in Game Five, giving the Senators a 3–1 Series lead. It looked as if Johnson would have a second feather to stick in his cap.

But the Pirates erupted for thirteen hits in a 6–3 Game Five victory, then eked out a 3–2 win behind Ray Kremer to knot the Series at three games apiece. For the second year in a row, the Series was coming down to the seventh game. Only this time Walter Johnson was slated to get the start.

By this point the Big Train's coal scuttle was pretty near empty…and yet the Senators would have, could have, should have won the game and the Series. Holding 4–0, 6–3, and 7–6 leads, they couldn't maintain their edge. Inning after inning, Johnson labored, his pitches lacking their usual heat, as the Pirate sluggers racked up fifteen hits.

Nor was he helped by his defense, especially shortstop Roger Peckinpaugh, who committed two of his Series record eight errors at crucial moments of the final game. But the true goat of the 1925 Series was the Senators' manager, Bucky Harris.

At a time when relief pitchers were usually washed-up veterans, Harris had come up with a brilliant innovation: Fred "Firpo" Marberry, the first true closer in the history of the game. Coming in late in tight games, he unleashed a fiery fastball that overpowered opposing sluggers—and he did it with all the insouciance characteristic of great relievers.

1925

PITTSBURGH PIRATES

4

WASHINGTON SENATORS

3

The Pirates' Pie Traynor helped doom the Senators' hopes of a second consecutive championship in 1925.

What the well-dressed superstar is wearing: Walter Johnson (third from right) with Ty Cobb, Babe Ruth, and John McGraw (center) and others prior to the 1924 Series.

"I credit my success in finishing up games partly to my nonchalance," Marberry said. "I just figure that my boss is paying me, win or lose."

Marberry had shone in relief in the 1924 Series, winning one game, saving another, and pitching three almost-perfect innings ahead of Walter Johnson's heroics in Game Seven. He was just as good in 1925, hurling a strong 2 $\frac{1}{3}$ innings in two Series appearances.

But in Game Seven, as Walter Johnson struggled, Harris never went to the fireballing Firpo. Instead, he left the Big Train in to give up nine runs, including three in the bottom of the eighth that enabled the Pirates to eke out the 9–7 win that decided the Series.

The only explanation was that Harris wanted to let Johnson pitch one more complete game. Instead, he gave the Pirates the championship.

"I CREDIT MY SUCCESS IN FINISHING UP GAMES PARTLY TO MY NONCHALANCE," MARBERRY SAID. "I JUST FIGURE THAT MY BOSS IS PAYING ME, WIN OR LOSE."

SIX RULES FOR FACING THE BABE

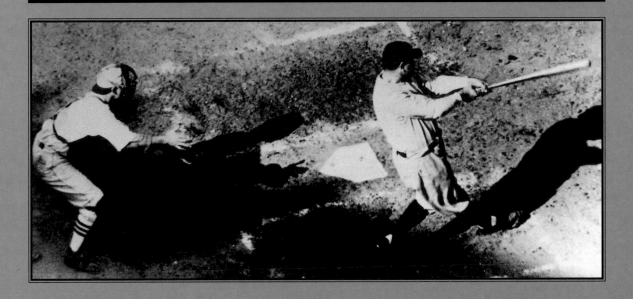

1 TRY NOT TO BE OVERAWED.

"Holy smoke! Does he do that often?"
— Pittsburgh's Emil Yde, watching Ruth hit a batting-practice home run, before the 1927 World Series.

2 PRETEND SELF-CONFIDENCE.

"Why shouldn't we pitch to Babe Ruth? We pitch to better hitters in the National League."
— Giants' Manager John McGraw before the 1921 and 1923 Series. McGraw went two for three: The Giants beat Ruth and the Yankees in 1921 and 1922, but Ruth slugged three home runs in the Yankees' 1923 Series victory.

3 PREPARE FOR THE WORST.

"He'd twirl that big 48-ounce bat around in little circles up at the plate as if he were cranking it up for the Biggest Home Run Ever Hit—*you felt that*—and when he'd hit one he would hit it like nobody has hit it before or since."
— Leo Durocher, in *Nice Guys Finish Last*.

4 DON'T EXPECT HELP FROM YOUR MANAGER.

"Donie Bush is going over the Yankees lineup.... 'Don't let Ruth beat you,' he says. But he doesn't offer any tips on how to avoid that fate. It's like sending somebody out in a hurricane without an umbrella and telling him, 'Don't get wet.'"
— Pirate infielder Dick Bartell, on 1927 pre-Series advice from Pittsburgh's manager, in *Rowdy Richard*.

5 BRING PROTECTIVE EARWEAR.

"There was a resounding report like the explosion of a gun."
— Sportswriter Richards Vidmer, describing Ruth's "called shot" home run in the 1932 Series.

6 BOW TO THE INEVITABLE.

"Yeah, I had a good day. But don't forget, the fans had a hell of a day, too."
— Babe Ruth, on the 1928 Series game in which he hit three home runs.

Like most seven-game Series, the 1926 battle between the resurgent New York Yankees and the first-time National League champion St. Louis Cardinals offered myriad delights. It had pitchers' duels, offensive explosions by Babe Ruth and others, fiery behavior by the Cardinals' pepper-pot player-manager, Rogers Hornsby, and enough controversial plays to keep the stove hot all winter.

But the 1926 Series, like so many others, has shrunk down to a single image as the years have passed: Grizzled old Grover Cleveland "Pete" Alexander trudging from the bullpen to the Yankee Stadium mound to face Tony Lazzeri with the bases loaded and the Cardinals clinging to a one-run lead in Game Seven. Coming in to pitch in relief after having thrown two complete games in the Series already—including one just the day before.

It's a strong image, all right, made even more vivid by the debate that has long surrounded that classic Series moment: Was Pete Alexander drunk when he faced the Yankees that day?

After his career ended, Alexander's struggles with alcoholism were so public, and so sad, that it became hard to remember anything else about him—including his 373 career wins as one of the greatest pitchers of all time. And even during his playing days, it was no secret that he was a drinking man who didn't always show up in the best condition.

So it's easy to understand why so many people thought Alexander was drunk when he made that walk in 1926 to relieve starter Jesse Haines in Game Seven. He even stumbled a little on the way to the mound.

But listen to those who were there, the people who knew Alexander in all his unmatched skills and un-

1926
PETE'S MOMENT

Tony Lazzeri fans with the bases loaded in Game Seven. "Funny thing, but nobody seems to remember much about my ball playing, except that strikeout," sighed Lazzeri in later years.

stoppable demons. Flint Rhem, who was also in the bullpen that day, claimed that Alexander was dozing with a pint of whiskey in his pocket when Rogers Hornsby called him into the game. But everyone else who was there refutes that claim.

Hornsby, for example, never one to mince words when it came to opinions about other players, swore until the end of his life that the way he told it in his autobiography, *My Kind of Baseball*, was the way it was:

"I left my position at second base and walked out toward the bull pen to meet him as he came in. I wanted to get a close look at him, to see what shape he was in. And I also wanted to tell him what the situation was, in case he'd been dozing. He was a great guy to relax, and probably had got himself a little shut-eye in the bull pen. But he was wide awake when I met him. His eyes were clear as usual, and he knew we were in trouble."

"I could have hit a dime with the ball had it been necessary," said Grover Cleveland Alexander of his control during his Game Seven confrontation with Tony Lazzeri.

1926

ST. LOUIS CARDINALS

4

NEW YORK YANKEES

3

Alexander himself was able to laugh about the rumors later. "One of the things they talked about afterward was my long, slow walk to the mound," he said. "Well, I didn't see any reason why I should run."

When they met out beyond second base, Hornsby filled the pitcher in on the crisis: "'We're still ahead, three to two,' I told Alex. 'It's the seventh inning, two out, but the bases are filled and Lazzeri's up.'

"Alex didn't say much. 'Bases filled, eh?' he said. 'Well, don't worry about me. I'm all right. And I guess there's nothing much to do except give Tony a lot of hell.'"

And that's what he did, as radio announcer Graham MacNamee reported to listeners: "Lazzeri batting. A hit means two runs. Alexander's arm goes up, here is the pitch, one ball, a little low. Here is the next one, and—strike!—a high, fast ball over the plate. Lazzeri didn't swing at it. One and one is the count, with three on. The next ball, a foul, a long shot into the left-field stand for the second strike—two strikes, one ball. And—he struck him out! Alexander the Great comes in and strikes out Tony Lazzeri, retiring the side. The entire Cardinal team has rushed over to Alexander, petting him and patting him on the back, and are simply wild over him."

They couldn't get too wild, of course: There were still two innings to go. Alexander got through the eighth in order and retired the first two men in the ninth. Then Babe Ruth strode to the plate. "This is a duel," said MacNamee. "There is electricity in the air." But Alexander walked Ruth, bringing down a hail of boos from the Yankee Stadium crowd.

Two outs, tying run on first. Bob Meusel, a fine clutch hitter, up. Alexander pitches…and Ruth tries to steal second. Bob O'Farrell throws him out. Game over. World Series over. "My biggest kick in that series," said Alexander, "was seeing the umpire with his arm pointing to the cloudy sky, calling Ruth out."

It was another great moment, centered on one of the best stories in the entire history of the World Series.

And it's just as good a story if Pete Alexander was sober.

More than a million fans poured into the streets of St. Louis to celebrate the Cardinals' stunning Series victory.

W hat was wrong with the Yankees? On paper, they had the most powerful team in either league throughout the 1920s. By the middle of the decade, Babe Ruth's supporting cast included such offensive luminaries as Lou Gehrig, Earle Combs, Tony Lazzeri, and Bob Meusel, as well superb pitchers such as Waite Hoyt, Herb Pennock, Bob Shawkey, and Urban Shocker.

The Bombers won pennants in 1921, 1922, 1923, and 1926 and just missed in 1920 and 1924. But with the sole exception of 1923, they always fell short of a World Series championship. Like the New York Mets in the 1980s and the Atlanta Braves in the 1990s, the 1920s Yankees seemed destined to be a team of might-have-beens, always good enough to see the ring, but never quite able to grab it.

Then came 1927, and all the disappointing seasons were forgotten. The Yanks' epochal year began with a dominating regular season: a 110–44 record that gave them the A.L. pennant by nineteen games. Ruth slugged his then-record sixty home runs while batting .356 with 164 RBI. Lou Gehrig hit .373 with 52 doubles, 18 triples, 47 home runs, and 175 RBI. Earle Combs hit .356 and Tony Lazzeri drove in 102 runs. Pitchers Hoyt (22–7), Pennock (19–8), Shocker (18–6), and Wilcy Moore (19–7) must have thought they were in heaven.

The Yankees' victims—that is, opponents—in the 1927 Series were the Pittsburgh Pirates, led by Paul ("Big Poison") and Lloyd ("Little Poison") Waner, future Hall of Fame outfielders. But the Waner brothers and the rest of the Pirates knew as clearly as every fan and sportswriter that they were outclassed in the Series…and the Yankees knew it too.

Call it the Sominex Series, guaranteeing a restful night to even the most committed insomniac. Rud Rennie set the tone in his lead article in the *New York Herald Tribune* as the Yankees headed to Pittsburgh for Game One. Datelined "In the Middle of the Night, Aboard the Yankees' Sleeping Car, En Route to Pittsburgh," the article didn't bother to interview Yankee manager Miller Huggins or detail the strengths and weaknesses of the Pirates' sluggers. Instead, Rennie compared and contrasted the Yankee stars' sleeping habits:

> There is usually an air of dim mystery about a strange sleeping car. One wonders who's behind the dark green curtains that move occasionally to the motion of the train. In this instance, however, one knows that the guttural noises up front betray the sleeping Ruth in lower 11. Those hissing sounds from lower 5 are the slumbering notes made by [Benny] Bengough, while lying on his back.
>
> From the depths of lower 3 comes nothing but a vast silence, for there lies Lou Gehrig. And when Gehrig sleeps, he sleeps with the quiet dignity of an Egyptian king long dead.
>
> Huggins has the drawing-room, a sound-proof place in which the mite manager might sing a paean of victory without disturbing a soul. But it is reasonable to suppose at this hour that Hug has knocked the ashes out of his bedtime pipe and is dreaming of the airtight pitching which will give him the championship of the world.

Airtight pitching Huggins wanted, but he didn't get it in Game One. Perhaps Waite Hoyt hadn't slept well, or perhaps the wild enthusiasm of the fans at Pittsburgh's Forbes Field (thousands of whom had to be turned away at the door) rattled him. Hoyt, struggling through 7 1/3 innings, gave up four runs and eight hits. But the Yankees, riding just enough offense, scored five to win. "It was scramble and rush and hullabaloo and stampede to look upon a gaudy spectacle which turned out to be one of the dullest games of the year," groused Grantland Rice.

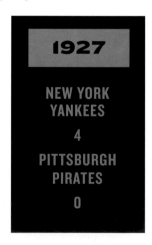

1927

NEW YORK
YANKEES

4

PITTSBURGH
PIRATES

0

Having lost Game One to a sloppy Yankee team, the Pirates seemed to realize they'd missed their best shot. When the Yankees' George Pipgras stopped them 6–2 in Game Two, the die was cast. As Damon Runyon put it in the *New York American*, "unless something nerve tingling transpires pretty soon, the several hundred inmates of the press section will be biting their telegraph operators in exasperation."

The headline in the *Herald Tribune* called it the "World's Dullest World Series"—after just two games! "Even Mr. Barney Dreyfuss, the Pirate owner, was seen to yawn openly in his box and did not even go to the trouble of concealing the yawn with his cash-calloused hand," noticed sportswriter W. O. McGeehan in the *Trib*. All was over, he added, "but the snoring of the wearied experts."

Game Three certainly didn't wake anyone up. Led by Ruth's three-run homer, the Yankees scored six runs in the seventh inning and cruised to an 8–1 win behind Herb Pennock. "Well, friends, I hope you won't expect much of a story out of me in regards to yesterday's game as I was too sleepy to watch what was going on," wrote McGeehan.

Game Four, at least, managed to keep fans alert. Pitting Wilcy Moore against the Pirates' Carmen Hill, it was a true pitchers' duel, tied 3–3 going into the bottom of the ninth inning. Then, in a welcome burst of drama, Pirate reliever Johnny Miljus proceeded to 1) put two men on; 2) throw a wild pitch to advance the runners; 3) walk Ruth to load the bases; and 4) strike out Gehrig and Meusel.

With the fans on the edge of their seats, Miljus threw a strike to Tony Lazzeri and then…hurled the next pitch to the backstop. Earle Combs scampered home with the winning run, and just like that the Series was over.

"The slapstick is mightier than the bludgeon, and for that reason your New York Yankees are the baseball champions of the world," wrote Paul Gallico in the *New York Daily News*, "and if ever a dramatic ball game came to a sillier ending, I would like to be informed."

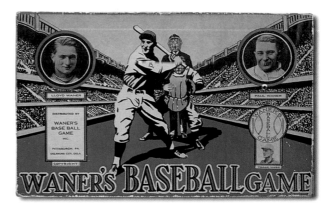

The 1927 Series was no game for Paul and Lloyd Waner, who watched their Pirates go down meekly in four games.

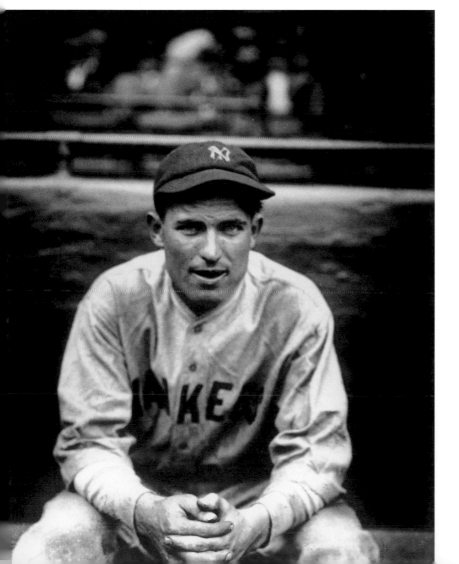

"UNLESS SOMETHING NERVE TINGLING TRANSPIRES PRETTY SOON, THE SEVERAL HUNDRED INMATES OF THE PRESS SECTION WILL BE BITING THEIR TELEGRAPH OPERATORS IN EXASPERATION."

In a line-up that included Ruth, Gehrig, and Lazzeri, the Yankees' leading hitter in the 1927 Series was shortstop Mark Koenig, who had nine hits in the four games.

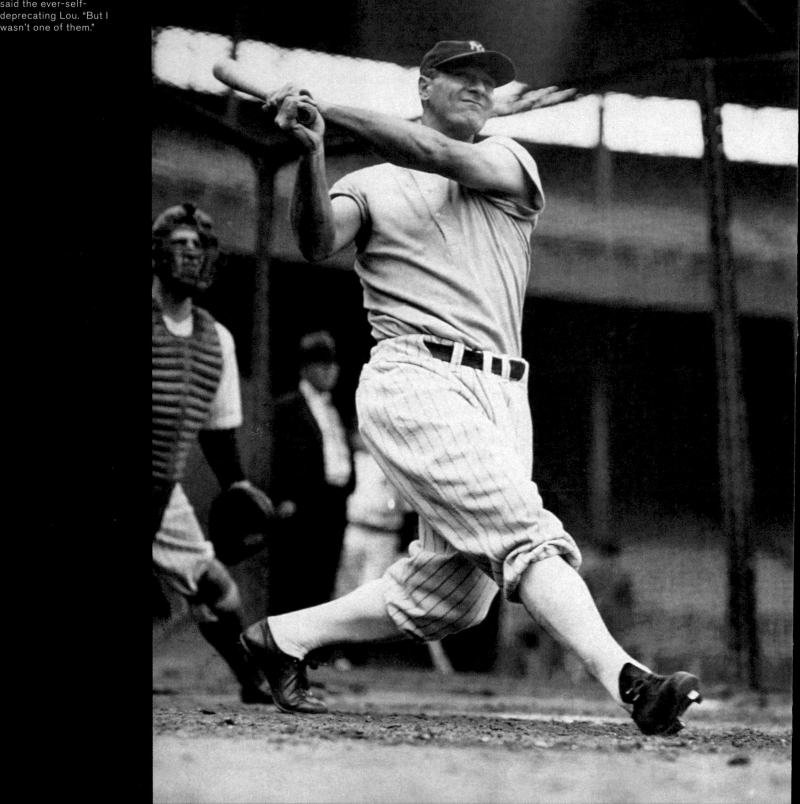

said the ever-self-
deprecating Lou. "But I
wasn't one of them."

1928

NEW YORK
YANKEES

4

ST. LOUIS
CARDINALS

0

No one was surprised to see the Bronx Bombers back in the Series in 1928. This time their opponents were the St. Louis Cardinals, who had defeated the Yankees in a seven-game classic just two years earlier. But two years can be a lifetime, and this Series was even less competitive than 1927's had been, a four-game sweep in which the Yankees outscored St. Louis 27–10.

The Yankees wielded an equal-opportunity bludgeon in 1928. Gehrig hit four home runs and drove in nine runs in the four games, while Babe Ruth hit only three homers—all in Game Four at Sportsman's Park in St. Louis. The last of the three was off old Pete Alexander, who gave up eleven runs in only five innings during the Series. It was a far cry from his dramatic Game Seven appearance in 1926.

After the last game, won 7–3 on the strength of Ruth's three home runs and sparkling defense, Manager Miller Huggins and the Yankees were joyful in the clubhouse, as Rud Rennie reported in the *Herald Tribune*:

Huggins was singing while he took his shower and the Babe was in such a good mood that he was a little bit silly.

"I never saw such a game," said Huggins. "What a ball club! Don't talk to me because I don't want to say anything. We won and I'm glad."

The Babe was bubbling over. He had pop bottles flung at him by the fans in left field. And he had kidded the throwers until they worshiped him. He had also smashed a few records.

"I told 'em I was going to hit two home runs," he said, "and I hit three. Haw, haw haw! I knew we could beat these guys. Am I happy—you tell 'em. Did ya see me catch that last one? What'ja think of that, huh? Oh, boy, what a day!"

You could hate the Yankees for their dominance, but you had to love the Babe.

Hat trick! The boaters fly as Babe Ruth celebrates his third home run in Game Four of the 1928 Series. "I told 'em I was going to hit two home runs, and I hit three," he crowed after the game. "Haw, haw, haw!"

S till Connie Mack endured. The only manager the Philadelphia Athletics had ever known was sixty-six years old by the time the 1929 season began. Gaunter and more reserved than ever, he had survived some of the worst years in modern baseball history after breaking up the A's 1910–14 dynasty, watching as the team plummeted to unimaginable last-place depths.

Was Mack through? Too old, past his time, unable to adjust to the action-packed era of the lively ball? A living anachronism, standing there calmly in the dugout in his business suit, while all the other managers wore uniforms and ranted and raved?

Nah. Connie Mack had a plan. Having torn down his great A's team, he slowly rebuilt it. Quietly, without attracting much notice, he started adding one great player after another: Jimmy Dykes and Jimmie Foxx in 1918, Rube Walberg in 1923, Al Simmons in 1924, Mickey Cochrane and Lefty Grove in 1925, George Earnshaw in 1928.

In the mid-1920s, for the first time in a decade, the A's began to win: eighty-eight games in 1925, ninety-one in 1927, ninety-eight in 1928. Then, in 1929, led by Simmons' .365 batting average, Foxx's 123 RBI, and Earnshaw's 24 wins, the A's went 104–46 to supplant the Yankees and capture their first American League pennant in fifteen years.

Their opponents were the Chicago Cubs, also making their first World Series appearance in more than a decade. The most dominant figure on the Cubs was itinerant Rogers ("Base Hit for Hire") Hornsby, who'd racked up 229 hits and a .380 batting average while playing for his fourth team. Short, squat Hack Wilson had also had a fine season, slugging thirty-nine home runs, but the conventional wisdom said that 1929 would be the Athletics' year.

1929

CONNIE MACK COMES BACK

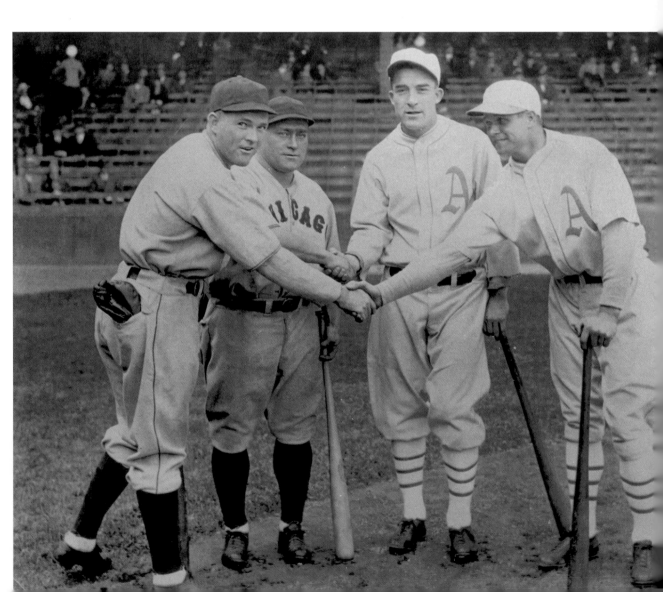

Four sluggers with 145 homers and 583 RBI among them in 1929: World Series combatants Rogers Hornsby and Hack Wilson of the Chicago Cubs and Al Simmons and Jimmie Foxx of the Philadelphia Athletics.

1929

PHILADELPHIA ATHLETICS

4

CHICAGO CUBS

1

Conventional wisdom, however, was confounded by Connie Mack's choice for a Game One starting pitcher: Not Lefty Grove, not George Earnshaw, not Rube Walberg, but Howard Ehmke. Ehmke had been a workhorse and a fine pitcher with bad teams in years past, even winning twenty games once when he was in the Red Sox. But by 1929 he was thirty-five years old and clearly in the waning moments of his career. He was the sort of pitcher who might get a mop-up inning or two in a blowout World Series game, but not a start.

Mack's selection of Ehmke plays a prominent role in nearly every history of baseball, and each book comes up with a slightly different explanation for what happened. The true inside story, however, comes from Ehmke himself, in an interview published in a 1931 book called *Play the Game*, edited by Mitchell Charnley:

In preparation for that game, Connie Mack left me in Philadelphia when the Cubs were playing a series with the Phillies. He told me to study the Cub batters....

I noticed, generally, that most of the Cub hitters pounded the ball into right field. This meant that they liked to hit the outside ball.

I watched Hornsby closely. He has a peculiar batting stance. His left foot is forward and his right one pretty well back. He's facing a bit toward right field. When the ball comes over, he steps toward the plate with his left foot. In other words, he steps into the path of the ball. That's how he gets his power. That, also, is how he gets hold of the outside ball and drives it to right field!

Hack Wilson, I noticed, squares away to the plate in orthodox fashion, but times his swing to hit to right field. Another thing that I learned was that the Cubs liked fast-ball pitching.

Connie Mack flanked by Mule Haas and George Earnshaw, two building blocks of the Mack's 1929–31 dynasty.

The guillotine falls: The Cubs' Pat Malone trudges off the mound as the A's celebrate a comeback 3–2 win and the 1929 World Series championship.

Armed with this information, I began working on a delivery. With practice, I can control any of the three deliveries—over-arm, side-arm, or under-arm. I hit upon the idea of delivering the ball out of my uniform. That is, I worked on an under-arm delivery in which my right hand came through close to my leg….

With that delivery, the batter won't be able to see the ball very clearly until it gets halfway to the plate. It's shaded by my uniform which is almost the same color as the ball. Only when it appears against a different background does the batter get a good look at it. I knew that the Cubs used a slightly colored ball that our blue-gray uniforms would shade nicely.

Armed with his strategy, Ehmke started retiring Cub batters in clusters in Game One. The Athletics scored a run in the seventh off Charlie Root and added two in the ninth to take a 3–0 lead. But when the Cubs rallied in the bottom of the ninth, scoring a run, putting men on first and third with two out and bringing up Chuck Tolson, Ehmke unveiled another trick:

Tolson, a pinch hitter, was at bat, and I didn't know anything about him. I gave him a strike, then a ball, and then another strike. The next one was close but outside. The next one was closer, and I thought the umpire might well have called it a strike, but he didn't and the count was now three and two. A walk would fill the bases.

Frankly, I didn't want to pitch to another batter. If Tolson let the next pitch go by, he might walk. I wanted him to swing at it, no matter where it went. And to get him to offer, I had to sell him an idea.

I called [catcher] Mickey Cochrane out and we talked for a moment.

"When you go back to the plate," I told Cochrane, "you tell Tolson my control is good."

That was to sell him on the idea that the ball would be over.

"When the ball comes over," I went on, "it'll be a fast one. Just as I deliver it, you yell *hit it!*"

Cochrane did that. When he wants to, he can be very convincing. Returning to the plate he walked by Tolson saying very seriously that my control was good, and when the ball came over he yelled "*Hit it!*" Tolson made a weak swing at the ball, missed by six inches, and the game was over.

The 1929 World Series ended up a runaway, with the Athletics winning in five games. But it wasn't as easy as it sounds. With the A's leading the Series 2–1, the Cubs jumped out to a seemingly insurmountable 8–0 edge in Game Four. But then, in the seventh inning, the A's started to come back. Al Simmons led off with a homer off Charlie Root, and the next four hitters all hit singles. After an out, another single brought in the run that made it 8–4.

Art Nehf came in to pitch for the Cubs. Mule Haas hit a liner to center field, which Hack Wilson let fly over his head. As the ball rolled to the wall, Haas motored around the bases for a three-run inside-the-park homer that brought the A's to within a single run.

The A's Jimmy Dykes was so excited by this that he slapped Connie Mack on the back, sending the slightly built manager flying onto a pile of bats. But all was forgiven a few moments later when Dykes hit a long double to drive in the last two runs of a stunning ten-run rally. When Lefty Grove came in to strike out four of the six batters he faced, the Athletics had their miraculous 10–8 victory and a 3–1 Series lead.

The Cubs, showing admirable (though snake-bit) fortitude, took a 2–0 lead behind Pat Malone into the bottom of the ninth of Game Five. Mule Haas' two-run home run tied the game, Al Simmons doubled with two outs, and then Bing Miller hit another double…and the Athletics were champions.

Said sportswriter Fred Lieb: "Connie's 1929 boys just didn't know how to lose."

onnie Mack was back in the Series again in 1930, calmly leading just as rough-and-tumble a group of Athletics as he had a year before. "Anything could happen in the clubhouse," star Jimmy Dykes told interviewer Donald Honig. "Shoes nailed to the floor. Sweat shirts tied into knots. Itching powder in your jockstrap. You're out there in front of thirty thousand people and dying to scratch… But on the ballfield, no fooling."

This year the Athletics met their match in the almost equally fiery St. Louis Cardinals. Led by George Watkins (.373), Frank Frisch (.346), and Chick Hafey (.336), the team also boasted take-no-prisoners pitchers Burleigh Grimes, Wild Bill Hallahan, and Jesse Haines.

1930

PHILADELPHIA ATHLETICS

4

ST. LOUIS CARDINALS

2

The Cardinals' irrepressible Pepper Martin, with Al Simmons at the 1931 World Series. "The greatest one-man show the baseball world has ever known," sportswriter Red Smith called Martin.

1930 1931

A TWO-YEAR PRIZEFIGHT

Thousands of fans lined the rooftops opposite Philadelphia's Shibe Park as the Series got underway. The tenor of the games was set right away, as the boos cascaded down on Cardinal starter Burleigh Grimes, who had earlier called the Athletics "a bunch of American League bushers," in the Philly newspapers.

Unfortunately, the quality of the early games didn't approach the rhetoric. Led by Mickey Cochrane's two home runs, the A's won the first two games easily behind Lefty Grove and George Earnshaw, only to see the Cardinals' Bill Hallahan and Jesse Haines win the next two, 5–0 and 3–1.

Game Five, at Sportsman's Park in St. Louis, was the turning point. Pitting Burleigh Grimes against George Earnshaw, the game was scoreless until the top of the ninth, when "I walked Cochrane on a 3–2 spitter with two out," Grimes said. "Geez, that pitch didn't miss by much. It was just a little tight. Then I threw Jimmie Foxx a curveball, and he knocked the concrete loose in the center-field bleachers. He hit it so hard I couldn't feel sorry for myself."

Lefty Grove, who'd come on in the eighth, shut down the Cardinals in the last of the ninth, and for all intents the Series was over. The A's, behind Earnshaw, cruised to a 7–1 victory in Game Six and their second consecutive World Championship.

The Cardinals and the Athletics were back for a rematch in 1931, but this was a different Cardinals team. The difference was Pepper Martin, "a plain-featured young man with a bristle of whiskers on a tanned and hawklike face—a young man who wears rumpled clothes and a broad-brimmed slouch hat," as Frank Graham described him.

No one could possibly have predicted that the World Series featuring Mickey Cochrane, Jimmie Foxx, Lefty Grove, Burleigh Grimes, and Frank Frisch would be dominated by Martin, a twenty-seven-year-old rookie out of Oklahoma. But it was. Observers marveled at the way

1931

ST. LOUIS
CARDINALS
4

PHILADELPHIA
ATHLETICS
3

Martin ran roughshod over the Athletics, batting .500 on twelve hits in twenty-four at bats, slugging four doubles and a home run and stealing five bases to boot. "This Pepper Martin is so fast," said Hearst columnist Bugs Baer, "that the first day in school, he stole the second grade."

Even with Martin's fireworks, the Series was a close, tense one, with neither team ever taking more than a one-game lead. Martin had three hits in Game One, but Lefty Grove pitched the A's to a 6–2 win. In Game Two, Martin, with two hits and two stolen bases, scored both runs in a 2–0 Cardinal win. He was back in Game Three, with two more hits and two more runs scored as the Cards won again, 5–2, behind Burleigh Grimes. Not letting a good thing go, Martin added two more hits in Game Four, but the A's George Earnshaw shut down the rest of the Cardinals, 3–0.

Game Five was Martin's glory: He had three hits in four at bats, with a home run and four RBI as Bill Hallahan tamed the A's 5–1. "There were seven wonders of the world before this World Series broke out and today there are nine," wrote Grantland Rice after Game Five. "The double wonder is Pepper Martin, who, after starring in the first four games of the Series, hit his real stride in the fifth today to step on past the Leaning Tower of Pisa, the Hanging Gardens of Babylon, and whatever wonders there are."

Walter Smith, a correspondent for the *St. Louis Star*, thought that Martin's exploits had broken the A's backs. "I am convinced that his thundering home run which featured his three hits as he led the Birds to a 5–1 victory in the fifth game whipt the Macks," Smith wrote. "They cracked visibly when the ball plopped into a customer's lap in the upper deck of the left-field stands."

If the A's cracked, they didn't fall to pieces in Game Six, which they won 8–1 behind Lefty Grove. But it was the Cardinals' and Burleigh Grimes' turn in Game Seven, a 4–2 victory saved by Wild Bill Hallahan, who came in to get the final out. Pepper Martin didn't star in this game, but he did add one more stolen base to his total and make a running catch to end the game with the tying runs on base—exclamation points to an extraordinary Series that brought Connie Mack's second and last dynasty to an end.

Even the taciturn Judge Landis was amazed by the rookie's exploits. "Young man," he told Martin, "if I could change places with one man in the world right now, that man would be you."

Replied Pepper: "It's all right with me, Judge. Just so long as we change salaries, too. My $4,500 for your $65,000.

Jimmie Foxx slamming the ball in Game Four of the 1930 Series. He gripped the bat, he said, "as if I wanted to leave my fingerprints on the wood."

The Cardinals' ornery headhunter Burleigh Grimes, pitching star of the '31 Series. "I was a real bastard when I played," he boasted.

METROPOLITAN
STUDIOS
ST. LOUIS

Some World Series sweeps are quickly and purposely forgotten. Sports fans and writers alike avert their eyes, as if from a grisly car accident, and move on. Maybe the next year will be better, they think. It can't be worse.

The problem with the Yankees' appearances in the World Series from the late 1920s through the 1930s is that the Bronx Bombers usually rolled over whoever was in their path. It's not much fun watching a dominant team crush the opposition—and not much fun writing about it, either.

Luckily, the 1932 Series between the Yankees and the Chicago Cubs came equipped with its very own (and highly entertaining) back story: the two teams loathed each other. At the center of the storm was Mark Koenig, shortstop on the great 1927–28 Yankee teams. After suffering from vision problems, Koenig had moved to the Tigers and then to the Pacific Coast League, a strong minor league.

Needing a shortstop for the 1932 stretch run, the Cubs signed Koenig, who proceeded to hit .353 and help the Cubs edge out the Pirates for the N.L. crown. But when the Cubs players voted World Series shares—the vote taking place before the Series started—they allotted Koenig only half a share.

According to Yankee shortstop Frank Crosetti, the Yankees were infuriated by what they saw as the Cubs' cheapness towards an old teammate. Babe Ruth, renowned for his generosity, was particularly incensed. "Did that burn the Babe!" Crosetti told Richard Lally in *Bombers*. "Not just because Mark was his friend, but because it went against his nature."

When the two teams met in the Series, Ruth wasted no time letting the Cubs know how he felt. "Babe would really razz them good," recalled Crosetti. "Called them cheapskates, pennypinchers, tightwads."

No one thought the nondescript Cubs could beat the Ruth- and Gehrig-led Yankees on the field, but they matched up pretty well at razzing. Led by notoriously hotheaded Burleigh Grimes, Guy Bush, Charlie Root, and others, the Cubs gave as good as they got. They commented loudly on the size of Ruth's ever-expanding belly ("Someone in their dugout offered to hitch a wagon to him," said Crosetti) and attacked him as personally as they could in other ways as well.

The Series was a mismatch from the start. In Game One, at Yankee Stadium, the Bombers cruised to a 12–6 victory. Game Two was a bit closer, but never in doubt, as Lefty Gomez pitched the Yankees to a 5–2 win.

When the teams moved to Chicago's Wrigley Field, emotions came to a boil. Ruth slugged a three-run homer off Charlie Root in the first inning of Game Three, but the Cubs had tied it 4–4 when the Babe came to bat in the fifth. The fans, seeing a comeback victory in the works, were howling.

What happened next is probably the most famous—and most disputed—moment in World Series history. Did Ruth, just before slugging his second home run off Root, point to a spot in the bleachers, or didn't he?

Reading through accounts of that moment remains peerlessly entertaining. Almost everything about the play has

1932

THE BABE IN CLOVER

Mark Koenig, Cubs shortstop in 1932—and an essential part of one of the most entertaining World Series moments of all time.

1932

NEW YORK YANKEES

4

CHICAGO CUBS

0

been argued, including where the ball landed. But by picking through dozens of accounts it is possible to develop a sense of what really happened. So here, in the spirit of a relay race, is a report from those who were there on that October Saturday in Chicago:

As the Babe walked up to the plate, "the Cubs' bench jockeys came out of the dugout to shout at Ruth," wrote Edward Burns in the *Chicago Tribune*. "And Ruth shouted right back."

"[A] concerted shout of derision broke in the stands," added Richards Vidmer in the *New York Herald Tribune*. "There was a bellowing of boos, hisses, and jeers…. But Ruth grinned in the face of the hostile greeting. He laughed back at the Cubs and took his place, supremely confident."

Root threw a pitch: Strike one! "The Babe held up his index finger and showed it to sundry and all," filled in Paul Gallico in the *New York Daily News*. "The implications were plain. It was the universal language that everyone understands—pantomime."

"Babe held up one finger as if to say, 'That's only one, though. Just wait,'" said Vidmer.

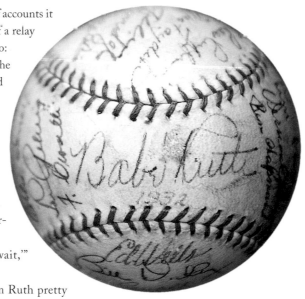

"Meet Babe Ruth's bat and see the world!" A signed ball from the notorious 1932 Series.

Root threw two balls, and then another called strike. "Our bench is on Ruth pretty heavy, with [Guy] Bush leading the tirading," recalled Cubs pitcher Burleigh Grimes. "After the second strike Bush yells, 'Now, you big ape, what are you going to do now?' So Babe holds up his finger as if to say, 'I've got the big one left.'"

"Ruth waved his hand across the plate toward the Cub bench," said Cubs catcher Gabby Hartnett. "At the same time he said—and I think only the umpire and myself heard him—'it only takes one to hit it.'"

"I have a distinct memory that once he pointed the bat at Bush who stood on the top step on the dugout," added columnist Joe Williams.

"The gestures were meant for Bush," agreed Lou Gehrig. "Ruth was going to foul one into the dugout, but when the pitch came up, big and fat, he belted it."

"There was a resounding report like the explosion of a gun," described Vidmer.

"BABE WAS LIKE A LITTLE KID RUNNING AROUND THE BASES."

"You've seen golf balls, how they take off, well that ball just went straight out and through a tree outside the ball park in center field," said Joe Sewell, Yankee third baseman. "The tree was loaded with youngsters up there watching the game, and as the ball went through the tree all those kids evaporated. They had all gone after the ball."

"Ruth resumed his oratory the minute he threw down his bat," wrote Edward Burns. "He bellowed every foot of the way around the bases, accompanying decisive roarings with wild and eloquent gesticulations."

"When Ruth rounded third base, cabbages and oranges and apples and all kinds of mess were thrown out there, and the grounds crew had to come and clean it up," said Joe Sewell.

"Babe was like a little kid running around the bases," added Ruth's teammate Frank Crosetti. "When he got into the dugout, he said, 'If anyone ever asks me what my greatest moment was, this is it!'"

So, by most accounts, that's what happened: great theater, lots of gestures from Ruth, but no definitive finger pointing at the distant bleachers.

And Ruth as much as admitted it…at least at first, before he began to enjoy the story and milk it for maximum appeal. In a 1933 radio interview, the Babe said, "Only a damn fool would do a thing like that. Root would have stuck the ball in my ear. And besides, I never knew anyone who could tell you ahead of time where he was going to hit a baseball."

The Babe's outsize personality was so overwhelming that few noticed Lou Gehrig's three home runs, 8 RBI, and .529 batting average in the four-game sweep.

Ruth's called shot, the way it didn't happen.

But the pressure to claim credit for having pointed—or at least not to deny it—grew to be more than the attention-loving Babe could resist. "I have met at least 850,000 people who saw that game," he said later. "Yeah, they were all there. Saw me do it. Big ball park in Chicago." Why disappoint those 850,000, and millions more beside?

The remainder of the 1932 World Series was little more than an afterthought. Lou Gehrig followed Ruth's blast with a home run of his own (his second of the game), and the Yankees went on to win, 7–5. In Game Four, they fell behind 4–1, then broke a 5–5 tie with eight runs in the last three innings for a crushing 13–6 win behind Tony Lazzeri's two homers. Yankee manager Joe McCarthy had his first-ever World Series championship, and Babe Ruth had his last.

While most of the memories of the 1932 Series remain big and noisy and garish (much like the Babe himself), the most telling of all comes from Yankee shortstop Frank Crosetti. "It was my first Series and I was only twenty-two years old. We were riding back to the Edgewater Beach hotel in Chicago on a chartered bus," he told Grantland Rice in 1949. "The players were singing 'On the Sidewalks of New York' and McCarthy would say 'Sing it again.' That was a thrill. In the pit of my stomach there was that feeling of excitement, a feeling that you cannot explain, a feeling of emptiness, a feeling of gladness, call it what you may."

For Carl Hubbell, just getting to the major leagues was a triumph. From the time he was a young prospect in the mid-1920s, Hubbell was looked upon with suspicion by coaches, scouts, and other players because he threw a bizarre pitch: the screwball, released with a sudden twist of the wrist and arm toward the body. The pitch, which spun and broke in the opposite direction of a typical curve, befuddled batters, but the stresses it placed on a pitcher's arm bothered the experts.

Even the young Hubbell knew that he had a mountain to climb just to get a fair shot to show his stuff with a major-league team. "The screwball's an unnatural pitch," he admitted. "Nature never intended a man to turn his hand like that throwing rocks at a bear."

Despite having a tremendous year throwing the screwball for a minor-league team in 1925, Hubbell never pitched a single inning for the big-league club in three years with the Detroit Tigers organization. Packed off to Beaumont in the Texas League—"I should have had the word 'reject' written over my uniform," he said—the twenty-five-year-old Hubbell finally caught a break.

1933

ONE FOR THE
MEALTICKET

"THE SCREWBALL'S AN UNNATURAL PITCH," HE ADMITTED. "NATURE NEVER INTENDED A MAN TO TURN HIS HAND LIKE THAT THROWING ROCKS AT A BEAR."

Dick Kinsella, a part-time scout for the Giants, was killing some time attending a Beaumont game when he found himself watching in astonishment as Hubbell pitched an eleven-inning masterpiece to defeat hot prospect Bill Hallahan. Kinsella hurried to the phone to call Giants' manager John McGraw, "and, by God, within about three or four days I was on my way to join the Giants," Hubbell marveled.

Once he made the Giants, Hubbell never left. He was a strong, steady pitcher, winning more than he lost every year, but he didn't come into his own until 1933, when he led the National League in wins (23), shutouts (10), innings pitched (308), and ERA (1.66).

So much for the theory that throwing the screwball would ruin his arm.

Hubbell's spectacular season helped carry the Giants to their first pennant since 1924—and their first ever with someone other than John McGraw as manager. An exhausted McGraw had retired after the 1932 season, with first baseman Bill Terry taking over as manager.

In the 1933 Series, Terry, Hubbell and such other Giant stars as slugging Mel Ott and pitcher Hal Schumacher faced the Washington Senators, their 1924 Series opponents. The Senators' Heinie Manush batted .336, player-manager Joe Cronin hit .309 with 45 doubles, and both General Crowder and Earl Whitehill won more than twenty games. The line-ups seemed to promise an intriguing, evenly matched World Series.

Unfortunately, it was not to be. This was Carl Hubbell's Series, with a little help from his supporting cast. Game One was typical: pitching against Lefty Stewart, the Mealticket

1933

NEW YORK
GIANTS
4

WASHINGTON
SENATORS
1

struck out ten and gave up just two unearned runs, Mel Ott had a home run as one of his four hits, and the Giants cruised
to an easy 4–2 win at the Polo Grounds.

The Senators' General Crowder gave up six runs in the sixth inning of Game Two to lose, 6–1. Having won the
first two games, the Giants were able to shrug off a 5–0 Game Three defeat, knowing that the Mealticket was slated to
pitch Game Four.

Hubbell didn't disappoint, but his pitching competition (Monte Weaver) was just as tough. Bill Terry hit a fourth-
inning home run to give the Giants a 1–0 lead, but the Senators tied the game on an unearned run in the seventh. Then
the innings rolled on, with no scoring until the top of the eleventh, when a single by the Giants' Blondy Ryan drove in
Travis Jackson with the go-ahead run.

In the bottom of the inning, Hubbell got into a jam, putting men on first and third with one out. But the pitcher
got Cliff Bolton to hit a sharp ground ball to shortstop Blondy Ryan. Easy double play; game over.

Game Five was another tense one. A three-run home run by the Senators' Fred Schulte tied the game at 3–3 in the
sixth inning, and again no one scored until extra innings, with the two relievers—the Giants' forty-three-year-old Dolf
Luque and the Senators' Jack Russell—shutting down the hitters.

In the top of the tenth Mel Ott hit a long fly ball that bounced off Schulte's glove deep in right-center and hopped
over the wall. The play was originally called a ground-rule double, but then changed to a home run—the home run that
won the Series, as Luque retired the Senators in the bottom of the inning.

The Giants had the championship, and Hubbell—a "reject" just a handful of years earlier—had his share
of baseball immortality.

President Franklin D. Roosevelt throws
out the first ball before the third game of
the Series on October 6, 1933. He
brought good luck to the Senators, who
won, 4–0.

Frustration, thy name is Tiger. In 1934, the Tigers had one of the greatest teams of what many think of as baseball's "golden age." Their powerful line-up included such future Hall of Famers as slugger Hank Greenberg, slick second baseman Charlie Gehringer, speedy outfielder Goose Goslin, and player-manager Mickey Cochrane, one of the greatest catchers of all time. They won 101 games in 1934, one of the best records of the era.

Yet, among all but baseball historians, avid fans, and residents of Detroit, the Tigers' burning-bright 1934 season has all but been forgotten. Why?

Because of one great pitcher's big mouth, that's why.

It is absolutely impossible to overstate the impact that Jerome Herman "Dizzy" Dean had on baseball's public relations in the

1934
1935

THE POWER
OF GAB

Detroit's stoical Schoolboy Rowe flanked by the Dean boys, Paul and Dizzy, just before Game Two. Rowe went on to pitch all twelve innings of the Tigers' 3–2 win. "He is never flustered," H. G. Salsinger wrote of Rowe. "He has proved an ideal pitcher in the crisis."

1930s. Even as a nineteen-year-old rookie in 1930, Dean was bursting with self-confidence, and not afraid to tell everyone about it. "Gee, I'll bet a lot of St. Louis people wish I was pitching every game," he told *The Sporting News*, after pitching a grand total of one game with the Cards. "I don't recall seeing any better than myself…. Don't think though that I'm bragging about all this. I'm just lettin' you in on some inside facts. Oh yeah, next year I'm going to be known as 'The Great Dean.'"

Of course, no one would have listened if Dean hadn't been able to back up his flood of words. He won eighteen games as a twenty-year-old in 1932, twenty games in 1933, and an astonishing thirty games in 1934, leading the Cardinals to a tight pennant victory over the defending champion New York Giants.

1934

ST. LOUIS
CARDINALS

4

DETROIT
TIGERS

3

Dizzy Dean wasn't the only star on the '34 Cardinals, of course. Nor was he the only talkative, brazen smart-aleck on the team. Any club featuring Pepper Martin, Frankie Frisch, Dazzy Vance, Dizzy's brother Paul, Joe "Ducky" Medwick, and a mouthy young shortstop named Leo Durocher had personality to spare.

But it was Dizzy who set the tone as the 1934 Series began, driving his teammates and the Tigers nuts alike with his chatter. "What makes you so white?" he asked Hank Greenberg, who'd merely hit .339 with 63 doubles, 26 home runs, and 139 RBI during the regular season. "Boy, you're shaking like a leaf. I get it; you done heard that Ol' Diz was goin' to pitch."

In Game One, the Great Dean put his money where his mouth was, pitching the Cardinals to an easy 8–3 win. Greenberg was able to control his tremors just long enough to slug a home run, but it wasn't enough.

In Game Two, the Cards' Wild Bill Hallahan matched up against the Tigers' star pitcher, Lynwood "Schoolboy" Rowe, a twenty-four-game winner in 1934. Through no fault of his own, Rowe epitomized the difference between the Tigers and the Cardinals in the 1934 Series. He was, in the words of the *Detroit News*' H. G. Salsinger, "very big and very phlegmatic...cold and calculating, as near to normal as you

"BOY, YOU'RE SHAKING LIKE A LEAF. I GET IT; YOU DONE HEARD THAT OL' DIZ WAS GOIN' TO PITCH."

will find a human, strictly unemotional, totally composed." Who are you going to interview, this man or the Diz?

Rowe might not have given a good interview, but his arm talked up a storm in Game Two. After the Cards grabbed a 2–0 lead after three innings, Rowe allowed only one hit the rest of the way, holding the Cardinals scoreless as the Tigers tied the game off Hallahan in the bottom of the ninth and won it on a Goose Goslin single in the twelfth.

Paul kept up with his big brother when he won Game Three, 4–1. But the Tigers took Game Four, 10–4, behind Elden Auker.

Neither Dean pitched that day, but Dizzy still made the news in what must be the most famous pinch-running moment in baseball history. Having convinced Manager Frisch to let him pinch run, Dizzy managed to get himself clocked on the noggin by a relay throw from second to first on a double-play grounder.

The ball, wrote Grantland Rice, "struck Dizzy Dean squarely on the head with such terrific force that it bounced thirty feet in the air and more than 100 feet away into Hank Greenberg's glove in short right field. The impact of the ball and glove sounded like the backfire of an automobile."

Dean fell to the ground like he'd been shot, and was carried off the field by his worried teammates. Sportswriter Tom Meany, writing in his book *Mostly Baseball*, reported:

Dashing to the clubhouse for information about the extent of Dean's injuries, I met [Dizzy's brother] Paul, who had been one of the stretcher-bearers. The report I got should have proved to me then and there that Dizzy was predestined to become a broadcaster. He was made for TV even before TV had been invented.

"Was Diz knocked out? Has he regained consciousness?" I asked Paul.

"He warn't unconscious at all," said Paul. "He talked all the time we carried him off the field."

"What was he saying?"

"He wasn't *saying* anything," explained Paul. "He was jes' talking."

Dizzy was well enough to pitch Game Five, but Detroit's Tommy Bridges was better, posting a 3–1 win that put the Tigers up 3–2 in the Series. Still, Dean didn't seem too worried. "Paul'll take them in the next one, and I'll set 'em back on their cans in the seventh game," he predicted.

Paul did his part in Game Six, riding three hits by shortstop Leo Durocher to a tight 4–3 decision over Schoolboy Rowe. That knotted up the Series at three games apiece and kept alive one of Dizzy's prophecies: that he and Paul would win all four games the Cardinals needed.

At first, though, Frankie Frisch hesitated to let Dizzy pitch Game Seven on just one day's rest, and considered pitching Bill Hallahan instead. Dizzy was outraged. "You gotta pitch me 'cause I'm the greatest pitcher you got," he pointed out. "Listen, Frankie. You string along with Ol' Diz and he'll make a great manager out of you."

Dizzy was right, as usual. He got the start in Game Seven against Elden Auker. The Cardinals scored seven runs in the third inning off Auker and three relievers—with Dean getting two hits in the inning!—on their way to an 11–0 rout and the 1934 World Championship.

1935

DETROIT TIGERS

4

CHICAGO CUBS

2

If ever a city needed a World Series victory, it was Detroit in 1935. Filled with frustration after having been defeated by the Cardinals in 1934, Detroit players and fans alike were eager for another chance. They won the A.L. pennant and found themselves facing the surprising Chicago Cubs. As a result, the Series pitted against each other two teams who had lost a combined nine World Series since 1907. In this case, though, one team had all the intensity.

With their simmering resentment spurring on Mickey Cochrane, Elden Auker, Schoolboy Rowe, and other holdover stars, the Tigers raced out to a three games to one Series lead. After a brief detour (a loss in Game Five), they went on to win Game Six at Detroit's Navin Field, 4–3, as Goose Goslin drove in Cochrane with a single in the bottom of the ninth to give the Tigers their first World Series title.

"It was something to see—Mickey Cochrane stabbing his spikes into the plate with the winning run," wrote Paul Gallico of the game's final moments, "and then going mad, like a young colt, leaping and cavorting about, shaking his bare, dark head."

The fans at Navin Field went mad as well. "That jungle-throated roar from 48,000 human throats as Goslin singled and Cochrane scored is one of the reverberations I won't forget," said Grantland Rice. "It was the pent-up vocal outbreak of nearly fifty years and it exploded with the suppressed power of nitroglycerine when the big moment came."

All of Detroit followed suit that night. The 1936 *Reach Guide* tried to do justice to the city's celebration, a rampage of emotions kept bottled up too long:

> There was a rush to the central part of the city. Pedestrians blew tin horns and motorists honked those on their cars as they snailed through the downtown streets almost hopelessly clogged with the product that has earned Detroit worldwide fame….
>
> Toward midnight the din increased instead of abating. The discharge of firearms and bombs, the staccato barks of backfiring cars and the shrieks of sirens and blasts of horns kept on a continuous roar until early in the morning. Guests of downtown hotels could not sleep until three hours after midnight.
>
> Even machine guns were rigged up in office windows to add to the noise. Natives of Detroit admitted that the noise and clamor were greater than on Armistice night.
>
> When merrymakers through sheer exhaustion finally decided it was time for bed, the city looked as if a cyclone had hit it. All the next day, the whitewings were employed cleaning up the litter.
>
> There never had been a night like that in Detroit, because the gallant victory of the Tigers in the supreme test of America's national sport had stirred the hearts of Detroiters more than ever before.

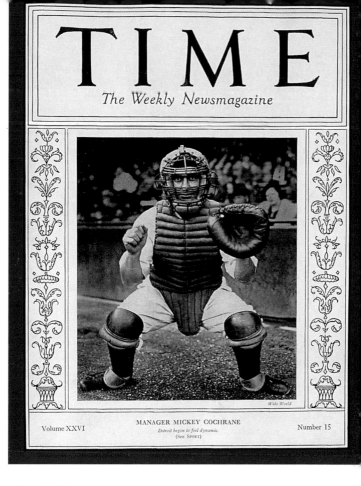

TIME
The Weekly Newsmagazine

Volume XXVI **MANAGER MICKEY COCHRANE** Number 15
Detroit began to feel dynamic.
(See SPORT)

Wide World

The Tigers' fiery Mickey Cochrane helped lead Detroit to its first World Series championship in 1935.

"IT WAS THE PENT-UP VOCAL OUTBREAK OF NEARLY FIFTY YEARS AND IT EXPLODED WITH THE SUPPRESSED POWER OF NITROGLYCERINE WHEN THE BIG MOMENT CAME."

The 1933–35 seasons were frustrating for the New York Yankees. Babe Ruth faded, leaving the team after the 1934 season, but the Yanks still had Lou Gehrig in his prime and such other stars as Tony Lazzeri, Bill Dickey, Lefty Gomez, and Red Ruffing. They posted records of 91–59, 94–60, and 89–60—good, but only enough for second place each season. Maybe the dominant Yankee team of 1932 was an anomaly, a flash in the pan.

In 1936, though, the Yankees put any such suspicions to rest. Featuring a highly touted rookie named Joe DiMaggio, they went 102–51, finishing a whopping 19½ games ahead of second-place Detroit. Their opponent in the World Series: their crosstown rivals, the New York Giants.

On paper, the Giants had only two true stars: Mel Ott, in his eleventh year but still only twenty-seven, and Carl Hubbell, coming off a 26–6 season. But these two were enough in Game One of the Series, as Ott went 2 for 2 and Hubbell pitched a complete game 6–1 victory. "Carl Hubbell," said Casey Stengel, then manager of the Brooklyn Dodgers, "is to the Giants what an onion is to a hamburger."

Unfortunately, the Giants could only pitch their onion once every four days, and in Game Two the Yankees turned Giant pitcher Hal Schumacher and four relievers into chopped meat in an 18–4 thrashing. This was the game in which Joe DiMaggio had his coming-out party as a budding superstar, with three hits, two runs scored, 2 RBI, and flashy defense in center field.

DiMaggio himself had a special memory of that game. "I got the last out by running for a ball Hank Lieber hit off Lefty Gomez," he told Ed Fitzgerald in 1952. "When I finally collared it, I was only a couple of steps away from the staircase leading up to the clubhouse. President Roosevelt had come to the game with Jim Farley, who was the Postmaster General then, and they made an announcement over the loudspeaker that no one should leave until the President was driven out. I wasn't sure if they meant the ballplayers or not but I wasn't taking any chances. I stood stock still, the ball still in my hand, while the car headed out the center-field gate. Just as they passed in front of me, the President gave me that big grin of his and waved at me. I gave him a kind of salute back and then I turned and ran up the stairs. That was quite a day for a kid from San Francisco."

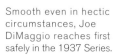

Smooth even in hectic circumstances, Joe DiMaggio reaches first safely in the 1937 Series.

A batboy and Bill Dickey (#8) greet Lou Gehrig after Gehrig's Game Three homer in the 1936 Series.

In Game Three, the Yankees' Bump Hadley and Pat Malone outdueled Freddie Fitzsimmons, 2–1, with one of the runs coming on a home run by Lou Gehrig. Just this one game, and a 2–1 Series lead, was enough to cause sportswriter Charles Segar in the *New York Sunday Mirror* to proclaim, "It was a Yankee season. It looks like a Yankee Series." The reaction from fellow writer Ken Smith: "Bah!"

Despite Smith's sparkling repartee, Segar was right. The Series was over as soon as the Yankees beat Hubbell in Game Four. Though the Giants' Hal Schumacher pitched the team to a gutty, ten-inning win in Game Five, no one was surprised when the Yankee hitters erupted for a Game Six 13–5 triumph and the Series title. The Bombers had outscored the Giants 43–23 in the six games.

Gehrig had a fine Series, with two home runs and 7 RBI, but the rookie DiMaggio was already beginning to grab the attention of onlookers. "Already baseball men accept the loose-limbed Italian as the best center-fielder in baseball, and he has been in the league only one year," wrote Joe Williams.

1936

NEW YORK
YANKEES
4

NEW YORK
GIANTS
2

1937

NEW YORK
YANKEES
4

NEW YORK
GIANTS
1

The same two teams faced each other in the 1937 Series. Everyone—including, it seemed, the Giants—thought the Yankees were prohibitive favorites going in. Even with Carl Hubbell pitching Game One, the Giants barely put up a fight, losing the first three games by a combined score of 21–3. The Yankees had time to focus on trivial matters, like the two walks their weak-hitting pitcher Lefty Gomez received in the Bombers' seven-run sixth inning in Game One. ("They sure treated me with respect," Gomez said after the game. "I guess those Giants know a real hitter when they see one.")

Hubbell and the Giants gained a bit of respect by winning Game Four, but Gomez bested Cliff Melton in Game Five for the championship. It was, in truth, one of the least scintillating Series of all time, and grumpy sportswriters covering it minced no words. "The Yankees in this series can be called great only by comparison," groused Rud Rennie. "The Giants were so bad they made the Yankees look good."

Unfortunately, despite a couple of close games, the 1938 Series was even worse. The Cubs, led by Bill Lee (twenty-two wins) and Stan Hack (.320), triumphed over Pittsburgh in a superb pennant race to become N.L. champs, but no one thought they had much chance against the Yankees, who'd cruised to the A.L. flag with ninety-nine wins.

It was true: this was no year for Cinderella, as the Yankees won in four straight games. What distinguished this otherwise forgettable Series was the sense of the inexorability of baseball mortality. How quickly time passes in the compressed horizon of a baseball career!

In Game Two, the Cubs wheeled out Dizzy Dean, once but no longer one of the most dominant pitchers in the league. Famously, Dean had broken a toe in the 1937 All Star game, and had ruined his arm trying to come back too quickly. He was still only twenty-eight years old when he was traded from the Cardinals to the Cubs before the 1938 season, but to the Yankees he looked like an old, old pitcher.

CHARLIE RUFFING

BIG LEAGUE CHEWING GUM

"We'd heard he lost his fastball but that sounded like an exaggeration," recalled Joe DiMaggio. "It was hard to picture Dean without that hard one. So all during the game we tended to keep looking for it up there. But it didn't come…mostly it was just a slow curve and control stuff."

Dean got away with slop for much of the game, but in the late innings the Yankees started to time his slow pitches better. Frank Crosetti and then DiMaggio tagged him for home runs, driving him from the game. "What a hand he got from the crowd!" DiMaggio said—the applause of a crowd for a once-great pitcher nearing the end of the line.

It was Red Ruffing's turn to manhandle the opposition in 1938, winning two games of the Yanks' four-game sweep. Ruffing, said writer Richards Vidmer, "laughingly toyed with the Cubs."

A familiar sight: the Yankees' Red Rolfe scoring as Joe DiMaggio looks on…and the Yankees move to another dominating Series victory.

VERNON "LEFTY" GOMEZ
NEW YORK YANKEES

There was even a more ominous foreboding over the 1938 Series. Lou Gehrig batted .286, but all four of his hits were singles, and it was clear that this wasn't the same Gehrig who'd slugged his way through five previous Series. Something was wrong…seriously wrong.

"Those four hits Lou got against us in that World Series had no oomph," the Cubs' Phil Cavarretta told Richard Lally in *Bombers*. "He didn't look quite right in the field and on the base paths. And whenever he took a lead, he wobbled. I kept looking at him to see what was wrong."

What was wrong, of course, was that Gehrig was already suffering from the progressive effects of amyotrophic lateral sclerosis, the disease that would bring his career to a halt early the next year, and end his life in 1941. Yankee fans would never have guessed as the 1938 Series drew to a close with an 8–3 Game Four win behind Red Ruffing, but they'd seen nearly the last of the great Lou Gehrig, a player everyone thought would somehow live forever.

The garrulous Lefty Gomez won five games in the four Series. The secret of his success: "I talk 'em out of hits."

"WHEN A TEAM SWEEPS YOU, IT'S LIKE YOU WEREN'T EVEN THERE. WHAT A NIGHTMARE!"

1939

NEW YORK YANKEES
4

CINCINNATI REDS
0

Minus Gehrig, the Yankees were back once again in 1939, having won 106 games to blast away the competition. For a change of pace, their N.L. opposition was the Cincinnati Reds, who had beaten out St. Louis in a tough pennant race.

This Series was over almost as soon as it began. All that the Reds had going for them were some superb pitchers, including Bucky Walters (twenty-seven wins) and Paul Derringer (twenty-five wins). When Red Ruffing bested Derringer in Game One, and Monte Pearson defeated Walters the next day, it was obvious that this would be another short Series.

Lefty Gomez lasted only one inning in Game Three, but Bump Hadley pitched eight strong innings and the Yankees got two home runs from Charlie Keller and one each from DiMaggio and Bill Dickey for a 7–3 win. Then, in Game Four, the Yankees scored two in the ninth to tie and three in tenth to win, sweep, and send everyone home.

"Four straight, four straight the Yankees beat us that World Series," Reds' second baseman Lonnie Frey told Richard Lally years later, the loss still bitter in his mind. "When a team sweeps you, it's like you weren't even there. What a nightmare!"

Except for Yankee rooters, fans everywhere could only say the same. With all due respect to the four-time champions, it was time for a more competitive World Series.

10 WORST SERIES
NO. 10
1939

ON BEING SWEPT

WHAT'S IT LIKE TO FACE A TEAM THAT IS CLEARLY SUPERIOR TO YOURS?

WHAT'S IT LIKE TO GO HOME FOUR GAMES LATER, KNOWING THAT YOU'LL BE ADDED

TO THE SHORT LIST OF TEAMS THAT DIDN'T END UP WINNING A SINGLE GAME?

"Gee! They're big guys."
   —Pittsburgh star Paul Waner, looking upon Babe Ruth, Lou Gehrig and the rest of the 1927 Yankee "Murderer's Row," who went on to sweep the Pirates in the Series.

"Out in right field, I was stunned. And that instant, as the run that beat us crossed the plate, it suddenly struck me that I'd actually played in a World Series. It's an odd thing, isn't it? I didn't think, 'It's all over and we lost.'"
      "What I thought was, 'Gee, I've just played in a World Series!'"
   —Paul Waner, after the Pirates were swept. From *The Glory of Their Times*.

"Spirit. Team Spirit. It is something you cannot buy and cannot learn. It is infectious, like a tonic. You don't know where it comes from when you have it and you don't know where it goes when you lose it. The Braves had that kind of spirit this year."
   —Philadelphia A's pitcher Chief Bender, after the A's were swept in 1914 by the "Miracle" Boston Braves.

"Four straight, four straight the Yankees beat us that World Series! When a team sweeps you, it's like you weren't even there. What a nightmare!"
   —Cincinnati infielder Lonnie Frey, bemoaning the Reds' 1939 sweep at the hands of the Yankees.

"It is a devastating way to lose, but when you score only two runs in four games and are shut out the last thirty-three innings, all you can do is go away and come to play another day.
      "In our case that other day would have to wait until the next year. And once again we were committed to a tour of Japan, a five-week jaunt that none of us looked forward to, especially after being skunked.
      "One of the writers asked me what I was going to say at all those press conferences in Japan about losing the Series in four straight.
      "' I'm going to tell them I can't understand what they're saying.'"
   —Los Angeles Manager Walt Alston, after his Dodgers were swept by the Baltimore Orioles in 1966.
   From *A Year at a Time*.

"I was so emotionally drained that my wife and I checked into the Statler Hotel in downtown Cleveland after the fourth game…and I slept for thirty-six hours, just tried to sleep it off. Oh, it was a horrible experience."
   —Cleveland third baseman Al Rosen, after the heavily favored Indians were swept by the New York Giants in 1954.

Slow misery for Manager Bruce Bochy and the Padres, on their way to being swept by the Yankees in 1998.

ooray! That was the reaction worldwide—except in parts of New York—as the Detroit Tigers survived a tense pennant chase to edge out the Cleveland Indians and the imperial Yankees and capture the American League crown. At last a World Series that wouldn't involve the hated Bronx Bombers running roughshod over some poor pretender from the N.L.

Facing the Tigers in the 1940 Series were the Cincinnati Reds, trounced by the Yankees in 1939. The Reds had bounced back by going 100–53 and trampling the National League behind terrific defense, stalwart pitching by Bucky Walters, Paul Derringer, and others, and timely slugging from massive catcher Ernie Lombardi and first baseman Frank McCormick.

On the surface, it had been a great year for the Reds. But dark shadows had gathered in August, when backup catcher Willard Hershberger committed suicide after holding himself responsible for several tough Reds losses. Then, in September, fiery shortstop Billy Myers, consumed with personal problems, jumped the team. Though Myers eventually came back, he was never the same.

Add to these woes disabling injuries to Ernie Lombardi and second baseman Lonnie Frey, and the Reds staggered into the World Series a wounded team, and no good bet to end the American League's streak of five consecutive World Series titles. The Tigers, by contrast, were healthy, with sluggers Hank Greenberg and Rudy York leading the way and Bobo Newsom (21–3) and Schoolboy Rowe (16–3) heading the pitching staff.

Game One pitted two of the majors' most notorious and entertaining characters, Newsom and Derringer, against each other. Derringer "loved good food and good whiskey," recalled his teammate, third baseman Bill Werber. Meanwhile, the round, noisy Newsom was "a bluff of a man, big and beefy, a buffalo out there," said Detroit sportswriter Joe Falls. "Or a rhinoceros. A wounded rhinoceros. He would snort and grunt and sweat and strain on every pitch."

The grunting Newsom had his best stuff in Game One. While he blew the ball past the unprepared Reds hitters, Derringer was driven from the game in the second inning as the Tigers cruised to an easy 7–2 win.

But the darkness that seemed to gather over this Series from the start now spread to include the Tigers as well. Instead of lauding Newsom's great pitching, the headlines the next day focused on something far more bitter: the sudden death of his father, Henry, after watching the game.

The Reds pounded Rowe in Game Two, with unsung left fielder Jimmy Ripple slamming a home run in a 5–3 win. The Tigers took Game Three, 7–4, but the Reds rode Paul Derringer's strong pitching to win Game Four, 5–2, and knot the Series 2–2.

Amazingly, there was Newsom on the mound again in Game Five. He pitched with uncharacteristic fierceness to hold the Reds to three hits while Hank Greenberg and the other Tigers slammed four Reds pitchers for an 8–0 win. But then the Reds' Bucky Walters pitched a five-hitter and hit a home run as the Reds won Game Six easily, 5–0.

1940

CINCINNATI REDS

4

DETROIT TIGERS

3

How could the hitters even see the ball? Paul Derringer, Cincinnati ace in the 1940 Series

Who else could pitch Game Seven for the Tigers but Newsom, on just one day's rest? And who else could be his opponent but Paul Derringer? And how could the game have turned out to be anything but a nail-biting pitchers' duel?

The Tigers scored an unearned run in the third to take a 1–0 lead. After that, grunting and sweating in the heat of Cincinnati's Crosley Field, Newsom struggled to hold the Reds scoreless. He succeeded until the seventh, when the Series was won and lost.

Frank McCormick began the Reds' rally with a double off the wall in left field. The next hitter, Jimmy Ripple, then hit a ball off the top of the right-field screen, just missing a home run. What happened next remains one of the most controversial moments in World Series history.

In his last Series appearance before heading overseas for World War II, Hank Greenberg batted .357— though in a losing cause.

The ball bounced to right fielder Bruce Campbell, who turned and threw it to shortstop Dick Bartell. Bartell got the ball when the slow-footed McCormick had barely made it past third base, but hesitated, one agonizing moment after another, before throwing home.

In his 1987 autobiography, Bartell recalls: "Everybody says they were all yelling, 'Home! Home!' at me—Gehringer, Newhouser out in the bullpen. The crowd was screaming—we're in Cincinnati, remember—and I don't hear any of them. I'm standing with my back to the infield with the ball in my hand for what I guess must have seemed like a day and a half to everybody else…. By the time I did turn around McCormick still hadn't scored. He must have gone by way of left field or stopped in the dugout for a drink on the way or something. But it was clearly too late to get him by then."

Backup catcher Jimmy Wilson followed with a sacrifice bunt, and Billy Myers' sacrifice fly then brought in Ripple to give the Reds a 2–1 lead. Derringer slammed the door on the Tigers, and somehow the Reds had come out on top. It was their first World Series victory since 1919—and their first untainted Series victory ever.

In the 1941 World Series, the Brooklyn Dodgers batted a collective .182. Their hitters—Dolph Camilli, Pete Reiser, and Ducky Medwick among them—combined for a single home run and 11 RBI. Kirby Higbe, who'd won twenty-two games during the regular season, lasted less than four innings in his single start and ended the Series with a 7.36 ERA. Future Hall of Famer Pee Wee Reese made three errors.

So who was the goat of the Series? Catcher Mickey Owen, of course.

World Series tend to shrink down to a single memorable moment as time passes, but never has the single chosen moment of a Series been less fair, more vindictive, than the missed third strike that doomed Owen to eternal notoriety on October 5, 1941.

1941

MICKEY OWEN'S NIGHTMARE

Riding great seasons from Camilli, Reiser, Higbe, and Whit Wyatt, Brooklyn won 100 games to get to its first Series in more than twenty years. The Dodgers' opponents, after a one-year hiatus, were the New York Yankees, who cruised to the A.L. flag on the back of superstars Joe DiMaggio (he of the fifty-six-game hitting streak) and Charlie Keller and strong pitching from Lefty Gomez, Red Ruffing, and others.

The 1941 Series was a taut struggle. The first three games were low-scoring contests, all decided by a single run, with the Yankees winning the first, 3–2, behind Ruffing, the Dodgers' Whit Wyatt taking Game Two, 3–2, and the Yankees scoring two runs off reliever Hugh Casey in the eighth inning of Game Three to go up two games to one.

Game Four, by comparison, was a slugfest. In front of the home crowd at Ebbets Field, Pete Reiser hit a two-run homer off the Yankees' Tiny Bonham, reserve outfielder

The fateful moment: Mickey Owen drops the third strike that would have given the Dodgers a Game Four victory, as Tommy Henrich heads for first. "I have no excuse for failing to catch that ball," said Owen after the game.

Jimmy Wasdell chipped in a two-run pinch double, and the Dodgers clung to a 4–3 lead entering the ninth. Again Hugh Casey was on the mound, and this time he got the first two men out.

The Yankees' last hope was Tommy Henrich, who'd had a poor Series thus far. The count went to 3–2, and then Casey reared back and threw one of the nastiest curve balls anyone had ever seen.

In Donald Honig's *Baseball Between the Lines*, Henrich recalled: "When I realized that was a bad ball I couldn't hold back. It broke down so fast I knew it was going to be ball four. You see, he didn't start it out chest-high; he started it out belt-high. It looked like a fastball. Then when it broke, it broke so sharply that it was out of the strike zone. So I tried to hold up, but I wasn't able to.

"But even as I was trying to hold up," Henrich added, "I was thinking that the ball had broken so fast that Owen might have trouble with it too."

And he did. "It had the wickedest inshoot I've ever seen," Owen told *Collier's Magazine* the next spring. "My glove was placed too near my body; that's how the ball got away."

"THE DODGERS WERE IN AGONY. I'VE NEVER SEEN SUCH A STUNNED CROWD. THEY COULD SEE WHAT WAS HAPPENING BUT THEY COULDN'T MAKE THEMSELVES BELIEVE IT."

Henrich took a quick glance and saw the ball bouncing toward the grandstand. "I saw that little white jackrabbit bouncing, and I said, *Let's go*. It rolled all the way to the fence."

By the time Owen retrieved the ball, Henrich had reached first. Frustrating for the Dodgers, but far from fatal. But the disaster that followed had nothing to do with the catcher, and everything to do with an onrush of events drowning a shell-shocked pitcher.

Forever after, Dodger Manager Leo Durocher blamed himself for not going to the mound to calm Casey down. Joe DiMaggio singled, bringing up the dangerous, left-handed Charlie Keller, and still Durocher didn't move. "Given everything that had been happening, the situation screamed for me to replace Casey," he wrote later. "I did nothing. I froze."

Calamity followed. With two strikes, Keller doubled in Henrich and DiMaggio. Shockingly, the Yankees suddenly had a 5–4 lead…and still the nightmare wasn't over. After Bill Dickey walked, Joe Gordon hit another double. Now it was 7–4 and as DiMaggio put it, "the Dodgers were in agony. I've never seen such a stunned crowd. They could see what was happening but they couldn't make themselves believe it."

The Dodgers went meekly in their half of the ninth, and just as quietly the next day, as Tiny Bonham bested Whit Wyatt, 3–1. The Yankees were crowned world champions for the fifth time in six years.

1941

NEW YORK YANKEES
4

BROOKLYN DODGERS
1

Back where they belong:
The Yankees' Art Fletcher,
Gerry Priddy, Earle Combs,
Phil Rizzuto, Red Rolfe,
Tommy Henrich, and Johnny
Sturm celebrate their 1941
Series triumph.

Who got blamed? Mickey Owen and Mickey Owen alone. Look at Richards Vidmer's take in the *New York Herald Tribune* the day after the game:

> The night watchman excitedly jingled his keys as he unlocked the Gallery of Goats last night. His hands twitched with excitement and there was a sinister gleam in his mean little eyes, for there was work to be done—the kind of work he loved most—the installation of a new member....
>
> "Move over there, Merkle," he murmured with fiendish delight. "Move over, Fred, and make room for a real goat. Hah! You forgot to touch second and lost a pennant. We got a fellow coming tonight who lost a World Series game—maybe the Series—after the game was over!"

With coverage like that, Owen's lifelong reputation was ensured. "The Mystery of the Missed Third Strike" was the title of an article in *Collier's Magazine* in 1942. "'I've Been Living With It a Long Time'" revealed a *Life Magazine* profile in 1966. "One that got away haunts Owen" said the headline in the *New York Post* in 1985. "Fifty Years Later: Mickey Owen Looks Back With a Smile" reported a piece in the official 1991 World Series program.

Smiling or not, Mickey Owen always handled his plight with patience, grace, and dignity. None of which obscures the fact that sometimes baseball—and history itself—is plainly, cruelly unfair.

You can't compare the World Series during World War II to any other Series. The Cardinals and Yankees, strong teams going in, dominated the war years, and other teams had their moments of glory, but no one at the time pretended that baseball was more than a pale shadow of its usual self.

The ball itself was different, as some of its components were needed for war products, leaving it as dead as a squishy Spaldeen. And with Joe DiMaggio, Ted Williams, Hank Greenberg, Bob Feller, Stan Musial, and dozens of lesser stars and everyday players heading overseas for the duration, the quality of play declined markedly as well.

As Bill James put it succinctly in his *New Historical Baseball Abstract*, "With most of the good players in the service, a collection of old men and children and men with one arm and seven dependents gathered regularly and batted around a dull spheroid, and this was called 'major league baseball' for three years."

None of which kept the players from playing hard, and nothing kept fans from going to the ballpark. In a famous letter, President Franklin Delano Roosevelt had decreed that baseball was essential to the war effort and should continue to operate. "I honestly feel," he wrote to Commissioner Judge Landis just five weeks after Pearl Harbor, "that it would be best for the country to keep baseball going." Millions of fans agreed.

Many of the Yankee players who would soon leave to join the armed forces were still on the team in 1942, and helped lead the Bombers to a 103–51 record and an easy American League pennant. It would be their sixth visit to the World Series in seven years. Their opponents, the Cardinals, had an even better year, going 106–48. It was one of the best records of all time—but barely enough to defeat the Brooklyn Dodgers, who won 104 games and finished two games behind.

But 1942 set the pattern for World Series during the war years: lots of fireworks, but not a lot of strong play. The Cardinals, for example, hit just .239, with two home runs and no stolen bases. Their fielders committed ten errors. One of their pitching stars, Mort Cooper, went 0–1 with a 5.54 ERA.

And they won in five games.

The Cardinals' hero was an unexpected one: a brash twenty-four-year-old pitcher named Johnny Beazley, who somehow had won twenty-one games in his first full season, pitching as both a starter and a reliever. But no one could have predicted that he'd dominate the Series, especially after the Yankees' Red Ruffing had a no-hitter through eight innings in Game One and held on for a 7–4 win.

The Cardinals' four-run rally in the ninth, which ended with the bases loaded, showed that they had no intention of going down easily. Beazley pitched a complete game in Game Two, withstanding a two-run home run by Charlie Keller in the top of the eighth (on "a damn good curve ball," according to Cardinal manager Billy Southworth) that tied the game, 3–3. But the young pitcher then shut down the Yankees in the ninth after Stan Musial's RBI single put the Cards ahead again in the bottom of the eighth.

"They say no pitcher ever beats the Yankees twice in a series, but Beazley's from Missouri and they'll have to show him,"

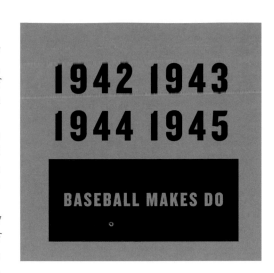

1942 1943 1944 1945

BASEBALL MAKES DO

Johnny Beazley (second from left) won two games for the St. Louis Cardinals in their 1942 Series triumph—but by 1943 he, Birdie Tebbets, World War I hero Hank Gowdy, and Hank Greenberg were in a different kind of uniform.

1942

ST. LOUIS CARDINALS

4

NEW YORK YANKEES

1

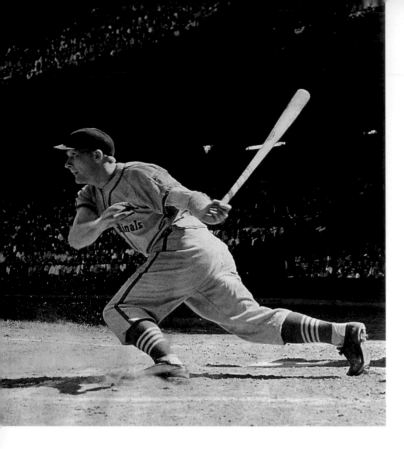

wrote Arthur E. Patterson in the *Trib*. "'Think I can beat them again? Why not?' he asked. 'Listen, I think I can beat any team.'"

Beazley had to wait a couple of days to find out if he was right. In Game Three, the Cardinals' Ernie White pitched a six-hitter, Stan Musial and Enos Slaughter robbed Yankee hitters of home runs, and the Cardinals won again, 2–0. Game Four was a completely different animal, a wild, messy, back-and-forth contest that ended with the Cardinals on top, 9–6.

In Game Five, played in front of 69,000 howling fans at Yankee Stadium, Johnny Beazley got to strut his stuff again. And strut he did, matching Red Ruffing inning for inning in a game that went into the ninth tied 2–2. Sportswriter Rud Rennie describes what happened next: "In a story-book finish to another million-dollar series of record-breaking proportions the incredible St. Louis Cardinals, National League Champions, defeated the lordly Yankees, 4 to 2, in the jam-packed Stadium yesterday afternoon with a two-run homer by George [Whitey] Kurowski."

The Cardinals were improbable champions of the world, and they were as surprised as anyone else. When the aging and ever-dignified Judge Landis entered the clubhouse after the game, he soon found himself borne atop the shoulders of the joyful St. Louis players—not a position he was used to!

Whitey Kurowski helped lead the aggressive, risk-taking Cardinals to two World Series championships during the war years. "The government's speed limit of thirty-five miles an hour doesn't stop the Cardinals," wrote Harry Cross in 1942. "The Cards are the most unstationary club that has been in the World Series in a blue moon."

Beazley, DiMaggio, Rizzuto, Ruffing, and others had gone into the service when the two teams met again in the 1943 Series. The war was raging at full throttle now, American and Allied casualties soaring even as the tide of the war turned against the Axis powers.

Even the ballpark was no refuge. On October 5, during Game One, an American Flying Fortress bomber buzzed the packed Yankee Stadium three times, interrupting play and terrifying fans. The roaring bomber drew an angry response from New York Mayor Fiorello LaGuardia and cast a pall over the proceedings, which the Yankees won, 4–2.

Sportswriters, well aware that the quality of play had diminished, were not entirely forgiving. "The annual high-priced autumnal baseball classic, as it is sometimes frivolously called, had many of the earmarks of a low-priced game in the Three-Eye League," complained writer Harry Cross.

The Cardinals bounced back with a 4–3 win behind Mort Cooper in Game Two, but their poor fielding (which hadn't hurt them in 1942) continued to bedevil them in Game Three, as they committed four errors in a 6–2 loss. Game Four was tighter, but Marius Russo pitched the Yankees to a 2–1 win. Then, despite strong pitching from Mort Cooper, the Cards could do nothing with the Yankees' Spud Chandler in Game Five, falling 2–0 as the Yankees claimed their sixth Series title in eight years.

Game Five was particularly sweet for Yankee catcher Bill Dickey, the team's last holdover from the days of Ruth and Gehrig. In his final season before joining the military, the thirty-seven-year-old Dickey hit a two-run homer to drive in the only two runs of the game. Dickey, Manager Joe McCarthy (celebrating his seventh World Series win), and the rest of the team burst into a rousing chorus of "East Side, West Side" in the victorious locker room…while thinking about all the teammates who weren't there to share their joy.

1943

NEW YORK YANKEES

4

ST. LOUIS CARDINALS

1

1944

ST. LOUIS CARDINALS
4

ST. LOUIS BROWNS
2

The Cardinals were back in the Series once again in 1944, but this time they had a new opponent: the ragtag St. Louis Browns, long a symbol of futility and a classic example of a team that won the pennant because most of the competition was decimated by wartime call-ups.

No one gave the Browns much of a chance, but everyone rooted for them. How could you not root for a team that had had only one winning season in the last fourteen? As Arthur Daley wrote in the *New York Times*, "This is easily the most astonishing ball club ever to reach the series. The Cardinals are a pre-war team of acknowledged strength and class. The Brownies are an ill-assorted collection of cast-offs."

Still, for three games, the Browns looked to be on the verge of pulling off a miracle against the Cardinals, who still had stars Stan Musial and Marty Marion on their roster. After Game Three, won by Jack Kramer (just returned from military service), the Browns held a 2–1 series lead. And no one had a home-field advantage, since all seven games were played in St. Louis' Sportsman's Park.

For the rest of the Series, however, talent would out. Superb pitching by the Cardinals' Harry Brecheen, Mort Cooper, Max Lanier, and Ted Wilks held the Browns to just two runs in the last three games, and the Cardinals marched to their second Series win in three war years.

"The bubble burst today for the Brownies," reported Daley after the last game, a 3–1 win by Lanier. "Their admirable fight of the past three weeks was at an end, and it was a bedraggled-looking ball club which lost out to the Cardinals in the final game of the Series…. Cinderella was back in shabby garb after a glorious whirl that carried her to her first American League championship."

Baseball versus Hitler: The war was never far from anyone's thoughts as the 1943 Series got under way.

Harry "the Cat" Brecheen, "hollow-cheeked, bandy-legged son of Oklahoma's red clay country"— and dominant pitcher in the 1944 and '46 Series.

"THE CARDINALS ARE A PRE-WAR TEAM OF ACKNOWLEDGED STRENGTH AND CLASS. THE BROWNIES ARE AN ILL-ASSORTED COLLECTION OF CAST-OFFS."

1945

DETROIT TIGERS

4

CHICAGO CUBS

3

By 1945, the war had come to an end, and a few of the stars who'd joined up were back in uniform. None was more prominent than the Tigers' slugger Hank Greenberg, who'd enlisted soon after Pearl Harbor (despite having already served his time in the military) and had seen combat in Europe while missing nearly four full seasons of baseball.

Was it anything other than Greenberg's due to return to the line-up late in 1945—and then hit the grand-slam home run that gave the Tigers the A.L. pennant on the last day of the season?

Led by Greenberg, and featuring such grizzled vets as Dizzy Trout, Doc Cramer, and Virgil Trucks, the Tigers ("the nine old men," as Fred Lieb dubbed them) entered the Series against the surprising N.L. champs, the Chicago Cubs.

The teams split the first four games before Detroit took a 3–2 Series lead with a messy 8–4 win behind workhorse Hal Newhouser. But if Game Five was messy, Game Six was more like a stickball game than a baseball championship. The final box score: nine pitchers, twenty-eight hits, four errors, fifteen runs, twelve innings, and one Cubs victory: 8–7.

So it was on to Game Seven, which was bound to be an anticlimax. "So many extraordinary things had occurred to date in this wackiest of post-season affairs that the grand finale left the spectators with a definitely deflated feeling," commented Arthur Daley.

Especially Cub fans. The Tigers scored five in the first and then cruised to an easy 9–3 win behind Hal Newhouser. The last of the wartime Series was over; by 1946 Williams, DiMaggio, and other stars would be back, and the game would begin to approach its prewar quality.

"There never was another World Series like the present one," wrote H. G. Salsinger in the *Detroit News* as the Tigers wrapped up the 1945 flag. "And there'll never be another like it until the next World War."

Hank Greenberg (right, with Hal Newhouser and Detroit Manager Steve O'Neill) made it back from the war just in time to lead the Tigers to the 1945 A.L. pennant—and then slammed two homers in Detroit's seven-game Series win.

I n 1946 the United States got back to the business of peace and prosperity, and the real baseball players took their rightful places on the diamond.

"Oh man, we were fearless," recalled Joe Garagiola, just starting his career in 1946. "Anything you did, you felt you were ahead of the game. Not that you'd been in the trenches necessarily. But you were so glad to be back."

In the American League, the Boston Red Sox, led by Ted Williams, jumped to an early lead and swept to a crushing pennant victory over the defending-champion Tigers. The National League, though, was something else again.

The St. Louis Cardinals and Brooklyn Dodgers finished the season with identical 96–58 records. Then St. Louis went on to win the first two of the best-of-three playoff series, breaking the oft-broken hearts of Dodger fans and sending the Cardinals to their fourth Series in five years.

The Series matched two players who had had MVP seasons: Stan Musial (.356 with 228 hits, including fifty doubles and twenty triples) and Ted Williams (.342 with 38 home runs and 123 RBI). It was Williams' first and only World Series…and, in one of the most heartbreaking turns of events in postseason history, he hurt his elbow in an exhibition game just before the Series started. Though he never used the injury as an excuse, it unquestionably contributed to his miseries at the plate.

1946

BOSTON'S HEARTBREAK

10 BEST SERIES

NO. 6

1946

One of the most famous World Series images of all time: Enos Slaughter completing his "mad dash" to clinch the Series for the Cardinals.

As so often happens, fate didn't choose either Williams or Musial to be the stars of this classic Series. Instead, lesser-known players got their chance to shine—or even to help pave their own roads to the Hall of Fame.

Game One was a thriller, a classic pitcher's duel between the Cardinals' Howie Pollet and Boston's Tex Hughson. Pollet pitched guttily in a game that went ten innings, but came up the loser when aging Sox slugger Rudy York hit a home run to win the game, 3–2.

The shining star of the 1946 Series made his first appearance in Game Two: St. Louis' Harry Brecheen. Harry the Cat, a long, lanky, quiet left-hander who'd pitched well but only gone 15–15 that year, threw a four-hitter and drove in a run with a single as the Cardinals evened up the Series, 3–0.

Boston's Boo Ferriss returned the favor, riding a three-run homer by Rudy York to an easy 4–0 Game Three victory. But if fans were expecting the rest of the Series to be a pitcher's duel…well, forget it. The Cardinals erupted for twenty hits in Game Four (including four each for Joe Garagiola, Whitey Kurowski, and Enos Slaughter) en route to a 12–3 win.

Game Five is usually pivotal, and when Boston's Joe Dobson shut down the Cardinals' offense in a 6–3 win, it looked like the Red Sox might have that elusive championship in hand.

"I HAD IT IN MY MIND THAT I WAS GOING TO SCORE. MAN, I DON'T THINK I EVER RAN THAT FAST."

Harry Brecheen was back again in Game Six, holding the Sox to a single run in the Cardinals' crucial 4–1 win. "When he's pitching, he's the kind of a guy who wouldn't even give his grandma a good ball to hit," marveled St. Louis captain, center fielder Terry Moore.

So it all came down to Game Seven, at St. Louis' Sportsman's Park. "The seventh game of the World Series," Slaughter told Donald Honig years later in *Baseball Between the Lines*. "Say it aloud—it's got a sound to it, doesn't it?"

And this was a great seventh game. The Cardinals jumped out to a 3–1 lead in the fifth, but Dom DiMaggio's two-run double tied the game for Boston in the top of the eighth. The hit came off, yes, Harry Brecheen, brought in to relieve starter Murry Dickson. But Brecheen then got Ted Williams to pop out to end the threat and the inning.

When Enos Slaughter, after a lead-off single in the bottom of the inning, remained at first after two outs, it looked like the game would go to the ninth tied. But then came one of those Top Ten Memorable Series moments, the kind that brand a ballplayer's career forever.

Every fan knows what happened: Harry Walker lined a base hit to left-center, where center fielder Leon Culberson (who'd just replaced the injured Dom DiMaggio, a brilliant fielder) retrieved the ball. Culberson fired the ball to Boston shortstop Johnny Pesky, the relay man, as everyone in the park expected Slaughter to stop at third.

1946

ST. LOUIS CARDINALS

4

BOSTON RED SOX

3

But Slaughter, who'd been running on the pitch and was now in the midst of what became known as his "Mad Dash," didn't stop. "I never broke stride," he said later. "I had it in my mind that I was going to score. Man, I don't think I ever ran that fast."

Pesky caught the relay with his back to the plate. With second baseman Bobby Doerr and others screaming at him to throw, he either did or did not hesitate before throwing home, far too late to get the sliding Slaughter.

At the time, Pesky took full blame, saying, "I'm the goat. I never expected he'd try to score. I couldn't hear anybody hollering at me above the noise of the crowd."

In later years, the warm and engaging Pesky was always willing to talk patiently about the play that tarnished his fine career. But he also told George Vecsey in 1974, "They say I took a snooze, but I can't see where I hesitated. Slaughter was at second when the ball was hit. He was twenty feet from home when I turned." But still, he added, "I guess you have to live with it."

There was still an inning to go after the Cardinals took the 4–3 lead. Harry Brecheen was still in the game ("I decided I'd rather have a tired Brecheen than a fresh anybody else," said Manager Eddie Dyer), but he had very little left. Rudy York and Bobby Doerr singled to lead off the inning, and a force play put runners on first and third with just one out.

But then the Cat stiffened. Roy Partee fouled out and Tom McBride grounded to second baseman Red Schoendienst, who almost booted the ball before throwing to Marty Marion for the force, the game, and the Series. Brecheen had his third win, and the Cardinals had their third World Series victory in five years. The Red Sox were bridesmaids once more, and in the most painful possible way.

More than half a century later, fans and players alike still marvel at the 1946 Series, and at Slaughter's mad dash. Joe Garagiola put it best: "You could almost say it was a dumb play that worked," he said. "You know the difference between dumb and smart—the word 'safe.'"

Has there ever been a World Series more filled with unforgettable moments than the 1947 classic? Even before it started, this Series had special meaning not only because it was a Subway Series (always a thrill, to New York fans at least), but also because it was the first Yankee-Dodger meeting since the 1941 Series, the one where Mickey Owen dropped the third strike and broke Brooklyn's heart. As if that wasn't enough, it was the Series that gave Jackie Robinson, the superstar who broke the major-league color line, his first national stage.

Unlike many supposedly fabled matchups, however, the 1947 Series lived up to all anticipation—and exceeded it. It was a stunning Series from beginning to end, packed with controversy and strategy and moments never seen in a World Series before, or since.

Among the glories of 1947:

Yankee left fielder Johnny Lindell, perhaps the most obscure member of a line-up that included Yogi Berra, Joe DiMaggio, Phil Rizzuto, and Tommy Henrich, outhitting them all with nine hits in eighteen at bats and seven RBI.

Little-known Spec Shea, starting three games for the Yanks, and winning two of them.

Jackie Robinson leaving a calling card for future years by stealing two bases.

Hugh Casey, the pitcher who threw the curve that Mickey Owen dropped in 1941, becoming the first ever to win two consecutive World Series games.

Al Gionfriddo making a mind-boggling Game Six catch of a seemingly certain home run hit by DiMaggio, causing the ever-stoical Yankee Clipper to kick the ground in disgust. "The reason I let my feelings show then was that I'd never had a Series where I'd been lucky," said DiMaggio many years later. "That catch by Gionfriddo was the straw that broke the camel's back."

Yankee relief ace Joe Page pitching five innings of one-hit ball in Game Seven as the Yankees finally (finally!) put away the Dodgers for good, 5–2.

And, of course, one more extraordinary moment, perhaps the single most famous World Series at bat of all time. In "Lavagetto's Double," an evocative 1990 piece—as pertinent today as when it was written—*New York Times* columnist Ira Berkow celebrates that moment and wonders why recent sports milestones don't live up to those of 1947.

Cookie Lavagetto, who died at age 77 in his sleep Friday morning at his home in Orinda, California, was famous for one thing: He was the Brooklyn Dodger who struck a celebrated pinch-hit in the 1947 World Series. Thoughts of Lavagetto the ballplayer led to the notion here that great moments in sports don't last as long as they used to.

The reason, I decided at first, was me. The older I become, the quicker life goes. More events are stuffed into a shrinking time frame. In the grade-school years, a summer vacation lasted forever. Now, a summer zips by nearly like a weekend. Yesterday it was July. Tomorrow it's September.

Jackie Robinson, out of position at first base, still made an impact in his first Series, driving in three runs and stealing two bases.

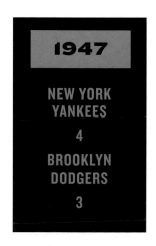

1947

NEW YORK YANKEES
4

BROOKLYN DODGERS
3

10 BEST SERIES

NO. 8

1947

Spec Shea's superb pitching made him an unlikely Series hero. Here, he receives congratulations from Joe DiMaggio.

Al Gionfriddo's spectacular catch off a Joe DiMaggio drive saved Game Six for the Dodgers. "It wasn't the greatest catch in baseball," said broadcaster Red Barber. "It was an impossible catch."

Yesterday, Cookie Lavagetto was batting against Floyd Bevens of the Yankees at Ebbets Field with two out in the bottom half of the ninth inning of the fourth game of the Series. Bevens had a no-hitter going. Just one more out. There had never been a no-hitter thrown in the 43 previous World Series. There were two runners on, by virtue of walks, the 9th and 10th that Bevens had given up in the game. Because of his wildness, Bevens had allowed a run in the fifth inning, but he was still ahead, 2–1.

Lavagetto was 34 years old and a 10-year big-league veteran when summoned by Manager Burt Shotton to pinch hit for Eddie Stanky. The capacity crowd of 33,443 was on its feet. Lavagetto swung and missed at the first pitch, and then hit the next pitch off the top of the right-field wall, breaking up Bevens' no-hitter, driving in the two runs and giving the Dodgers a 3–2 victory.

Brooklyn erupted. Lavagetto was pummeled by his teammates. Fans and vendors pummeled one another. In his book "1947—When all Hell Broke Loose in Baseball," Red Barber recalled announcing the game on radio, which dwarfed the television coverage, because it was the first televised World Series, and seen only on the Eastern seaboard.

"I remember the final sentence I said," Barber wrote. It was: "I'll be a suck-egg mule."

I was a boy when all this was going on, although I don't remember the game or the broadcast. What I remember is that the Lavagetto hit, the Bevens failed no-hitter and the sensational catch by Al Gionfriddo to rob Joe DiMaggio of a home run in the Series all became part of the lore of baseball for me, as famous as anything Paul Bunyan did, or Tom Sawyer, or even George Washington.

There are still a lot of great achievements going on all over the place these days in sports, but somehow they fail to stick in the brain as they once did.

Who won Wimbledon last year, or this? Who won the Super Bowl three years ago? Who'd they beat? If not for the earth rhumba in California last year, some of us would hardly remember the 1989 World Series. Who was the m.v.p., anyway?…

Once, great moments seemed to last longer. Fred Merkle's bonehead play in 1908, Ruth's supposedly called home run in the 1932 Series, Dizzy Dean's Gashouse feats in the '34 Series remain a vivid part of our national heritage.

There were, too, no instant replays, nor the continual replays on the evening news of all those moments. Today, everything is a sound bite, or a visual bite. Once, there was only a picture in a newspaper, or a book. Or the description on the radio. And the imagination did the rest. The special moment hung like a painting in the mind's eye, and for all time.

Perhaps, too, that was a simpler time, when the world wasn't so crowded and close, and America was like a small town. "Come out and smell the heliotrope in the moonlight," said Mrs. Gibbs to her husband in Thornton Wilder's "Our Town." For some of us, it was a little like that.

We had time to savor our exceptional moments, to smell the heliotrope in the moonlight, to ruminate on Lavagetto's double. And even to remember the bittersweet ironies of something like the 1947 World Series. Neither Gionfriddo, Bevens nor Lavagetto ever played another season in the major leagues.

Game Four hero Cookie Lavagetto (left) with victim Floyd "Bill" Bevens. "Looking back," Bevens said later, "I'd keep that pitch to Lavagetto down and inside."

B aseball continued its breathless, bizarre, down-to-the-last-minute course during the 1948 season. For the second time in three years, two teams ended the season in a tie. This time the teams were the Cleveland Indians and the Boston Red Sox, and this time it was determined that the pennant would be decided on the strength of a single game.

It was Cleveland's year. Behind the knuckleball of rookie pitcher Gene Bearden, the Indians, an exciting young team owned by brash (some would say madcap) entrepreneur Bill Veeck, added to the litany of Red Sox woes with an 8–3 victory.

The 1948 Indians' greatest strength was the pitching of Bob Lemon (20–14), Bearden (20–7), and Bob Feller (19–15). Their opponents in the 1948 Series were the Boston Braves, no slouch in the pitching department either, with Johnny Sain (a league-leading twenty-four wins) and Warren Spahn leading the way.

No surprise: Game One was a classic pitchers' duel, with a run-scoring single by the Braves' Tommy Holmes providing the difference in Sain's 1–0 win over Feller. Bob Lemon evened the score in Game Two, 4–1, and then the Indians grabbed a 2–1 Series lead with yet another pitching gem, a five-hit shutout by Gene Bearden and a 2–0 win.

Game Five featured yet another masterpiece, as Steve Gromek (who'd started just nine games all year) threw a seven-hitter and the Indians won yet again, 2–1. The game was also notable for a home run by the Indians' Larry Doby, Jackie Robinson's American League counterpart.

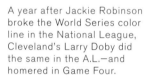

1948

THE PITCHERS' SERIES

A year after Jackie Robinson broke the World Series color line in the National League, Cleveland's Larry Doby did the same in the A.L.—and homered in Game Four.

Thus far, every game had been excruciatingly close—and also too quiet, too mono-chromatic. Baseball thrives on variety, on noise, as Bill Veeck knew well. Famous in later years for his crowd-pleasing stunts (such as sending the midget Eddie Gaedel up to bat in a game), Veeck was already in fine form during the 1948 Series, as Red Smith reported from Cleveland Stadium in the *New York Herald Tribune*: "This is written between hot licks on a trumpet while a man in a pale blue derby beats on a bull fiddle and four fat clowns howl 'Show me the way to go home' into a microphone.... A siren is screeching somewhere and an airplane is buzzing the park.... Let's see now. Oh, yes, about the third game of the World Series, which was won by—oops, half a moment 'til things quiet down."

Things didn't quiet appreciably in Game Five, a blessedly slam-bang affair before a record crowd of 86,288 at Cleveland Stadium that ended 11–5 Braves. Bob Feller got lit up for seven runs ("I couldn't have struck out my own two-year-old kid," Feller said after the game. "That's how bad I was."). All-time Negro League great Satchel Paige contributed two-thirds of an inning for the Indians while becoming the first African American to pitch in a World Series game. And Warren Spahn held the Indians scoreless for 5 2/3 innings while the Braves rallied to win.

For most of the way, Game Six regained the pattern set by the first four: Bob Lemon pitched brilliantly through seven innings as the Indians moved to a 4–1 lead. "Great echoing gobs of silence" rose from the crowd at Braves Field in Boston, said Red Smith. "It was a smothered silence, depressed and dismal."

But in the eighth, the silence turned to shrieks and cheers as the Braves rallied for two runs and knocked Lemon from the game. Boston even had the tying and go-ahead runs in scoring position before Gene Bearden got the final out in the inning, turning away the threat.

In the ninth the Braves' Eddie Stanky led off for a walk, but then Sibby Sisti bunted into a double play, and a moment later the game was over. The Indians had won their first World Series since 1920.

1948

CLEVELAND INDIANS

4

BOSTON BRAVES

2

The Braves hoist Gene Bearden, who won the Series-clinching Game Six in relief.

CUE THE JAWS THEME, PLEASE

Two days after the World Series ended, while the Indians were still celebrating their victory and dreaming about a 1949 repeat, the New York Yankees made an announcement. As John Drebinger put it in the *Times*: "Meet the new manager of the Yankees: Charles Dillon (Casey) Stengel, one-time hard-hitting outfielder, manager of both major and minor league clubs, sage, wit and gifted raconteur."

Stengel, at the press conference announcing the move, sounded a bit shaken. "This is a big job, fellows, and I barely have had time to study it," he said. "In fact, I scarcely know where I am at."

Little-remembered today, but big news in 1948, was the rumor that Joe DiMaggio, not Stengel, would replace Bucky Harris as the Bombers' manager. But DiMaggio showed up at the press conference to say, "You know me, boys. I'm just a ballplayer with only one ambition, and that is to give all I've got to help my ball-club win."

Asked about what moves he planned for his new team, Stengel was uncharacteristically modest. "There'll likely be some changes," he said, "but it's a good club and I think we'll do all right."

It would be six years before any American League team but the Yankees got a taste of World Series play.

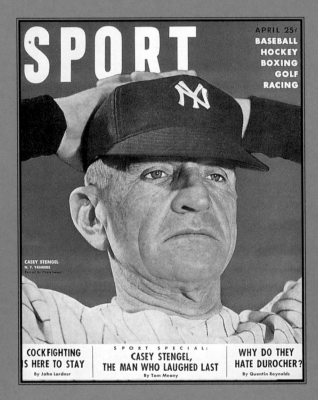

Casey Stengel at the height of the Yankee dynasty. "Baseball is my very life," he said, "my one consuming interest."

At first glance, 1949 wasn't a vintage year for the Yankees. Joe DiMaggio, hobbled with a bad heel, had only 272 at bats during the season. Tommy Henrich, one of the team's stalwarts, was nearing the end of the line. The budding superstar Yogi Berra lost nearly thirty points off his batting average from the year before. New manager Casey Stengel made for good press, but there were many who wondered whether he was all talk, no action.

Still, these were the Yankees. Led by a pitching staff that included Allie Reynolds (17–6), Vic Raschi (21–10), Ed Lopat (15–10), Tommy Byrne (15–7), and star reliever Joe Page, the Bombers managed to edge out the Red Sox—again—by a single game for the A.L. pennant. The National League pennant, after an equally tight race, went to the Dodgers, led by Jackie Robinson (.342 with 124 RBI).

Game One, at Yankee Stadium, was terrific pitchers' duel, with Allie Reynolds and the Dodgers' Don Newcombe matching zeroes through eight innings. The old warrior Tommy Henrich then slammed a home run leading off the ninth, giving the Yankees a 1–0 win.

The Dodgers' Preacher Roe returned the favor in Game Two, holding the Yankees to just six hits in what he called "the best game I ever pitched." Jackie Robinson scored on a Gil Hodges single in the second, and Roe made it hold up.

Game Three provided more of the same: Great pitching and no hitting, as the game remained tied 1–1 till the ninth, when the Yankees scored three times, then hung on for a 4–3 win. The star of the game, and developing star of the Series, was Yankee reliever Joe Page, who pitched the final 5 2/3 innings for the win.

After that, the Series went downhill fast. The Yankees jumped out to a 6–0 lead in Game Four (a bases-loaded triple by third baseman Bobby Brown was the big blow), then turned to Allie Reynolds to nail down a 6–4 win. Game Five was even worse, as the Yankees jumped out to a 10–2 lead. When the Dodgers scored four in the seventh, Joe Page came in to slam the door again, giving the Yankees their twelfth World Series trophy.

The Bronx Bombers' greatest dynasty had begun.

In 1950, the Yankees reinforced their reputation as the big scaly guy in an ongoing version of *Bambi Meets Godzilla*. Got yourself a miracle team in the National League? Have your fun winning the pennant, because the Yanks are going to flatten you in the World Series.

The 1950 pancakes were the Philadelphia Phillies, the brash young Whiz Kids. Led by burgeoning stars Richie Ashburn and Robin Roberts, the Kids entranced fans throughout the season by racing to a big lead and then, gasping and struggling, holding on to beat out the onrushing Dodgers on the last day of the season.

But the Yankees, who'd survived a four-team pennant race of their own, were waiting. And though every game of the Series but the last was close, it was obvious from the start that

1949–1953

THE PINNACLE

1949

NEW YORK YANKEES

4

BROOKLYN DODGERS

1

Portrait of a dynasty reborn: the 1949 Yankees celebrate their first World Series championship under new manager Casey Stengel.

the battle-tested Yankees and their cold-eyed tactician, Casey Stengel, would rule over the inexperienced Whiz Kids and their manager, affable Eddie Sawyer.

Vic Raschi shut down the Phils on just two hits in Game One as the Bombers won, 1–0. Yogi Berra broke up a pitchers' duel between Robin Roberts and Allie Reynolds with a tenth-inning homer to give the Yankees a 2–1 win in Game Two. And then, in Game Three, the Phils held a 2–1 lead going into the eighth, only to see a succession of misplays, bad breaks, and questionable moves by Sawyer give the Yankees two runs for a 3–2 win.

1950

NEW YORK YANKEES

4

PHILADELPHIA PHILLIES

0

Watching the Series, the *New York Post*'s Milton Gross couldn't stand what he was seeing. "The tendency is to work lightly over the bleeding remains of Eddie Sawyer," he wrote. "As nice a manager as you'd want to meet, he is belabored and beleaguered after seeing his brain waves boomerang or otherwise fail to prevent the Yankees from sneaking away with the first three games of a World Series that could go down as the dreariest of all time."

Things didn't get any less dreary in Game Four when the Yankees jumped out to a 5–0 lead on the strength of timely hits by Joe DiMaggio, Yogi Berra, Bobby Brown, and other reliables, while rookie Whitey Ford shut down the Philly stars (Richie Ashburn went 3 for 17 in the Series, Dick Sisler 1 for 17). The final score: Yankees 5, Phillies 2, Yankees four games, Phillies none.

"We'll be back, all right," said Sawyer after the sweep. But the Philly Whiz Kids never did make it to another Series. Once Godzilla crushed Bambi, Bambi stayed flat.

In 1951 the onrushing New York Giants came back from a 13 ¹/₂-game deficit to tie the Dodgers—and then went on to beat Brooklyn in the third game of a best-of-three playoff when Bobby Thomson slammed his "shot heard 'round the world." For the second year in a row, the N.L. had hosted one of the greatest pennant races of all time, and for the second time, the team that survived the race had to face the Yankees.

Though each team had plenty of holdover stars from earlier years (Joe DiMaggio, Vic Raschi, Yogi Berra, et al. for the Yanks; Sal Maglie and Eddie Stanky on the Giants), the 1951 Series was noteworthy for the appearance of two extraordinary rookies: Willie Mays and Mickey Mantle. Both had arrived borne on floods of hype, and both had struggled to establish themselves. "We kept an eye on each other, Willie and me," Mantle said.

Mantle and Mays' first World Series, 1951 was also notable for being DiMaggio's last. Old before his time, struggling annually against injury, the great Yankee was getting ready to hang up his pinstripes. Fittingly, both his first Series, in 1936, and this one were against the Giants. "The only difference was that I was the only player on the field who had played in the earlier Series, and I was fifteen years older," DiMaggio said.

The Giants, adrenaline still pumping from their playoff victory, came into Yankee Stadium and took Game One easily, 5–1, behind pitcher Dave Koslo and four hits (and a steal of home) by Monte Irvin, a Negro League star finally getting a chance in the majors. It was the first time the Yankees had lost Game One of a World Series since they played the Giants in 1936.

Ed Lopat handled the Giant batters in Game Two, a 3–1 Yankee win most notable for the freakish leg injury Mantle suffered when he caught his spikes in a sprinkler head while chasing a Willie Mays fly ball. Mantle, who would eventually post the greatest World Series numbers of all time, was out after only seven plate appearances and one hit.

When the Giants won Game Three, 6–2, to take a 2–1 Series lead, it looked like this Series might differ from the last two. But it was not to be. The Yankees beat up on old warhorse Sal Maglie in Game Four, winning 6–2. And then, scenting the kill, they rampaged over five Giant pitchers in Game Five, riding home runs by Phil Rizzuto and Gene Woodling and three hits by DiMaggio to a 13–1 rout.

Game Six was closer, especially after the Giants scored two runs in the ninth to draw within a run. But Yankee Hank Bauer (Mantle's fill-in) made a diving catch with the tying run on base in the ninth inning, and the Yankees held on for a 4–3 win to earn another set of World Series rings.

"Magic and sorcery and incantation and spells had taken the Giants to the championship of the National League and put them into the World Series," Red Smith wrote after it was over. "But you don't beat the Yankees with a witch's broomstick. Not the Yankees, not when there's hard money to be won."

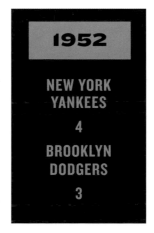

1951

NEW YORK
YANKEES
4

NEW YORK
GIANTS
2

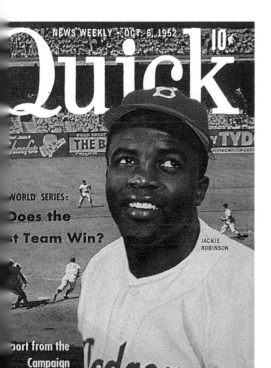

The World Series of 1952 between the Yankees and Dodgers was one of the best of all time. No, really, it was. A great Series, filled with rhubarbs and controversy, terrific fielding and mental lapses. Awesome offensive displays by hometown favorites like Duke Snider and Mickey Mantle and peerless pitching by Vic Raschi, Joe Black, and Allie Reynolds. Even Red Smith called it "the liveliest baseball show in eighteen years," since the great Cardinal-Tiger series of 1934.

But it was hard to get anyone outside New York to pay attention. To most fans, the 1952

1952

NEW YORK
YANKEES
4

BROOKLYN
DODGERS
3

It didn't matter how quick Jackie Robinson was—his Dodgers just kept losing to the Yankees.

Ebbets Field, Brooklyn—home to Dodger heartbreak in 1949, 1952, and 1953.

Series was just another rematch between the Godzilla Yankees and the perennial pancake Dodgers. As Smith put it before the Series started, "The simplest objective argument to support a belief that the Yankees will win is to point out that they always do."

But by all objective standards, this Series was a stunner. Joe Page, winner of the Rookie of the Year Award as a reliever, started Game One for the Dodgers and outdueled Allie Reynolds, 4–2, as Pee Wee Reese, Jackie Robinson, and Duke Snider slammed home runs. The Yankees, who *never* allowed themselves to fall two games behind, rode superlative pitching by Vic Raschi to a 7–1 Game Two win. Billy Martin, the Bombers' hotheaded new second baseman, took center stage in this game with a home run and four RBI. ("It kind of bugged me that Billy hit a World Series homer before I did," said Mickey Mantle later.)

Using his cut fastball (or, perhaps, his spitter), Preacher Roe carried the Dodgers to a tense 5–3 Game Three win that wasn't decided until the last out was made. Even though he had three hits, this was one of the worst games of Yogi Berra's career. Reese and Robinson worked a double steal off him in the ninth, and then his passed ball allowed both to score the runs that provided the winning margin.

It was Black against Reynolds again in Game Four, and both of them pitched beautifully. But Black gave up a home run to thirty-nine-year-old Johnny Mize (a late-season Yankee acquisition) and the Bombers won, 2–0.

Game Five was a classic. The Dodgers jumped out to a 4–0 lead, then saw the Yankees score five in the fifth. (Mize hit another home run.) But Brooklyn's young pitcher Carl Erskine stiffened then, retiring the last nineteen Yankees while the Dodgers tied the game and then won it, 6–5, in the eleventh on a double by Snider. But even this run almost wasn't enough against the deadly Yanks: Carl Furillo had to leap high to reel in a blast by Mize that would have tied the game in the bottom of the inning.

Somehow, amazingly, the Yankees had lost a fifth game, and were now trailing the Series, 3–2, with the last two games to be played at Ebbets Field. Could this be the Dodgers' year, finally, after so many disappointments?

No chance. The twenty-year-old Mickey Mantle finally drew even with Billy Martin by hitting a homer that gave the Yankees a 3–1 lead in Game Six. Duke Snider's second homer of the game brought the Dodgers within a run, but that was all they got as Allie Reynolds ("who seemed to be on twenty-four-hour call," said Mantle) came in to save the game for Vic Raschi.

Game Seven: another nail-biter. Joe Black, arm weary, didn't have it, giving up three runs in 5 $^1/_3$ innings, the third coming on Mantle's home run completely out of Ebbets Field. The Yankees took a 4–2 lead into the bottom of the seventh, but when Vic Raschi came in to relieve an exhausted Allie Reynolds, he immediately loaded the bases with one out.

Little-known Bob Kusava came in to try to save Raschi's bacon. Kusava was no melon in his only appearance of the Series, getting the dangerous Snider and then, after running him to an agonizing full count, inducing Jackie Robinson to hit a pop-up on the infield. Easy out, right? Well, no…first baseman Joe Collins couldn't see the ball in the sun, Kusava seemed frozen on the mound, and for a heart-stopping moment it looked as though the ball might drop, allowing the tying runs to score.

"THIS TIME THEY WERE PUSHED TO THE LIMITS OF THEIR MAN POWER AND THEIR ENDURANCE."

But then Billy Martin streaked into the picture, fierce concentration on his pointy face, and grabbed the ball just above knee-level for the third out. The threat was over, and when Kusava stifled the Dodgers for the last two innings, so was the great Series.

"Every year is next year for the Yankees," grouched the Bard of Brooklyn, Roger Kahn, the next day. The Dodgers' only consolation: "Never before has a Yankee team managed by Stengel had to scramble so hard to win," Kahn wrote. "This time they were pushed to the limits of their man power and their endurance."

For the true Dodger fan, of course, this was cold comfort.

Everybody back in the pool!

Yes, 1953 saw the Yankees cruise to another A.L. flag, their fifth in a row, but this was not a vintage Yankee team. Mantle had suffered through a subpar, injury-plagued year, and no Yankee pitcher had won twenty games, though Whitey Ford, Ed Lopat, and Johnny Sain had all had strong seasons.

The Dodgers, on the other hand, had one of their best years, going 105–49 and winning the pennant by thirteen games. This may have been the most powerful Dodger team of all: Duke Snider hit forty-two home runs, MVP Roy Campanella added forty-one (with 142 RBI), and Gil Hodges wasn't far behind with thirty-one homers and 122 RBI. The team as a whole hit 208 home runs, forty-eight more than any other team in the majors.

None of which meant a thing once the Series started. For this was Billy Martin's Series, as the pesky second-baseman made himself the star of "Pepper Martin: the Sequel." He had three hits, 3 RBI, and a stolen base in the Yankees' 9–5 Game One win; two more hits, including a home run, in Ed Lopat's 4–2 conquering of the Dodger bats in Game Two; another hit as the Dodgers won Game Three, 3–2, behind Carl Erskine's fourteen strikeouts; two more, including a triple, as the Dodgers evened the Series, 7–3, in Game Four; and another home run as the Yankees romped to an 11–7 victory in Game Five, a game highlighted by Mantle's grand slam.

So the Dodgers were down three games to two going into Game Six at Yankee Stadium, which must have felt familiar to the eternal also-rans. But this Dodger team would not go without a fight. After the Yankees jumped out to a 3–0 lead off the weary Erskine (making his third start of the Series), the Dodgers battled back. They scored a run off Whitey Ford in the sixth and then, with one out in the ninth, Carl Furillo hit a two-run homer off Allie Reynolds to tie the game.

But the joy of Dodger fans was short-lived. Clem Labine gave up a walk to Hank Bauer to start the bottom of the ninth. With one out, Mantle singled to move Bauer to second. And then who should come up but Billy Martin, the "brash, combative, fist-slinging little hellion," as Red Smith described him. All Martin did was lash a single through the middle—his twelfth hit of the Series—to score Bauer with the deciding run.

The Yankees had won their fifth straight Series under Casey Stengel. "I felt bad when Casey took me out," said Whitey Ford after being yanked following the seventh inning. "Then I thought, well, he hasn't been wrong in five years."

Nor had any of the other Yankees.

Mickey Mantle's grand slam in Game Five of the 1953 Series sent the Yankees on their way to their fifth straight title. "Every year is next year for the Yankees," mourned Dodgers fan Roger Kahn.

1953

NEW YORK YANKEES

4

BROOKLYN DODGERS

2

The Yankees had their best year in more than a decade in 1954, going 103–51. Their only problem: a buzzsaw called the Cleveland Indians, who blasted to the amazing total of 111 wins and the A.L. pennant.

Grateful non-Yankee fans worldwide gave thanks.

The Indians were led by one of the best pitching staffs of all time. Their team 2.78 ERA was far better than any other in the league, and star pitchers Bob Lemon and Early Wynn won twenty-three games each, with Mike Garcia not far behind with nineteen. Meanwhile, Larry Doby led the league in home runs and RBI, while Bobby Avila took the batting crown with a .341 average.

The Indians' opponents in the World Series were the New York Giants—yes, still a New York team, but you couldn't have everything. The Giants had been carried by Willie Mays' MVP season (.345, 41 home runs, 110 RBI) and superb pitching from Johnny Antonelli (twenty-one wins). But no one thought the Giants had much of a chance against the Indians' juggernaut.

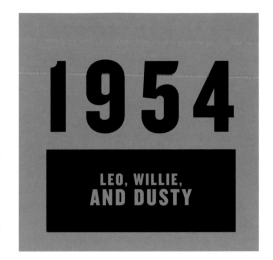

1954

LEO, WILLIE, AND DUSTY

"PRESSURE? THEY SPIT AT IT."

In fact, by 1954 the National League had lost seven straight World Series: six to the Yankees and one (in 1948) to Cleveland. There was no question in most minds that baseball had entered one of those eras in which one league is clearly superior to the other. The consensus said that the American League had it all over its older sibling and that 1954 wasn't going to be any exception.

One man, however, didn't buy into the consensus: Giant manager Leo Durocher. The Lip *always* thought he could win, and he entered the Series with no fear of the Indians. His weapons? An obvious one named Willie Mays and a secret one, pinch-hitter extraordinaire James "Dusty" Rhodes, an easygoing Alabama boy who had won several games for the Giants in 1954 with late-inning hits.

"Between Willie Mays and Dusty Rhodes there was nothing but laughter in our clubhouse all season," Durocher recalled in his autobiography, *Nice Guys Finish Last*. "Pressure? They spit at it."

Rhodes was a terrible fielder, but he was always grabbing a bat when the Giants needed to be rescued from an almost certain loss. "He thought he was the greatest hitter in the whole world," Durocher said. And in the 1954 World Series, he behaved like it.

Game One was a barn-burner, exciting enough that the great sportswriter Arnold Hano wrote a superb book about it (1955's *A Day in the Bleachers*). This was the game in which Indians slugger Vic Wertz hit the most famous fly out of all time: the monster blast that Willie Mays ran down 450 feet from home plate with an over-the-shoulder catch with two men on in the eighth inning of a 2–2 game.

Dusty Rhodes facing joyful teammates and fans after smacking his second homer of the Series, the Game Two blast that gave the Giants a 3–1 victory at the Polo Grounds. "The big fuss they made over me was a little embarrassing," said the unassuming Rhodes.

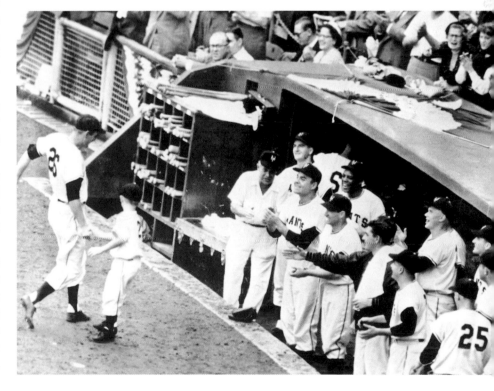

Here's Arnold Hano on the catch and the amazing throw that followed:

> He had turned so quickly, and run so fast and truly that he made this catch look—to us in the bleachers—quite ordinary. To those reporters in the press box, nearly six hundred feet from the bleacher wall, watching Mays run and run until he had become the size of a pigmy and then he had run some more, while the ball diminished to a mote of white dust and finally disappeared in the dark blob that was Mays' mitt.
>
> The play was not finished, with the catch....
>
> Mays caught the ball, and then whirled and threw, like some olden statue of a Greek javelin hurler, his head twisted away to the left as his right arm swept out and around. But Mays is no classic study for the simple reason that at the peak of his activity, his baseball cap flies off. And as he turned, or as he threw—I could not tell which, the two motions were welded into one—off came the cap, and then Mays himself continued to spin around after the gigantic effort of returning the ball whence it came, and he went down flat on his belly and out of sight. But the throw! What an astonishing throw....the throw of a giant, the throw of a howitzer made human.

The Indians didn't score in that inning. The game remained tied, 2–2, until the bottom of the tenth, when Leo Durocher had the chance to bring in his second weapon to face dominating Cleveland starter Bob Lemon. With two

1954

NEW YORK GIANTS

4

CLEVELAND INDIANS

0

Indians' right fielder
Dave Pope trying—and
failing—to catch Dusty
Rhodes' tenth-inning,
game-winning, three-
run home run in
Game One.

"I MEASURED IT OFF JUST RIGHT, SKIP."

men on, Dusty Rhodes popped a ball down the right-field line, barely 265 feet but just far enough to make it into the seats of the oddly proportioned Polo Grounds. Somehow the Giants had won Game One, 5–2.

Rhodes' comment to Durocher after the game: "I measured it off just right, Skip."

Rhodes measured off a couple more in Game Two. Coming up to pinch hit for Monte Irvin in the fifth inning, he singled to drive in the tying run against Early Wynn. This time, though, Rhodes went out to play left field after his at bat. "I was tickled when Leo let me stay in," he said later. "It gave me the chance to show a few guys I could hit the ball beyond 265 feet, because in the eighth inning I belted one against the right-field roof that made it 3–1."

Of course, Leo still had to survive watching Rhodes play in left field. He'd warned Mays to catch everything he could reach—but then, with two outs in the ninth and the tying runs on base, Vic Wertz hit a long drive to left-center. "A monster of a drive, but it's in the park and all is right with the world because Mays is racing over," Durocher recalled with a shudder. "And then, all of a sudden, I see Rhodes coming into the scene, pounding his glove and driving Mays away. *Oh no!* I dropped down on my knees and covered my head. I wouldn't look."

But somehow Rhodes caught the ball. ("I had it all the way," he told Durocher.) The game ended 3–1, leaving the stunned Indians wondering how they could be two games down to such as Dusty Rhodes. But things didn't improve in Game Three, as the Indians started to struggle and writhe like a creature caught in a tar pit. Rhodes came in to pinch hit in the third (!) inning of this game and singled with the bases loaded to drive in two. The Giants cruised to a 6–2 win.

By Game Four the Indians were almost paralyzed with disbelief. The Giants pounded Bob Lemon to jump to a 7–0 lead, and though the Indians got as close as 7–4, there was never any doubt that this was to be the Giants' year—and the year the National League got its groove back.

TALES OF THE GLOVE

A REMARKABLE NUMBER OF WORLD SERIES HAVE HINGED ON SPECTACULAR FIELDING PLAYS.

HERE'S THE INSIDE STORY ON A FEW OF THE MOST MEMORABLE.

"If I had played straightaway like I should have played, it would have been easy for me to catch the baseball. But everybody says to play all the way to center field. So Berra hits the ball to the corner down the left-field line. Well, I had to do something. I run like a hawk. I run to the wall and I figure, 'I can get it,' and so I catch it, and Pee Wee, he tells me, 'Give me the ball, give me the ball,' and Pee Wee is standing on the line down third base, and I throw it to Pee Wee, and we caught McDougald on second base, so we throw to Gil Hodges at first, and they make a double play. We finish the inning, 2–0, we play the ninth, and they don't do nothing in the ninth, so it finish 2–0. We win the championship."

— Brooklyn's Sandy Amoros, describing his catch in Game Seven of the 1955 World Series, which preserved Johnny Podres' shutout and gave the Dodgers their first championship. From *Bums*.

"I had no time for conscious thought or judgment. The ball was out there too fast. I took off with the crack of the bat and dove. My body was stretched full out, and I felt as if I was disappearing into another world. I can't remember thrusting my glove across my body—I must have; the ball was in it. Then I turned over, bounced up, and threw it in….

"When I see it on film now I'm still amazed by it. When they slow it down it seems impossible that I could reach the ball. It was just hit too hard. Somehow it happened. Somehow I got it. A miracle? Wasn't the entire season a miracle?"

— New York Mets' Ron Swoboda, whose Game Four catch in 1969 saved the game for the Miracle Mets, who went on to win the Series in five. From *After the Miracle*.

"Otto Miller was on first base and Pete Kilduff was on second. They had both singled, Miller to center and Kilduff to left. Clarence Mitchell, a relief pitcher, and a pretty good left-handed hitter, was the next batter.

"I was playing deep—back on the grass—and Mitchell hit the second pitch, a line drive to my right. I guess everybody thought it was headed for center field. I took a step to my right and jumped. The ball stuck in my glove and my momentum carried me to second base.

"Well, Kilduff, who took off for third when the ball was hit, was easy. All I had to do was touch second with my toe…

"Miller apparently didn't see what happened because I looked at first base and saw him within five feet of me. He stopped running and stood there, so I just tagged him…. Just before I tagged him, he said, 'Where'd you get that ball?' I said, 'Well, I've got it and you're out No. 3.' Then I trotted off the field."

— Bill Wambsganss, on his unassisted triple play in Game Five of the 1920 World Series.

"I played Wertz to pull the ball slightly…. And that's what happened. He swung at Liddle's first pitch. I saw it clearly. As soon as I picked it up in the sky, I knew I had to get over toward straightaway centerfield. I turned and ran at full speed toward center with my back to the plate. But even as I was running, I realized I had to be in stride if I was going to catch it, so about 450 feet away from the plate I looked up over my left shoulder and spotted the ball. I timed it perfectly and it dropped into my glove maybe ten or fifteen feet from the bleacher wall. At that same moment I wheeled and threw in one motion and fell to the ground. I must have looked like a corkscrew. I could feel my hat flying off, but I saw the ball heading straight to Davey Williams on second. [Larry] Doby had tagged up at second after the catch. That held Doby to third base, while [Al] Rosen had to get back to first very quickly."

—Willie Mays, whose Game One catch off Vic Wertz (probably the most famous catch of all time) sent the Giants on their shocking four-game sweep of the Cleveland Indians in 1954.

1955

AT LAST

1955

BROOKLYN
DODGERS

4

NEW YORK
YANKEES

3

Time was running out for these Dodgers. National League champions in 1941, 1947, 1949, 1952, and 1953, they had lost to the Yankees every year. And now, in 1955, they were getting old. Jackie Robinson, twenty-eight when he finally got the chance to break the color line, was thirty-six now, white-haired and injury-prone. Roy Campanella was only thirty-three, and coming off a year in which he hit .318 with thirty-two home runs, but catchers age fast, and he could feel the end approaching as well. Duke Snider, Gil Hodges, Pee Wee Reese, Clem Labine, Don Newcombe—all were close to thirty or past it. If they were going to win a World Series from the Yankees, it was going to have to be soon.

The first two games of the Series didn't make it seem likely. Whitey Ford beat Don Newcombe in Game One, 6–5, in a game marked by two home runs by the Yankees' Joe Collins. Then Tommy Byrne beat Billy Loes, 4–2, and it seemed like the usual Yankee-Dodger mismatch.

But then, at Ebbets Field, everything began to change. Pitching on his twenty-third birthday, rambunctious young Johnny Podres outdueled Bob Turley in the Dodgers' crucial 8–3 win. When homers by Duke Snider, Gil Hodges, and Roy Campanella carried Brooklyn to an 8–5 victory in Game Four, the Series was all even.

And then the Dodgers rode Snider's two home runs to a 5–3 win in Game Five, and suddenly they were just a game away from their first World Championship. For the second time in four years, Brooklyn needed just one win in two games to capture the Series. In 1952, they couldn't do it. How about this year?

Uh-oh. Cool as ice, Whitey Ford shut them down in Game Six, 5–1. That left only one game to play, at Yankee Stadium, with Johnny Podres facing off against thirty-five-year-old Tommy Byrne. Youth versus experience. A team that always won versus a team that never did. It didn't look good.

The result was a stunning pitchers' duel and an indelible World Series game. In the third, Roy Campanella doubled and Gil Hodges drove him in with a single. Hodges drove in the second run with a sacrifice fly in the sixth, and after that it was up to Podres.

It seemed like the lead might not last past the sixth, as the young pitcher, looking shaky, put two men on with nobody out. Then Yogi Berra, one of the great clutch hitters of all time, drove the ball toward the left-field corner. Dodgers' outfielder Sandy Amoros, who'd just been inserted into the game for defensive purposes, was playing over toward center, and as he raced after Berra's blast it seemed impossible that he could catch up with it. But somehow he did, snaring the ball one-handed near the foul line. A spin, a throw, and he'd turned what had looked like a game-tying double into a double play.

"Lucky, lucky, I'm so lucky," Amoros kept saying after the game. But luck had nothing to do with it—and it had nothing to do with the Dodgers finally getting the championship they'd long craved, as Podres set down the Yankees to complete the 2–0 win.

Sportswriters, thrilled to have a "Man Bites Dog" story to write, outdid themselves trying to put the feelings of Brooklyn into words. "At precisely 3:43 in Yankee Stadium yesterday afternoon a king died and an empire crashed," wrote Joe Williams, "and from Greenpoint to Red Hook, from Sea

Finally, something for the Dodgers to wear.

Gate to Bushwick, from Coney to Flatbush, in fact, all over the teeming, turbulent borough across the bridge, joy was at once unconfined and unrefined."

In the fullness of time, the novelist and columnist Pete Hamill wrote about what the Dodgers' triumph meant to him and other young fans in 1955. The following essay, entitled "Faith, Hope, and Charity," first appeared in the 1989 World Series program:

The pitching form of Johnny Podres, forever enshrined in the Brooklyn pantheon.

> When I was a boy growing up in the slums of Brooklyn, the World Series was an elusive, glittering dream. The long season started in the spring, with Red Barber's voice coming to us from the Florida of the imagination. There was no television then, in the first years after the war, so we constructed images of ballplayers among the palm trees from Barber's voice and the stories in the newspapers. In all the years that have followed, baseball was never so alive.
>
> The year that started in the spring ended in the fall. Around Labor Day, the two most majestic words in the American vocabulary began to be whispered in the streets of Brooklyn: World Series. The season became a kind of Yellow Brick Road, full of twists and turns, surprises and ambushes; and at the end of the road was Oz.
>
> To get to that Oz was in many ways more of a religious experience than a pennant race. We prayed for the boys of our summers. Oh, how we prayed. I remember praying during one angst-ridden series with the Cardinals, promising God that if only Enos Slaughter would strike out, if only He could prevent the big man from parking one over the pavillion roof in Sportsmen's Park, then I would be kinder to old people, obey my parents, forsake all temptations to wickedness; if only Stan Musial would pop up to short, I would banish all impure thoughts forever, make a hundred novenas, send my pennies to the missions in Africa.

My Jewish and Protestant friends made their own prayers. Together, we bombarded Heaven itself. In the fall, when the shadows in the ballparks started growing longer, and the impossible goal of the World Series actually seemed within reach, we must have offered God a thousand deals. Alas, we sometimes fell short; somehow, God inexplicably granted his benevolence to the Cardinals or Phillies, or, far worse, to the Giants.

Faith, we soon learned, was never enough; you still needed left-handed pitching. And if you came from Brooklyn, you were forced to live with the heartbreaking knowledge that man is imperfect. All of us, for example, were haunted by what happened in 1941. Some terrible events took place in the world that year; most terrible of all was Pearl Harbor. But if you were a kid from Brooklyn, the year would forever be remembered for one additional infamy: it was the year that Mickey Owen Dropped The Third Strike.

The Dodgers had battled and scrapped and played brilliantly to get to the World Series against the hated Yankees. When they won the pennant, their first since 1920, Brooklyn went insane; there were block parties, fireworks, pots and pans banging on fire escapes; there was a roaring parade up Flatbush Avenue to Ebbets Field. My father and his friends all believed that the long, gray twilight was over, the Depression had ended, we (our identities were always merged) had won the pennant, and now we would show the Yankees what National League baseball was about. We'd run them crazy, we'd slash line drives off the concave outfield wall, we'd…And Mickey Owen Dropped The Third Strike and the Yankees beat us, four games to one. That was the first time I saw grown men sobbing. It would not be the last, as the young men of the neighborhood went off to the war. For some of them, there would be no next year.

After the war we discovered that hope was an intricate part of our lives; we needed it more than most other fans to fight off the darkness of depression, a darkness that usually endured throughout the winter. In 1947, we went up against the Yankees once more, and lost four games to three. "Wait'll Next Year!" became the slogan. Alas, we had to wait until '49, and lost four games to one, again to the Yankees, and were defeated again in '52 and '53, extending them to seven games the first time, going down in six the following autumn. To us, the Yankees became the faceless, automated doom machine. We prayed sometimes now for Cleveland or Boston, hoping that we could for once play some other team; but it was always the Yankees. Years later, in a darkened movie house, I saw Darth Vader for the first time, and shuddered, thinking of Mr. Stengel's muscular charges.

Those years marked all of us who rooted then for the Dodgers. This wasn't simply a matter of a baseball team losing; it was about character and fate, the essential components of tragedy. And the often profound depression that set in after still another losing effort had to do with the nature of the World Series itself. The best-of-seven series was, and remains, the greatest single test in team sports. By comparison, the Super Bowl is a mere gang fight. Anybody can be a hero in May; the truest test of talent, heart, and will always comes in October.

It is made more vivid by the beauty of the season. Everywhere in America, October is the most beautiful month. The skies are chilly and clear. The light seems somehow more grave. May can be silly; August is a torment; but October belongs to serious men. During the long season, attention is dispersed among all the teams of both leagues. In October, all attention falls upon these two, the last teams standing on a field. They have at once arrived in Oz and are prepared to bid it farewell. What they do upon these green fields will be remembered through the winter and in some cases, for life. And the players surely know this. If they disgrace themselves, the disgrace will follow them into old age. And if they rise to this final occasion, if they go past mere talent into that remote and mysterious realm where champions dwell, they might become ornaments of their time. Nothing else in American life is like this, not even war.

Which is why I carry 1955 around with me all of my days. That, at last, was Next Year. That was

Clash of titans: Jackie
Robinson doubles up Yogi
Berra in Series action.

"FAITH, WE SOON LEARNED, WAS NEVER ENOUGH; YOU STILL NEEDED LEFT-HANDED PITCHING."

the year the Dodgers finally beat the Yankees in the World Series. It didn't matter that they lost to the Yankees again the following year, or that the year after they abandoned Brooklyn forever. In 1955, the year of Johnny Podres, they went to seven games with the Yankees and emerged as champions of the universe. The past was indeed prelude. Starting in 1941, the heroes had submitted to all of their tests, like a collective Odysseus; they had sipped the bitter dregs of defeat; they'd had the taste of ashes in their mouths; they'd been slandered and vilified and laughed at; they'd made men and women weep and cast themselves into the wine-dark sea. And there they were on the autumn fields at the end, still fighting, still struggling, still hoping. Until they had triumphed at last.

There are some people who insist that baseball is a boy's game, and that it proves something or other about the permanent adolescence of American men. I disagree. All of us—men and women—spend our lives moving toward October. Not all of us are winners in the conventional sense nor do we all handle pressure with grace. But it is not some foolish whim to believe that there will always be a Next Year, another chance, one more at bat, an opportunity to hold on to that third strike.

Such desires are the essence of being human. And if we can come away with such knowledge from the playing fields of autumn, then the World Series is as good a guide to conduct as any we've devised.

Of course, a little left-handed pitching wouldn't hurt.

I f history tends to reduce every World Series to a single moment, at least in 1956 it picked the right moment. Going into the contest, the big question was whether the Dodgers could miraculously make it two Series victories in a row, or whether the Yankees could reassert the dominance they'd shown before 1955. Most bets were on the Yankees, who rode a triple-crown year from Mickey Mantle (.352, 52 home runs, 130 RBI) to a typically easy pennant victory over the Indians.

1956

PERFECTION

The Dodgers, on the other hand, were now definitely old. Jackie Robinson and Roy Campanella were shadows of their former dominant selves, and only big years from Duke Snider (forty-three home runs) and Don Newcombe (twenty-seven wins) enabled the Dodgers to edge Milwaukee and repeat as N.L. champions.

The Series started as the mirror image of 1955, with the Dodgers blasting Whitey Ford in Game One for a 6–3 win and then running roughshod over starter Don Larsen and six relievers to slam the Yankees again, 13–8, in Game Two. Just like that, the Dodgers were only two games away from another Series victory.

Yankee Manager Casey Stengel, desperate for a well-pitched game, went back to his workhorse, Whitey Ford, in Game Three. And Whitey responded, working out of several jams to win, 5–3, with help from homers from Enos Slaughter and "Mini-Mr. October," Billy Martin. Then, when Tom Sturdivant outpitched Carl Erskine in Game Four (a 6–2 Yankee win), the Series was knotted up—just as it had been a year earlier.

The pitching matchup for Game Five pitted the Dodgers' thirty-nine-year-old Sal Maglie (the Game One winner) against Don Larsen, who'd been yanked in Game Two after giving up four runs in less than two innings. It seemed an act of desperation on Casey's part, since Larsen—a notorious party animal who'd "made most of his headlines off the field as an after-hours playboy," as *The Sporting News* put it—was the last person to trust in a pressure situation. What's more, his

estranged wife was in court a few blocks away from Yankee Stadium, seeking to have his Series money withheld until he paid her back alimony. And the pitcher had slept only an hour the night before the game.

But Casey Stengel loved to play hunches, and his hunch was that Larsen had a good game in him. So out went the big right-hander to start Game Five.

Everyone knows what happened next. With some strong fielding behind him, Larsen faced twenty-seven Dodger batters and set them all down as the Yankees won, 2–0, on the strength of a Mickey Mantle home run. Mantle also made a great running catch on a long fly by Gil Hodges, Sandy Amoros hit a drive that just went foul, and the rest was Larsen, who went into the ninth inning having thrown fewer than ninety pitches.

Years later, Yogi Berra still marveled at the tense quiet that took over the Yankee bench as Larsen's gem progressed. "It was like everybody went out of their way to say nothing and just go about their business," Berra said. "Larsen didn't change anything in the late innings. He was always able to get the ball up there pretty good but he was a different pitcher when he

Gil Hodges' strong Series helped keep the Dodgers close—but couldn't overcome the Yankees.

1956

NEW YORK YANKEES

4

BROOKLYN DODGERS

3

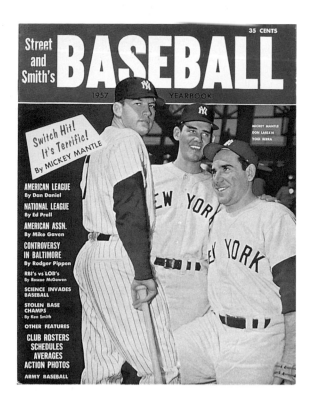

could get his great breaking pitch over. That's what he was throwing—and he just didn't miss that day."

In the ninth, Carl Furillo led off. "This guy's got good stuff, huh?" Yogi, crouched behind the plate, said to him. "Yeah, not bad," Furillo replied, before flying out. Then Campanella grounded out to Martin at second. One out to go, Dale Mitchell up. Ball one, strike one. Strike two. Larsen turned away from the plate, took off his cap, rubbed the sweat away from his brow. Then got ready and threw one more pitch—called strike three!

"Berra ran out and leaped into Larsen's arms like a small boy greeting his father," said *Sports Illustrated*. Berra said it even better: "I was on Larsen's back like a bear in a tree."

And Larsen himself? He might have looked calm out there at the end, but "in the ninth I was so nervous I almost fell down, my legs were so rubbery," he said the next day. "My fingers didn't feel like they were on my hand."

Still two games to go, amazingly. A World Series still to be won. Game Six was Clem Labine's forgotten masterpiece, the ten-inning, 1–0 game decided when Yankee left-fielder Enos Slaughter misplayed Jackie Robinson's line

"THE MILLION-TO-ONE SHOT CAME IN.

HELL FROZE OVER."

drive into a hit that drove in Jim Gilliam with the only run. "That was heartbreaking," said hard-luck loser Bob Turley, still hurting decades later.

Sadly, Game Seven wasn't the classic this classic Series deserved. The Yankees beat up Don Newcombe for five runs in the first four innings, cruising to a 9–0 win and adding to Newcombe's list of postseason miseries. (149–90 in his major-league career, he went 0–4 with an 8.55 ERA in five Series appearances.)

"Newk was throwing good in the game. He just got hit, that's all," Roy Campanella said in defense of his friend. "That could happen to anyone." But it usually happened to Newk.

Still, if Labine's gem has been forgotten, so have Newcombe's mound miseries. The 1956 Series belonged to one man, and one man only: a bad boy named Don Larsen.

After the final pitch of Don Larsen's unprecedented World Series perfect game. "The million-to-one shot came in," wrote Shirley Povich. "Hell froze over."

Major-league baseball struck out for terra incognita after the 1952 season, when the ramshackle Boston Braves resettled in Milwaukee. The nation's population was on the move, and after years of declining attendance in crumbling old ballparks, baseball recognized the inevitable and went where the fans and the shiny new stadiums were.

The Braves' move was just the first: by the end of the decade, the St. Louis Browns became the Baltimore Orioles; the storied Philadelphia Athletics became the Kansas City A's; and, of course, the Dodgers and Giants flew over the Midwest entirely and landed on the West Coast.

Through all the turmoil, the Yankees, though not quite the team they'd been earlier in the decade, kept on winning. In the N.L., stepping into the void of the rebuilding Dodgers, were the Milwaukee Braves. Their biggest stars had big years: Hank Aaron, just twenty-three, hit .322 with forty-four home runs and 132 RBI, while Eddie Matthews weighed in with thirty-two homers. Meanwhile, the Braves' trio of superb starters, Bob Buhl, Lew Burdette, and Warren Spahn, combined for fifty-six wins.

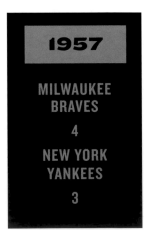

WORLD SERIES BATTING FOES
MICKEY MANTLE ∘ HANK AARON

Cream of the crop.

Still, and understandably, the Yankees were heavy favorites going in against an inexperienced team making its first visit to the Series. And they knew it, jockeying the Braves from the first inning of the first game. "They rode us pretty hard, taunting us with cries of 'choke up' and 'cheese champs,'" recalled Lew Burdette in a *Saturday Evening Post* article published after the Series. "They held up four fingers, indicating they were going to beat us four straight."

The Yankees' confidence gave the Braves just what they needed: the righteous anger of the underdog. And though Whitey Ford out-dueled Warren Spahn, 3–1, in Game One, Burdette (who'd been traded away from the Yankees seven years earlier after pitching just one inning for them) wasn't too impressed. "The Yankees weren't as good a ballclub as I expected them to be," he said.

Burdette had a chance to put his arm where his mouth was, so to speak, in Game Two—and he did, pitching the Braves to a 4–2 win in a game where the bad blood spilled over into a bean-ball war. "Everybody says I fooled the Yankees," Burdette said. "Well, they fooled me. I thought they were better hitters."

The Series moved to Milwaukee for Game Three, which turned into a 12–3 Yankee rout before 45,000 disappointed fans. But Game Four was a classic, a contest that saw the Braves leap out to a 4–1 lead (Hank Aaron hit a three-run home run) before the Yankees tied it in the top of the ninth on a blast by Elston Howard. The Yankees then went ahead, 5–4, in the tenth…but Eddie Matthews crushed a Bob Grim pitch for a two-run home run in the bottom of the inning to give the Braves a 7–5 win. Warren Spahn, with less than his best stuff, pitched the entire game for Milwaukee.

Game Five was Burdette's turn again, and this time he was even better than he had been in Game One, pitching a shutout to best Whitey Ford in the Braves' crucial 1–0 victory. "I especially enjoyed retiring Yogi Berra for the final out with a man on first,"

1957

MILWAUKEE BRAVES

4

NEW YORK YANKEES

3

Lew Burdette, facing the dangerous Moose Skowron with the bases loaded, delivers the last pitch of the 1957 World Series.

After Moose Skowron hit into a force play on a great backhand stop by third baseman Eddie Mathews, Lew Burdette celebrated his third victory—and the Braves' first Series triumph in Milwaukee. Burdette's philosophy: "I think pitching is seventy percent luck and thirty percent control."

Burdette wrote. After throwing Berra screwballs and sinkers all afternoon, the pitcher decided to cross up the Yankee catcher with a slider that broke in over the plate. "He let out a 'whoof' in amazement as he swung half-heartedly. The result was a puny pop-up halfway between third and the plate which Mathews caught."

The Series moved back to New York, "which isn't the most gracious place to try to win a World Series," as Hank Aaron put it. Game Six was another classic won by the Yankees, 3–2. So, for the third year in a row, the Series was heading into a seventh game.

"LEW COULD MAKE COFFEE NERVOUS."

Braves Manager Fred Haney sent out Burdette on two days' rest. On the mound and off, Burdette was a bundle of nerves. "I'm fidgety," he said. "I touch my cap, tug at my pants, pull my sleeves loose from under my arms, wipe the sweat off my eyebrows." Added his roommate, Bob Buhl: "Lew could make coffee nervous."

In and around his fidgets, Burdette pitched a masterpiece in Game Seven, dissecting the Yankees for his second shutout and third win of the Series, 5–0. "My pitches didn't have much steam behind them," he admitted after the game. He was saved, he said, by his control and by the Braves' fine fielding, including a backhand stab of a grounder by Eddie Mathews at third that turned into the final out with the bases loaded in the ninth.

The unlikely Braves were the champions of the world. After the Series, Burdette revealed that he and Warren Spahn planned to win fifty games between them in 1958. "We expect to share another four victories over the Yankees," he crowed, "*if* they make the Series again!"

Of all the Yankee super-stars—Mickey Mantle, Yogi Berra, Bobby Richardson, Whitey Ford—who would have guessed that the most important Yank in the 1958 Series would be pitcher Bob Turley?

1958

NEW YORK YANKEES

4

MILWAUKEE BRAVES

3

They did, and so did the Braves, bringing the two teams into a rematch in the 1958 Series. The Braves won the first two games, 4–3 for Warren Spahn and 13–5 for Burdette, and after Don Larsen pitched a shutout for a 3–0 Yankee win in Game Three, Milwaukee moved within a game of their second championship when Spahn pitched a two-hitter in a 3–0 victory.

But then the Brave bats went silent. Bob Turley shut them down, 7–0, and an array of Yankee relievers held on to win, 4–3, in the ten-inning Game Six.

Game Seven matched previous Series stars Don Larsen and Lew Burdette. Larsen was gone in the third, replaced by Bob Turley (who had pitched a complete-game shutout in Game Five and gotten the save in Game Six!). Turley held the Braves to one run in 6 $2/3$ innings, while the Yankees broke a 2–2 tie in the eighth with four runs off Burdette for the clincher.

Burdette was heartbroken. "I thought we were going to blow them away," he said.

But even when the Yankees were pushed to the limit, no one ever blew them away.

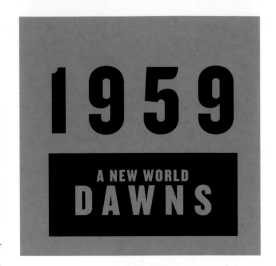

Palm trees. The wind sweeping in from the desert. Polite fans giving opposing players a respectful round of applause before leaving in the seventh inning. Seating capacity for 90,000 plus. It was a long way from Brooklyn.

As anyone within earshot of forty-five years of laments and protestations knows, the Dodgers and Giants left New York after the 1957 season and headed for the West Coast. While waiting for their ballparks to be built, the Giants moved into San Francisco's Seals Stadium, while the Dodgers settled into Los Angeles' Memorial Coliseum, a behemoth park with such a short left-field fence (250 feet) that the team had to erect a forty-two-foot-high screen to cut down on the cheap home runs.

The Dodgers made it right back to the World Series. A few of the familiar Brooklyn faces were still there: stoical Gil Hodges at first, Carl Furillo patrolling right field, Duke Snider still blasting the occasional mammoth home run. But this was a transitional time for the Dodgers, a team soon to be dominated by such younger stars as Sandy Koufax, Don Drysdale, and Maury Wills.

The Dodgers' opponents in the 1959 World Series were even less familiar to fans across the country. After a forty-year punishment for the sins of 1919, the Chicago White Sox were back in the Series at last. Led by monster years from Early Wynn (22–10) and Bob Shaw (18–6), the Sox also boasted a player who helped shake baseball from its "walk, don't run" torpor of the 1950s: Luis Aparicio, who decimated unprepared A.L. catchers with fifty-six stolen bases.

In Game One, the "Go-Go Sox" were more like the "Go-Yard" Sox, as Ted Kluszewski blasted two homers and Early Wynn handled the Dodgers easily in an 11–0 Chicago win. But, as Dodger pitcher Stan Williams told Danny Peary in *We Played the Game,* the Dodgers weren't that impressed. "Don Zimmer came into the clubhouse and said, 'Boys, the Go-Go Sox are dead. They've got no chance.' Everybody laughed though we'd just got bombed. We knew what he was saying was true. We had looked at them as a ballclub and knew we were better."

Los Angeles began to prove it in Game Two, as Johnny Podres (just turned twenty-seven, though it seemed he'd been around forever) and Larry Sherry combined to hold the Sox to three runs in the Dodgers' crucial 4–3 victory. Journeyman Dodger second baseman Charlie Neal hit two home runs as Sherry—who'd been in the minors as recently as midseason—began a journey that would make him the Series' unlikely star.

Don Drysdale got most of the ink in Game Three, giving up eleven hits and four walks in seven innings but somehow emerging with a 3–1 win. But it was Sherry again who kept the ship afloat, pitching two shutout innings in front of a record Coliseum crowd of 92,394 for his second save in two games. "The Sox just couldn't figure out his slider," Stan Williams recalled.

The Dodgers drove Early Wynn from the box early in Game Four, but when Roger Craig gave up four runs in the seventh the game was tied, 4–4. Here came Sherry, pitching two hitless innings and getting the win when Gil Hodges hit a home run in the eighth. Now the Dodgers were just a game away.

They had to wait an extra game, as Chicago's Bob Shaw and two relievers held on for a 1–0 Sox victory over Sandy Koufax. But back in Chicago Comiskey Park, the Dodgers erupted for eight runs in the first four innings in Game Six. Neal went 3–5, Snider hit a home run, and Sherry pitched 5 $\frac{2}{3}$ innings of scoreless relief for the 9–3 win.

"Every body but Mrs. O'Leary's cow got into the act today," wrote Red Smith, "when a howling pack of savages from the West, cutting, shooting and burning, breached Comiskey Park's tall green stockade and laid waste to the championship dream which American League baseball fans here had clutched to their bosoms through forty barren years."

All the Dodgers' Larry Sherry (#51) did in the 1959 Series was appear four times in relief, garnering two wins and two saves. That's Gil Hodges (#14) looking like an imposter in a uniform that doesn't read "Brooklyn."

The "Go-Go" White Sox were founded on speed and defense, but they also had Ted Kluszewski, who provided muscle with two home runs in Game One.

THE MOMENT

WHAT DOES IT FEEL LIKE TO WIN A WORLD SERIES? SOME STARS PUT US IN THE KNOW.

"I was still thirteen days shy of my twenty-first birthday and my heart was almost orbiting the earth."
   —Mickey Mantle after the Yankees' 1952 Series victory over the Brooklyn Dodgers.

"I could feel tears smarting in my eyes as Ruel came home with the winning run. I'd won. We'd won. I felt so happy that it didn't seem real."
   —Walter Johnson, after shutting down the Giants over four innings to give his Washington Senators their first World Series victory, in 1924.

"I had it all today. I just had everything—fastball, curveball, and change-up. I just had the feeling from the start, and now I know I'll remember this day as long as I live."
   —Johnny Podres, after pitching the Game Seven shutout that gave the Brooklyn Dodgers their long-awaited first championship in 1955.

"Imagine…a grown man crying."
   —Dodger Clem Labine, after the same game.

"Nine big ones in the kick—nine great big thousand bucks!"
   —Gino Cimoli, claiming the winners' share after the Pittsburgh Pirates came back to beat the Yankees 10–9 and capture the Series on Bill Mazeroski's famous ninth-inning home run.

"I will light my cigars with hundred dollar bills."
   —Art Shamsky, after his Amazing Mets dispatched the Baltimore Orioles in the 1969 Series.

"All my life it's been the other guys who were heroes while I just plugged along and tried to do my job. And now it's me who is the hero!"
   —Mickey Lolich, whose three wins carried the Detroit Tigers to an upset Series victory over the St. Louis Cardinals in 1968.

"Right now, I don't really know what this means to me, except that we're the best. Maybe when I've settled down a bit, maybe when I see my wife's face, then I'll know just what this means."
   —Joe Morgan, after his Cincinnati Reds wrapped up their Game Seven win over the Boston Red Sox in the thrilling 1975 Series.

As unlikely as a man walking on the moon: Ed Charles, Jerry Koosman, and Jerry Grote celebrate the Mets' championship. "I know there were people who changed their lives because of the Miracle Mets," Charles said. "People felt better. It was a good thing."

"You realize you are world champions, that you've won the World Series, but the importance of that doesn't really sink in until you've had the chance to think about it over the winter. And you hear people talk about it and how special it is, and how few people are able to enjoy that as a player…. And the luster of that memory continues to grow, and it was something in your life that can never be taken away. You were on a team that was so special for that frozen moment in time."
—St. Louis Cardinals' pitcher Nelson Briles, on his team's 1967 championship. From *The Spirit of St. Louis*.

"You guys can ask me all the questions in the world and I'll tell you just one thing: It's done."
—Chili Davis, after the Minnesota Twins' 1–0, Game Seven victory over the Atlanta Braves in the 1991 Series.

At a quick glance, the years 1960 through 1964 look like just another era when the Yankees ran roughshod over major-league baseball. They captured the A.L. pennant every season, never winning fewer than ninety games, and won the World Series in both 1961 and 1962. Any other team would consider such a run the highlight of its history.

But in truth 1960–64 contain the final rise and crashing fall of a dynasty, the years in which a Yankee team that had functioned with machine-smooth precision for nearly four decades began to come apart. The seeds were there from 1960—Mickey Mantle's injuries, a weaker supporting cast, increasing questions about Casey Stengel's age—even as the inevitable outcome was postponed.

1960

PITTSBURGH PIRATES
4

NEW YORK YANKEES
3

As the 1960 Series began, doubts about the Yankees' longevity seemed far away. Mantle and Roger Maris topped the A.L. with forty and thirty-nine home runs, while Yankee pitchers led the league in ERA, shutouts, and saves. Although their opponent, the Pittsburgh Pirates, won ninety-five games on the strength of N.L. MVP Dick Groat's league-leading .325 batting average and Vern Law's twenty wins, they seemed at first just another patsy for the powerful Yanks.

The Series' raw numbers seem to support this. The Yankees outhit the Pirates .338 to .256 and outscored them 55–27. Yankee pitching held Dick Groat to a .214 batting average, while Mickey Mantle hit .400 (with three homers and 11 RBI), Bobby Richardson drove in a Series-record twelve runs, Elston Howard hit .462, Whitey Ford pitched two complete-game shutouts…and so on.

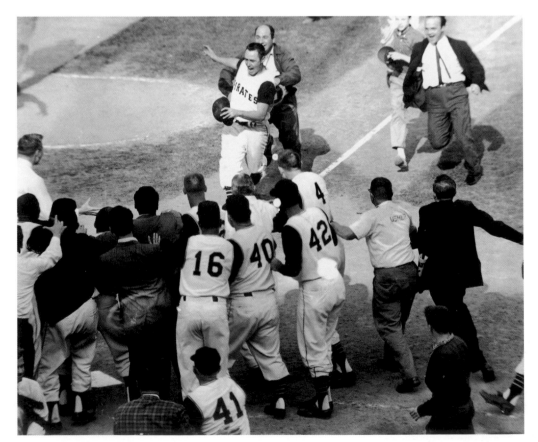

Unbelievable! Teammates and fans swarm Bill Mazeroski after his ninth-inning home run gave the Pirates the 1960 championship.

A Yankee rout, except for one thing. When the seventh game was over, somehow the Pirates were World Champions and the stunned Bombers were headed home.

After Game Three (Ford's first shutout), the pattern of the Series had been set: the Yanks had outscored the Pirates, 30–9, but had only a 2–1 Series lead. Then the Pirates went on to win Games Four and Five, 3–2 and 5–2, and suddenly the dominant Yankees were one game away from a shocking Series defeat. They postponed that moment with a 12–0 blowout behind Ford. Then came Game Seven in Pittsburgh, perhaps the single most famous Series game of all time.

For the first time the Pirates kept pace with the Yanks' hitting barrage. It was a seesaw contest that saw the Pirates take a 4–0 lead, the Yankees go ahead 7–4, the Pirates come back for a 9–7 lead, and the Yankees tie it 9–9 with two runs in the top of the ninth.

Starting the bottom of the ninth, Yankee pitcher Ralph Terry knew he was in trouble. "Everything I threw was high," he said later. "I couldn't get the ball down."

The Pirate lead-off hitter, second baseman Bill Mazeroski, was just trying to get on base. Mazeroski was famous for his incomparable glovework, but he had some pop in his bat as well. Enough pop that, when he hit Terry's second pitch toward the wall in left-center, he thought he might have an extra-base hit.

"When I rounded first, I was at full speed," he said later. "I wanted to end up on third where a fly ball could score me. When it did get over the wall it surprised me so much."

Though Mazeroski tried to keep a stoic demeanor as he rounded the bases, his excitement was too great to hide. "All I could think about was 'We beat 'em, we beat 'em, we beat the great Yankees!'" he said. "And that's when I started jumping around." As did all his teammates and a significant proportion of the population of Pennsylvania.

For the Pirates, it was their first World Series championship since 1925. For the Yankees, it was a galling defeat. And for the aging Casey Stengel, it was the last hurrah: Just two days after Mazeroski smashed his home run, the Yankee owners fired Stengel, who had brought the team nine pennants and seven World Series victories in twelve years, and replaced him with Ralph Houk.

"I'll never make the mistake of being seventy again," Casey said.

All that time in the batting cage must have paid off: Bobby Richardson, a meek hitter during the regular season, totaled an astounding twenty hits in the 1960 and '61 Series.

1961

NEW YORK
YANKEES

4

CINCINNATI
REDS

1

"You would have thought that going from Casey Stengel to Ralph Houk required an adjustment so great, the Yankees in 1961 would need counseling more than spring training," Mickey Mantle said in *All My Octobers*. "But it wasn't that tough…. Ralph wasn't colorful and he wasn't complicated. He was strong as pig iron, firm, direct, sure of himself, a straight shooter."

Under Houk's steely guidance, the Yankees went 109–53 in 1961, leaving the rest of the league in the dust. Of course, it didn't hurt Houk's freshman year that a couple of Yankee sluggers named Roger Maris and Mickey Mantle combined for 115 home runs and 264 RBI to lead the world in both departments.

Still, by the time the World Series rolled around, the Yankee sluggers were reeling. Mantle was battling a serious leg injury, and Maris had withstood almost unbearable pressure

10 WORST SERIES

NO.
7

1961

Casey's "banty rooster" Whitey Ford, a World Series master throughout his career. "You kind of took it for granted around the Yankees that there was always going to be baseball in October," he said.

as he succeeded in toppling Babe Ruth's twenty-four-year-old mark of sixty home runs. Neither was nearly at full strength at any point in the Series.

Not that it mattered. The Yanks' opponents, the Cincinnati Reds, were just the latest in a roster of Cinderella teams (cf. the 1927 Pirates, 1932 Cubs, 1950 Phillies) who triumphed over fierce opposition in the N.L. race only to realize, once the Series began, that playing against the big boys was a whole 'nother kettle of fish. Frank Robinson, a true superstar, led the Reds—but neither he nor any other Red, including twenty-game–winners Joey Jay and Jim O'Toole, had ever played in a World Series before.

In Game One, Whitey Ford picked up where he'd left off in '60, throwing an easy two-hit shutout as the Yankees won, 2–0, over Jim O'Toole. (Endearingly, O'Toole called the loss "the highlight of my career.") In what would become the Series' trademark, the Yankees' big hitters were quiet, while the supporting cast—in this case, Elston Howard and Moose Skowron, who both homered—got the crucial hits.

The Reds came back to win Game Two, 6–2, behind Jay, to send the Series back to Cincinnati tied, 1–1. "Shop windows were decorated in red; girls wore red dresses, scarves, sweaters. I saw a puppy wearing a bright red sash," Ralph Houk recalled in *Ballplayers Are Human Too*. "All Ohio was behind the underdog Reds, who'd bitten us and liked the taste of our blood."

But then Johnny Blanchard hit a home run in the eighth inning of Game Three and Maris followed with one in the ninth (his only homer of the Series) to give the Yankees a 3–2 win, and the air went out of Cincinnati's red balloon. Few except the most emotional rooters thought the Reds had much chance of coming back.

Having eked out a couple of close wins, the Yankees seemed to sit up and shake off their lethargy. Whitey Ford pitched five shutout innings in Game Four, Jim Coates came in to complete the game, and the Yankees cruised to an easy 7–0 win. Game Five was even less suspenseful (despite the fact that Mantle and Yogi Berra were out with injuries) as the

Yankees scored eleven runs in the first four innings en route to an easy 13–5 win.

Ralph Houk, emerging from Casey's shadow, had his first World Series championship. "That was the greatest year I ever had in baseball," Houk said a quarter of a century later. "It was a pleasure managing that team."

In 1962 the Yankees cruised to a relatively easy pennant, then rested and watched as the N.L. engaged in a brutal fight to the finish. The Giants and Dodgers ended the season in a tie— with the Giants making up a four-game deficit in the last eight days. The Giants prevailed in the three-game playoff, and then staggered into the Series against the rested Bombers. "We weren't prepared to play," said Giant pitcher Billy Pierce. "We didn't even have tickets for our wives."

Still, this was a strong Giant team, one that boasted Willie Mays in his prime and such up-and-coming stars as Willie McCovey, Orlando Cepeda, and Matty and Felipe Alou. Everyone predicted that the Yankees would win— everyone always predicted that Yanks would win—but the pundits also said it would be a high-scoring Series featuring offensive explosions from both teams.

The pundits were wrong. In the words of sportswriter Roy Terrell, "Somebody took the rabbit out of the ball and put spaghetti in the bats." The "somebodies" included Whitey Ford, Ralph Terry, Juan Marichal, Jack Sanford, and others, who held the two offensive line-ups to a combined total of eight home runs and 41 runs in seven games.

When Whitey Ford won Game One, 6–2, it looked like more of the same old same old. But the Giants came back behind Sanford for a tense 2–0 win in Game Two, and after that the Series was nip and tuck, with the teams alternating hard-fought wins. Game Three: Yankees, 3–2. Game Four: Giants, 7–3. Game Five: Yankees, 5–3. Game Six: Giants, 5–2. For the second time in three years, the Yankees had been extended to a seventh game.

Game Seven of the 1962 World Series belongs in the pantheon. The Yankees scored a single run off Jack Sanford in the fifth (on a double-play grounder by Tony Kubek), while Ralph Terry—the man who'd given up Bill Mazeroski's heartbreaking home run to end the 1960 Series—retired the first seventeen Giants in order and gave up only two hits through eight.

10 BEST SERIES

NO. 10

1962

Yankee pitching dominated Willie Mays during the 1962 Series, holding him to just a lone RBI in seven games.

" WE HAD CURLED UP LIKE A SHRIMP ON A HOT GREASED GRILL."

1962

NEW YORK YANKEES

4

SAN FRANCISCO GIANTS

3

Not until the ninth did the Giants mount a threat. Matty Alou led off with a pinch-hit bunt single. Terry then struck out Felipe Alou after Alou failed to lay down a sacrifice bunt. (Forty years later, in a *New York Times* interview with Murray Chass, Felipe called his failure "the lowest point of my life.") When Chuck Hiller struck out as well, the Yankees were only an out away.

But then Willie Mays doubled to right field, with Roger Maris making a fine play to cut off the ball and prevent Matty Alou from scoring. Now there were runners on second and third, with the dangerous Willie McCovey coming up. "I cherish being up in that spot," Willie McCovey said later. "I dreamed about it as a kid."

Then he added: "But the results were different from what I dreamed about."

With the count 1–1, Terry threw McCovey a fastball up and in. "For an instant in time, all the world seemed to stand still," reported Jack Murphy in the *San Diego Union*. "A baseball had been struck violently and the man who threw it watched with sinking heart as it sped toward the emerald turf of right-field in Candlestick Park. Then the scream died in the throats of a crowd of 44,948 as the ball smashed into the glove of Bobby Richardson and stuck there. Suddenly Ralph Terry was able to breathe again."

So the stunned Giants had to watch Terry and the Yankees celebrate their ninth world championship in fourteen years—with only the cold comfort of knowing they'd pushed the Bombers to the limit.

Sandy Koufax and John Roseboro exult in their 1963 Game One win.

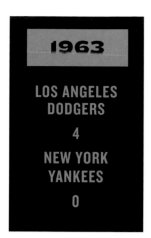

1963

LOS ANGELES DODGERS

4

NEW YORK YANKEES

0

It was the Dodgers' turn to face the juggernaut in 1963. The Yankees had won 104 games despite injury-plagued years from both Mantle and Maris. Stepping into the breach were the Yankee pitchers: Whitey Ford, Jim Bouton, and Ralph Terry all had strong years against weak A.L. competition.

The Dodgers also had an inoffensive offense but terrific pitching. Sandy Koufax (25–5, 1.88 ERA), loving the high mound and spacious dimensions of newly opened Dodger Stadium, had his first great year, and Don Drysdale, Ron Perranoski, and others helped the Dodgers to a team ERA of 2.85.

Still, everyone expected the Yankees to be able to figure out the Dodgers' pitchers. No one in a million years could have guessed what was about to happen. The Series, in the words of Roger Angell, turned out to be like "an economy display of back-yard fireworks. Four small, perfect showers of light in the sky, accompanied by faint plops, and it was over."

In Game One, Koufax struck out fifteen Yankees and bested Whitey Ford, 5–2. The Dodgers' Johnny Podres, thirty-one now and finishing up his last good year, gave up just one run and rode a home run by ex-Yankee Moose Skowron for a 4–1 Game Two win. Then, in Game Three, Jim Bouton gave up a lone first-inning run, but Don Drysdale was better, surrendering just three hits in the 1–0 victory.

Somehow the Dodgers had scored just ten runs in three games, but had a 3–0 Series lead.

In Game Four it was Koufax's turn again, never a good sign for the opposition. The Yankees scored a run off him (on Mantle's home run), but Whitey Ford gave up two. The first was on a blast by Frank Howard, and the second—the run that clinched the Series—was set up by an egregious error by Yankee first baseman Joe Pepitone. Jim Gilliam hit a grounder to third. Clete Boyer fielded the ball and threw to first, but the ball "went through the Yankee first baseman as if he had been made of ectoplasm," in Angell's words.

Gilliam then scored on a sacrifice fly, Koufax shut the Yankees down, and the Dodgers had a 2–1 victory and a Series sweep. The Yankee Series totals: two home runs, four runs scored, thirty-seven strikeouts (twenty-three by Koufax), a .177 batting average. "We had curled up like a shrimp on a hot greased grill," was how Mickey Mantle put it in *All My Octobers*. "I can't express how embarrassed we were."

The Yankees handled Bob Gibson in Game Two of the '64 Series…but the Cardinal great came back to beat them in Games Five and Seven. The Bombers' unprecedented four decades of success had come to an end.

1964

ST. LOUIS
CARDINALS
4
NEW YORK
YANKEES
3

By 1964, the string was running out for this Yankee team. Only last big years from Mickey Mantle, Whitey Ford, and Jim Bouton enabled the Bombers to nip the White Sox and Orioles for the A.L. pennant.

In National League champion St. Louis Cardinals (who'd overcome the collapsing Philadelphia Phillies on the last day of the season), the Yankees were facing a young, aggressive, hungry opponent. Bob Gibson, Lou Brock, Curt Flood, and the rest of the Cardinals weren't just happy to be there. They intended to win.

The teams split the first four games. For eight innings of Game Five, Bob Gibson clung to a 2–0 lead—only to see the Yankees tie the game with two unearned runs in the bottom of the ninth on an error and a home run by Tom Tresh. Almost immediately, the Cardinals' Tim McCarver untied it with a three-run blast. "I couldn't believe it," the always irrepressible McCarver said after the game. "By the time I got to third I was laughing out loud."

Home runs by Mantle, Maris, and Pepitone gave Bouton and the Yankees an 8–3 win in Game Six, setting up a classic confrontation—Gibson versus Stottlemyre—in Game Seven. Unfortunately, the game itself was no classic, as the Cards jumped to a 6–0 lead and the arm-weary Gibson (making his third start in five games) hung on for a 7–5 win. Mantle slugged a home run, the eighteenth and last Series homer of his career, but it was the Cardinals who got—and deserved—the accolades.

"When I had time to think about what we had accomplished, I realized that dethroning the Yankees was incredibly rewarding," McCarver told Danny Peary years later. "They weren't the New York Yankees of the '50s or even '61, but they still had the name and tradition."

Name and tradition were soon all the Yankees had left. After the 1964 Series they descended into chaos, a maelstrom of losing seasons and rotating managers that would continue for more than a decade. After an unprecedented run that had lasted more than four decades, the dynasty had come crashing down.

Mickey Mantle (with Roger Maris and Joe Pepitone) celebrates a homer during the 1964 Series—the last post-season appearance of his career.

Following a decision by the Baseball Rules Committee to expand the strike zone after the 1962 season, baseball entered a dead-ball era. Great hitters struggled to keep their batting averages above .300, while even mediocre pitchers found that they suddenly possessed overpowering stuff.

This was not a vintage era for baseball fans, but there were pleasures to be had. One of the greatest of those pleasures was watching Sandy Koufax at work.

In 1965 Koufax had his third straight spectacular season, going 26–8 with a league-leading 2.04 ERA and an astonishing 382 strikeouts. Don Drysdale added twenty-three wins to carry the Dodgers to the top of the National League for the second time in three years. Their opponents, gratefully leaping into the void left by the collapsing

1965
1966

WHEN THE MOUND SEEMED
TEN FEET HIGH

The 1965 Series went the full seven—but with Sandy Koufax on the mound for the last game, who thought the Twins had a chance?

Yankees, were the Minnesota Twins, led by Tony Oliva (.321), Zoilo Versalles (forty-five doubles, twelve triples, sixteen home runs), Jim "Mudcat" Grant (twenty-one wins), and Jim Kaat (eighteen wins).

The young, enthusiastic, talented Twins showed the Dodgers right away that 1965 would be no repeat of '63, when L.A.'s pitchers shut down the Yankee hitters in four straight. Mudcat Grant and Jim Katt outpitched Drysdale and Koufax as the Twins dominated the first two games, 8–2 and 5–1, at Minnesota's Metropolitan Stadium.

Twins fans and sportswriters began to count their chickens: "Can you back guys away from the plate who see T-bones on the dish?" wrote Don Riley in an "Open Letter to Sandy Koufax" in the *St. Paul Pioneer Press.* "Can you overpower people who carry sticks in their hands and belong to a cause? Can you win with two runs? I don't believe so."

The coolly efficient pitching motion of Jim Palmer.

Taunting Koufax and the Dodgers doesn't seem like a very good idea mid-Series, does it? Once the teams returned to Los Angeles, the Dodgers' pitching reasserted itself. Claude Osteen shut down the Twins with a complete-game five-hitter in Los Angeles' crucial 4–0 Game Three win. Sandy Koufax called it "the key game for us," because it gave him and Drysdale the chance to start again with the Series still in reach. And who would bet against those two twice in a row?

Drysdale was in full command in Game Four, an easy 7–2 victory. Game Five was even easier, 7–0, as Koufax held the Twins to four hits and struck out ten, with Maury Wills going 4–5 and Willie Davis stealing three bases. "Two runs had, it seemed, been more than ample," said Koufax.

The Twins rallied in Game Six before their home crowd, as Mudcat Grant hit a home run and outpitched Claude Osteen, 5–1. This set up Game Seven and a great pitching matchup: Jim Kaat versus Sandy Koufax, both pitching on two days' rest.

It was an excruciatingly tight, tense game, played (as Koufax recalled) "in something remarkably close to absolute silence." Koufax was arm-weary, he admitted in a 1966 article in *Sport Magazine*. "In the first inning, I had a curve," he said. "It wasn't much of a curve. All I can say is that it was a better curve than I had for the rest of the day."

In the sixth inning of a scoreless game, the Dodgers' Lou Johnson hit a high fly that slipped over the left-field wall of Metropolitan Stadium, just fair. As Koufax recalled, "Up in the press box, they tell me, some of the writers closed their typewriters and said, 'One run, that's enough.'"

The Dodgers got Koufax one more run, and that was more than enough in his complete-game, ten-strikeout, three-hit victory. The Dodgers took Game Seven, 2–0—in what turned out to be the last World Series victory of Sandy Koufax's magnificent career.

Koufax and the rest of the Dodgers were back in the Series in 1966, having once again weathered a draining pennant race against the San Francisco Giants. Koufax had won twenty-seven games during the season, with a 1.73 ERA—perhaps his greatest year, and also his last, as he shockingly retired after the season due to an arthritic pitching elbow.

The battle-weary Dodgers faced another young, eager, and well-rested opponent. This time it was the Baltimore Orioles, carried to an easy pennant by the fine pitching of Jim Palmer and Dave McNally and the spectacular play of Triple Crown winner Frank Robinson (.316, 49 home runs, 122 RBI) and preeminent third baseman Brooks Robinson.

Triple-crown winner Frank Robinson's Game Four home run put the cap on the Orioles' sweep.

Just as the Twins had done a year earlier, the Orioles immediately showed that they wouldn't roll over against the Dodgers' dominating pitchers. They drove Don Drysdale from the mound in Game One with four runs in the first two innings, including home runs by both Robinson boys, Frank and Brooks.

Then, when the Dodgers started to come back against Dave McNally, Baltimore Manager Hank Bauer brought in free-spirited reliever Moe Drabowsky—and that was the game. Drabowsky later said, "I would have been happy just to have faced one or two batters so that years later I could see my name in a World Series box score." Instead, he pitched the final 6 ⅔ innings, giving the Dodgers no runs while striking out eleven (including a record six in a row) as the Orioles won, 5–2.

Shockingly, the Dodgers' two runs in Game One were the last they would score in the entire Series. In Game Two, Koufax, pitching on guts alone in the last start of his career, was at less than his best, centerfielder Willie Davis committed three errors in the fifth inning, and Jim Palmer shut down the Dodgers, 6–0. Game Three was tighter—extremely tight, in fact, as Paul Blair's home run was the only tally in the Orioles' 1–0 win for Wally Bunker.

That brought Game Four. Don Drysdale pitched brilliantly, but Dave McNally was even better, and Frank Robinson's homer gave the Orioles a 1–0 lead in the fourth. After that, nothing but zeroes, for another shocking 1–0 Baltimore victory and a Series sweep.

"Now we all knew how the Yankees felt when we ripped them in 1963 in four straight," Dodger Manager Walt Alston, clear-thinking as always, wrote later in his autobiography, *A Year at a Time.* "It was a devastating way to lose, but when you score only two runs in four games and are shut out the last thirty-three innings, all you can do is go away and come to play another day."

"I WOULD HAVE BEEN HAPPY JUST TO HAVE FACED ONE OR TWO BATTERS SO THAT YEARS LATER I COULD SEE MY NAME IN A WORLD SERIES BOX SCORE."

Moe Drabowsky mows 'em down: the Oriole reliever strikes out Jim Lefebvre for his sixth consecutive strikeout in Game One of the '66 Series. "I would have been happy to just to have faced one or two batters," he said later.

B efore 1967–68, how many pitchers had started six games in two successive World Series? Two. The Philadelphia Athletics' George Earnshaw in 1930–31 and the Milwaukee Braves' Lew Burdette in 1958–59.

In 1967 and 1968, Bob Gibson made it three.

Gibson was one of the giant figures of the 1960s dead-ball era. A fierce competitor who never hesitated to knock down an opposing hitter, he seemed to dominate every game he was in. He'd won two games in the Cardinals' 1964 victory over the Yankees, and when the Cardinals won 101 games and the pennant in 1967, he got another chance to strut his stuff on the big stage.

As the Series started, though, few were focusing on Gibson and the Cardinals. Onlookers were still breathless over the A.L. pennant race, perhaps the most exciting of all time, in which the perennial doormat Boston Red Sox (in what came to be known as their "Impossible Season") edged out the Twins and Tigers on the last day for the pennant. Led by a Triple Crown season from Carl Yastrzemski and twenty-two wins from ace Jim Lonborg, the Red Sox entered the Series exhausted, thrilled to be there, and a decided underdog.

Gibson was masterful in Game One, striking out ten in the Cards' 2–1 win. In Game Two, Lonborg returned the favor, riding two home runs from Yaz and pitching a one-hitter in an easy 5–0 victory. But Red Sox Manager Dick Williams wasn't satisfied. "I realized that this World Series was missing something," he wrote in *No More Mr. Nice Guy*. "There wasn't any fire. There wasn't any hate."

1967 1968

TOWERS
OF STRENGTH

Lou Brock, Julian Javier, and Bob Gibson celebrate their seven-game victory in the 1967 Series.

Bob Gibson, perhaps the most frightening pitcher of all time. "A brushback has its place in baseball," he said—and proved it again and again.

When Cardinals' pitcher Nelson Briles hit Yastrzemski with a retaliation pitch in the first inning of Game Three, the final component was in place. "From that point on, we had a Series," Briles said.

Gibson was masterful again in Game Four, a 6–0 rout. Suddenly, after the miracle season, the Red Sox were a game away from going home. But they had Lonborg going for them in Game Five, and he pitched another masterpiece, a three-hitter. Roger Maris hit a home run and the Red Sox stayed alive, 3–1. Then the Sox tied the Series in Game Six, 8–4, scoring four runs off four Cardinal pitchers in the seventh inning to break a 4–4 tie.

The deciding game matched the staff aces, but with one crucial difference. Bob Gibson would be pitching on three days' rest, Jim Lonborg on only two. "I knew, and I think everybody else at least suspected, that Game Seven could be the most lopsided tiebreaker in Series history," Williams wrote later. "No matter. I'll be damned if I lose a Game Seven with anybody but my ace."

Williams' forebodings were on the mark. Gibson was dominating yet again, giving up just three hits and two runs and striking out ten. Lonborg had nothing left, leaving after six innings with the Red Sox trailing, 7–1. The final score was 7–2.

When the game was over, the Cardinals celebrated their second championship in four years. The Red Sox had only the bittersweet knowledge that they had come so far in their Impossible Season—but not quite far enough.

1967

ST. LOUIS CARDINALS

4

BOSTON RED SOX

3

Unlikely hero Mickey
Lolich celebrates his
third Series win and the
Tigers' championship.

In 1968, Lonborg was hurt, Yaz's numbers declined, and the Red Sox finished seventeen games behind pennant-winning Detroit. But Gibson (twenty-two wins, an eye-opening 1.12 ERA), Lou Brock, Curt Flood, and others were healthy, and the Cardinals won the pennant easily for the second year in a row.

Unlike the Sox of 1967, the Tigers were no miracle team. They were a battle-tested, dangerous opponent, led by noisy, self-confident Denny McLain (31–6), the first pitcher to win thirty games in thirty-four years.

Fans expected an austere series of pitchers' duels between Gibson and McLain. What they got was a lot more fun: a combination of pitching gems and slugfests, with Gibson towering as always—and matched not by McLain, but by Mickey Lolich, a large man with a physique a million miles removed from Gibson's sculpted frame.

Another highlight of the Series was Tiger Manager Mayo Smith's brave decision to get slugger Al Kaline (in his first Series after sixteen years in the bigs) into the line-up in right field. Kaline had been injured during the season, and while he was out the Tiger outfield had become set without him.

But, as Smith told Donald Honig in *The Man in the Dugout,* Kaline "deserved to be there, I wanted him in there, and we needed him in there." The manager's solution: moving centerfielder Mickey Stanley to shortstop, shifting right fielder Jim Northrup to center, and putting Kaline in right. Talk about opening yourself up to second-guessers! But it worked, as Stanley survived in the field and Kaline had a spectacular Series.

In Game One, Gibson struck out a Series-record seventeen men and held the Tigers to five hits in a 4–0 victory over McLain, who was victimized by some shoddy defense. In Game Two, it was Lolich's turn: he spun a gem and hit a home run (the only one of his career!) as the Tigers won, 8–1.

Games Three and Four were all Cardinals, though: 7–3 behind Ray Washburn and 10–1 for Gibson, who struck out ten more Tigers for twenty-seven in two games. Just as they had in '67, the Cards had a 3–1 Series lead—and just as they had the year before, they immediately gave it away.

As late as the seventh inning of Game Five, the Cardinals held a 3–2 lead. But then Lolich singled to start the seventh, the Tigers were off on a three-run rally. The 5–3 final gave Lolich his second win of the Series. "And do you know who got the base hit that drove in the fourth and fifth runs?" Mayo Smith exulted. "Mr. Al Kaline."

After a season of heavy work, Denny McLain had a sore arm—sore enough that Smith didn't know if he could pitch in Game Six. The day before the game, though, just as Smith was speculating to the sportswriters over who he might start instead, the unpredictable left-hander walked by and gave him a wink. "Doesn't say anything, just keeps on going," Smith recalled. "I watched him go. I didn't say anything to the reporters, but I thought to myself, 'By God, there's my pitcher.'"

Pitcher and winner. McLain got his first World Series win in Game Six, a 13–1 laugher that evened the Series.

So it all came down to Game Seven for the fifth time in seven years. It was inevitable that the game would match the Series' aces: Bob Gibson and Mickey Lolich.

It seemed an ideal stage for Gibson, perhaps the preeminent big-game pitcher of all time. "Nobody beats Bob Gibson," is the way Joe Falls put it in *Baseball's Great Teams: Detroit Tigers.* "He always wins the big ones. Always. It is a simple fact of life."

But Lolich was just as good on this day. For six innings the game was scoreless, as neither pitcher gave the opposing team anything to hit. Then, in the seventh, two Tigers singled. The next man up, Jim Northrup, hit a line drive toward Curt Flood in center. Flood, one of the best fielders in the league, misjudged the ball, slipped on the wet outfield grass (sportswriter Bob Broeg called it his "$100,000 slip"), and watched the ball go over his head for a two-run triple.

Northrup scored a few moments later, and the Tigers were on their way to a 4–1 win. Lolich had bested the seemingly invincible Gibson, and Detroit had its first World Series victory since 1945.

1968

**DETROIT TIGERS
4**

**ST. LOUIS CARDINALS
3**

No World Series in history has been written about in such numbing detail as the Cinderella Mets' five-game dismantling of the powerful Baltimore Orioles in 1969. Within a year of the stunning upset, at least a dozen books and countless magazine articles on the Mets were published—a multi-angled view of the great events from the perspectives of players, Manager Gil Hodges, radio voice Lindsey Nelson, a plethora of sportswriters, and at least a few literary types overcome with joy.

In his book *The New York Mets: The Whole Story,* Leonard Koppett even created a celebration up in heaven, attended by George Bernard Shaw, Dante (who could only say "Amazing…amazing"), Immanuel Kant ("To all the K's," he shouted. "Kranepool, Koosman, Koonce…Kleon-Chones"), Leo Tolstoy, Saint Francis of Assisi ("For the very first time I found myself rooting against the Birds"), and even God himself ("Let it be said, one more time: 'Let's Go Mets'").

Why all this hullabaloo? Because the Mets' pennant made many fans in the New York area feel young again…as if the clock had been turned back fifteen years, to the halcyon days of the mid-1950s.

It seemed as if every Dodgers and Giants rooter took the Mets to heart. And not just them: For anyone who believed that baseball required a National League alternative to the hated Yankees, watching the Mets rise to the top of the league was like emerging after a decade's wandering in the desert, and being offered not just a glass of cool water but a five-course meal as well.

The terrific 1969 N.L. pennant race, in which the Mets overcame a big lead by Leo Durocher's self-destructing Cubs,

Table-setter Tommy Agee struggled at bat during the Series—but saved Game Three with two outstanding catches.

was an unexpected treat. So was the Mets' three-game dismantling of the favored Atlanta Braves in the new divisional playoffs. Even so, few were willing to dream that the Mets would have much chance against Earl Weaver's magnificent Orioles, one of the best teams of its generation.

The Mets' pitching staff, led by Cy Young winner Tom Seaver (25–7) and Jerry Koosman (17–9), was the best in the league. But Baltimore's was even better. Mike Cuellar and Dave McNally both won more than twenty games, while Jim Palmer went 16–4.

And there was no comparison in the teams' offenses: The Mets' leading slugger was midseason acquisition Donn Clendenon (who hit sixteen home runs that year, twelve with the Mets), while the Orioles had a couple of guys named Boog Powell (37 home runs, 121 RBI, .304) and Frank Robinson (32, 100, .308), and a supporting cast that included Brooks Robinson (twenty-three homers), Davey Johnson, Paul Blair, and others, who made the Mets' Al Weis, Ed Charles, and Bud Harrelson look like holdovers from 1962.

When Don Buford, the first man up in the top of the first inning of Game One, slugged a home run off Seaver, Mets' fans would have been forgiven for gulping in anticipatory horror. The rest of the game wasn't much better for Seaver and the Mets, who lost lifelessly to Cuellar, 4–1.

But Jerry Koosman shut down the potent Oriole offense on a run and two hits in Game Two, while the Mets rampaged for two runs on a homer by Clendenon and three little singles in the ninth inning for the win. Maybe the Amazin's could play with the big boys!

1969

HOME ARE THE WANDERERS

1969

NEW YORK METS

4

BALTIMORE ORIOLES

1

The tenth man: the Mets' Sign Man and other fans let Baltimore know what they thought of them.

Then, in Game Three, young Met right-hander Gary Gentry teamed up with a scatter-armed twenty-two-year-old fireballer named Nolan Ryan on a four-hit shutout which the Mets won, 5–0—a deceptive score, since Met centerfielder Tommy Agee saved at least five runs with two spectacular catches.

As so often is the case, Game Four was pivotal. Either the Mets would take a dominating 3–1 lead or the Series would be knotted up, with the Orioles holding the momentum.

The game featured a rematch between Mike Cuellar and Tom Seaver, and this time Seaver had full command of his stuff. In the ninth inning, Seaver saw his 1–0 lead disappear on a sacrifice fly by Brooks Robinson—a sac fly that would have been a game-breaking double, if not for an almost unbelievable diving, rolling catch by Ron Swoboda in right field. ("It was a thousand-to-one shot," said Swoboda of his dive for the ball, "but I had to gamble.")

With the game now tied, the Mets failed to score in the bottom of the ninth. Weary but unwilling to leave the game, Seaver—who'd already thrown 135 pitches—came out to try to hold the Orioles one last time. In a 1970 book called *The Perfect Game* (written with Dick Schaap), Seaver gives insight into perhaps the most crucial inning he ever pitched. "Obviously, in extra innings, I was under greater mental strain than usual," he wrote. "I knew that if I made one large mistake, we'd have only one more time at bat to get even. I had to be more than careful."

Baltimore's first man up was Dave Johnson. Johnson hit a hard grounder to third baseman Wayne Garrett, who booted it. Mark Belanger, trying to bunt, popped the ball up for the first out. But then pinch hitter Clay Dalrymple singled, putting runners on first and second.

Don Buford, who had homered off Seaver in Game One, was up next—and he hit another long fly ball to right. "Actually Buford hit the ball just as well as he had hit his home run four days earlier," Seaver commented, "but in Shea

Stadium, much deeper down the foul lines than Baltimore's Memorial Stadium, Ron Swoboda had enough room to move back and catch the fly ball."

Dave Johnson moved to third on the fly ball, but now there were two out as Paul Blair stepped to the plate. "I knew that he was likely to be the last man I'd face in the fourth game, perhaps the last man I'd face in my first World Series," Seaver said. "If Blair got a hit, Gil would possibly bring in a relief pitcher. If I got Blair out, Gil would probably pinch-hit for me in the bottom of the tenth."

Blair struck out, and the great game remained tied. As Seaver walked into the dugout, having thrown his last pitch, he said, "Let's get a run. No use fooling around any longer."

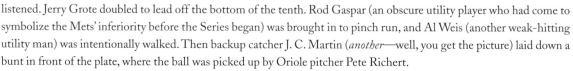

When Tom Seaver spoke, his teammates listened. Jerry Grote doubled to lead off the bottom of the tenth. Rod Gaspar (an obscure utility player who had come to symbolize the Mets' inferiority before the Series began) was brought in to pinch run, and Al Weis (another weak-hitting utility man) was intentionally walked. Then backup catcher J. C. Martin (*another*—well, you get the picture) laid down a bunt in front of the plate, where the ball was picked up by Oriole pitcher Pete Richert.

Martin hustled down the line. ("I ran wide," he said later. "I was trying to swell up.") Richert fired the ball toward first—only to see it deflect off Martin's wrist. The ball bounced away as Gaspar raced around third. "I knew right then, as soon as I spotted the loose ball, that we had won the game," Seaver said.

Despite the fact that Martin had left the running lane and could have been called out, the play stood. The Mets suddenly had a 3–1 Series lead over the stunned Orioles.

"Shove the bats down their throats," Seaver told starter Jerry Koosman before Game Five. Koosman was shaky early, and the Orioles leaped out to a 3–0 lead after three innings, but these Mets were unstoppable. In the sixth—in yet another all-time famous play in a Series packed with them—Cleon Jones was awarded first base after showing shoe polish on a ball, proving that an errant pitch had actually hit him on the foot. Donn Clendenon then homered. Mighty Mite Al Weis' home run in the seventh tied it up, and after that, Koosman was indomitable. "I don't care if it goes twenty innings," he told his teammates, "nobody scores off me."

He was as good as his word, and in the eighth the Mets scored two runs to take a 5–3 lead. Koosman came out to pitch the ninth inning, as Mets fans everywhere realized that this Impossible Dream was about to become reality.

"'The METS,' I thought, 'are about to be champions of the WORLD,'" broadcaster Lindsey Nelson wrote in his foreword to Larry Fox's *Last to First*. "I wasn't alone in that thought. Thousands of people, with the same realization, were about to pour forth into the city streets—laughing, crying, dancing, tossing tons of confetti, newspapers, ticker tape, phone books in the air. Soldiers in Vietnam and Thailand were hanging onto every word of the overseas broadcast. Car drivers all across this land pulled over to curbs to listen. Schoolchildren with smuggled transistors squealed uncontrollably in classrooms."

With two out, Dave Johnson lifted a fly ball to Cleon Jones. "Come to me, baby," Jones said to himself as the ball descended. "Come down to me, baby." He squeezed the ball, went down on one knee, and tried to comprehend that the Mets, yes, the Mets, were world champions.

Watching the final out, the novelist Wilfrid Sheed, one of the National League fans cast into the wilderness when the Dodgers and Giants left town, finally felt as if he'd come home. "That afternoon, with the shadows lengthening, cheerfully for once, over our little miracle, baseball was giving us all it had to give," he wrote in *My Life As a Fan*. "And it was plenty."

Orioles Manager Earl Weaver in a familiar stance. "I think there should be bad blood between all clubs," he once declared.

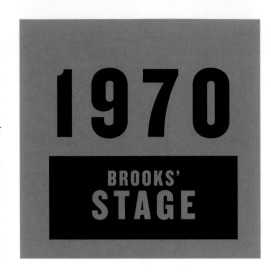

Only a great team, in the hands of a great manager, can come back from bitter defeat and ascend to the top of the mountain again. The Baltimore Orioles were a great team, and Earl Weaver was one of the finest managers in baseball history—a tactician, emotional leader, and problem-solver supreme. The 1970 Orioles, still reeling from their devastating defeat at the hands of the Cinderella Mets, might have been Weaver's finest creation.

Driven by Weaver, the Birds came to play in 1970. Led by pitchers Jim Palmer, Dave McNally, and Mike Cuellar and superstars Frank and Brooks Robinson, they racked up 108 wins (including the last eleven games of the season), capturing the A.L. East by fifteen games and taking apart Minnesota in the playoffs. "We played the entire 1970 season with one thought in mind—redemption," was how Weaver put it.

Baltimore's opponents in the World Series were the Cincinnati Reds, not yet the Big Red Machine but already blessed with a tremendous offense. Catcher Johnny Bench led the majors with 45 home runs and 148 RBI, while receiving strong support from many players, including Pete Rose (205 hits), Tony Perez (forty home runs), and Bobby Tolan (fifty-seven stolen bases).

The Reds' biggest problem was their pitching staff, a mediocre group beset with injuries. "Against the Mets all you had to worry about each game was one man—the one on the mound," Weaver said. "Against the Reds you had to worry about every man in the lineup except one—the pitcher."

Both teams got pretty good pitching in Game One, a tight struggle between Gary Nolan and Jim Palmer that Brooks Robinson won, 4–3, with a home run in the seventh. Robinson, already famed as the best-fielding third baseman in the game, made an error on the first ball hit to him in that game. "It was the second inning, we were already behind 1–0, and I made an error on my very first grounder," Brooks recalled in *My Greatest Day in Baseball.* "'Maybe you can't handle the pressure,' I thought."

But then, in the sixth inning, Robinson showed the world that the pressure didn't faze him at all. The Reds' Lee May hit a smash down the line, seemingly headed for the corner. "I had to lunge for the ball, and it was actually past me by the time I backhanded it, about a foot off the ground," Robinson said. Yet somehow he got to his feet and threw May out.

It was a stunning play, and just the first for Brooks as he made the Series his own. It was that day that May dubbed him "Hoover," a nickname that stuck. (When Robinson retired, May's gift to him was a Hoover vacuum cleaner.)

The Reds jumped out to a 4–0 lead in Game Two, but again the Orioles came back. Boog Powell jump-started the offense with a home run in the fourth, and then the Orioles pounded Jim McGlothlin and Milt Wilcox for five runs in the fifth. Forty-year-old Dick Hall pitched 2 1/3 innings of hitless relief, Brooks robbed Lee May of another double with a diving stop that ended up as a double-play, and Baltimore had a 6–5 victory and a 2–0 Series lead.

Game Three was a laugher. Brooks hit two doubles and

Brooks Robinson making one of his innumerable stunning plays during the Series. "When Brooks Robinson retires," said columnist Jim Murray, "he's going to take third base with him."

1970

BALTIMORE
ORIOLES

4

CINCINNATI
REDS

1

robbed Johnny Bench of a hit, while Oriole pitcher Dave McNally blasted a grand-slam home run in Baltimore's 9–3 win. The Orioles had a 3–0 Series lead, and looked poised for a sweep.

But momentum can be a tricky thing. When Lee May hit a three-run homer in the eighth inning of Game Four to give the Reds a 6–5 win and their first Series victory, Earl Weaver was distraught. "I suddenly felt sick," he said. "I got a premonition that the Reds were going to win it. I had everything figured in their favor."

But when he entered the locker room before Game Five, Weaver found that his team wasn't nearly as downbeat. Jim Palmer took him aside. "I know we're going to win it today," he told Weaver. "But if we don't win it today, McNally will win it. And you can bet your life on this. If neither of them win it, we'll win it in seven, because they've scored their last run off me."

The Series didn't have to go seven. After giving up three runs in the first inning, Mike Cuellar settled down. The Orioles scored two runs in each of the first three innings, and ended up winning 9–3. "There can be little doubt," said Reds pitcher Clay Carroll after the game, "that we came in with a crippled staff and that the Orioles crippled what was left of it."

Brooks Robinson hit a single in Game Five, giving him a .429 average for the Series, and made yet another spectacular play at third base to rob Johnny Bench of a hit. "That guy," marveled Cincinnati's Pete Rose, "can field a ball with a pair of pliers." Added Bench: "I hope we can come back and play the Orioles next year. I also hope Brooks Robinson has retired by then."

So late in his career, so late in his life, Roberto Clemente finally had the chance to show the world what he was capable of. Clemente had been a star for fifteen years by the time his Pittsburgh Pirates went to the World Series in 1971, hitting over .320 eight times and playing right field with unparalleled brilliance. Yet he never received the attention he felt he deserved. The many articles about him focused on his outspoken ways, his tendency to complain about his physical ailments, and even his accent, giving short shrift to his magnificent ability.

Clemente was certain that he was treated differently not only because he was a Latin player, but because he was a black Latin—at the bottom of the totem pole, in his opinion. "I play as good as anybody," he told sportswriter Wells Twombly. "But I am not loved. I don't need to be loved. I just wish that it would happen."

If being loved was beyond Clemente's grasp, in the 1971 Series, pitting the Pirates against the defending champion Baltimore Orioles, he finally got the spotlight he craved.

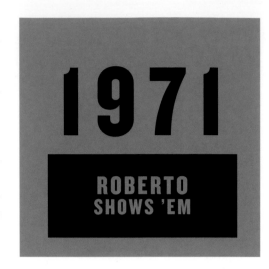

1971

ROBERTO
SHOWS 'EM

1971

PITTSBURGH
PIRATES

4

BALTIMORE
ORIOLES

3

Clemente, Willie Stargell (forty-eight home runs, 125 RBI during the regular season), Steve Blass (fifteen wins), and other Pirate stars certainly had the motivation they needed to play hard. Conventional wisdom gave the Series to the powerful Orioles before it even began—and the scornful voices reached cacophonous levels when the Orioles won the first two games easily behind Dave McNally and Jim Palmer.

"This World Series is no longer a contest, it's an atrocity," said Jim Murray in the *Los Angeles Times*. "It should rank with such other great contests of history as the St. Valentine's Day Massacre, the yellow fever epidemic, and the bombing of Rotterdam." Added the *New York Times'* Arthur Daley: "Although euthanasia is not a practice that merits approval, this World Series may present an exception."

Nor did the Orioles treat Clemente and the Pirates seriously. When Clemente complained about the quality of the outfield in Baltimore's Memorial Stadium, Frank Robinson scoffed at him. "If he can't adjust," said Robinson, "tell him to watch the way I play right field—or buy a ticket and sit in the stands."

But the *Pittsburgh Press'* Roy McHugh, who watched Clemente play every day, warned: "Goading Roberto Clemente would seem to be a foolhardy business…. [A] pinch of incitement lifts him two feet off the ground."

"ALTHOUGH EUTHANASIA IS NOT A PRACTICE THAT MERITS APPROVAL, THIS WORLD SERIES MAY PRESENT AN EXCEPTION."

And not only him. In Game Three, Steve Blass carried the Pirates back to respectability with a three-hitter and a 3–1 win. Then, in Game Four (the first Series game ever played at night), the Pirates' Bruce Kison came in to relieve an ineffective Luke Walker in the first inning, with the Bucs already behind 3–0, and proceeded to pitch 6 ⅓ innings of one-hit relief while his team clawed their way back, coming out on top 4–3. Suddenly the Series was tied 2–2 and no one was talking about the Orioles embarrassing the Pirates.

In Game Five, it was the Pirates' Nelson Briles' turn. Briles pitched a two-hitter. Bob Robertson slugged a home run, and the Pirates won easily, 4–0.

The complicated, brilliant Roberto Clemente. "Nobody does anything better than me in baseball," he said.

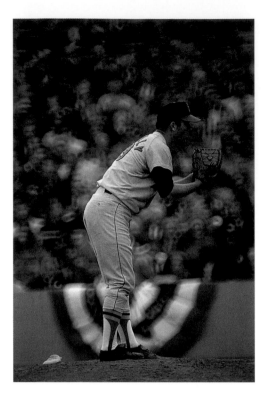

Dave McNally pitched brilliantly four times in the 1971 Series—but came up on the short end of the Series.

The Orioles had one more shot left in their gun. Despite Clemente's triple and home run, the Orioles scored a run in the tenth to win a classic Game Six, 3–2. As it should have, a magnificent Series was going the full seven games.

By this point, Roberto Clemente's skill, desire, and big-game brilliance was no secret any longer. Clemente was, in Roger Angell's words, "playing a kind of baseball that none of us had ever seen before—throwing and running and hitting at something close to the level of absolute perfection, playing to win but also playing the game almost as if it were a form of punishment for everyone else on the field."

In the fourth inning of Game Seven, Clemente hit a home run (his twelfth hit of the Series) to give the Pirates a 1–0 lead off Mike Cuellar. Then Willie Stargell led off the eighth with a single and scored on Jose Pagan's double. Steve Blass, the pitching star of the Series, gave up a run in the bottom of the inning, but that was all—a complete game four-hitter, a 2–1 win, a thrilling vindication for Clemente, for the Pirates, and a treat for every fan who loved the game of baseball.

After the World Series, Clemente, clear-eyed as always, knew the perfect use for his hard-won celebrity status: to bring better schools and sports facilities to his homeland, Puerto Rico, and to inspire others to help as well. "Through me lots of people maybe can be helped," he told a reporter from the *San Juan Star*. "People look up to you when you are in sports. They try to imitate you. That's why this World Series was the most important thing ever to happen to me."

During the 1971 Series, Roberto Clemente played "a kind of baseball that none of us had ever seen before—throwing and running and hitting at something close to the level of absolute perfection," in the words of Roger Angell.

It's almost impossible to believe now, in the midst of the latest Yankee Generation, but at the dawn of the 1970s the American League was considered almost embarrassingly inferior to the National. As *Sports Illustrated's* Ron Fimrite explained, "The National League has all the superstars, the batting averages, the stolen bases, the home runs and the crowds. American League stars—such as they are—are merely recycled National Leaguers."

Some of this perception was based on reality. It represented the bill finally coming due for the A.L. owners' racism and recalcitrance after the 1947 breaking of the color line by Jackie Robinson. While there were exceptions on both sides (Bill Veeck's Cleveland Indians were among the first to integrate, while the N.L.'s St. Louis Cardinals took forever to do so), there was no doubting that A.L. lagged far behind when it came to seeking out and signing black and Latin players. By the 1960s, the National League was playing a more exciting, creative, and diverse brand of baseball, riding the talents of Willie Mays, Hank Aaron, Roberto Clemente, Joe Morgan, Lou Brock, and a host of others.

Something needed to be done to increase interest in the A.L. And the Oakland A's, the ragged, rowdy, contentious A.L. champs, were just the ticket.

At first, though, the A's didn't get any respect. "Well, the National League playoffs between Cincinnati and Pittsburgh brought together the two best teams in baseball," Sparky Anderson, manager of the N.L. champion Cincinnati Reds, told sportswriters. "So that makes this year's World Series an anticlimax."

The A's stars, including Reggie Jackson, Joe Rudi, Vida Blue, and Blue Moon Odom, had big ears, long memories, and hot tempers. After they clinched the American League playoffs against Detroit, Vida Blue and Blue Moon Odom got into a locker-room fistfight. "[T]he message was clear," said Manager Dick Williams later: "We had to get to the World Series before we killed ourselves." And playing for notoriously erratic and egocentric owner Charlie Finley ("Twenty-two out of the twenty-five guys on our team hate him," said A's third baseman Sal Bando) left them ready to face any challenge.

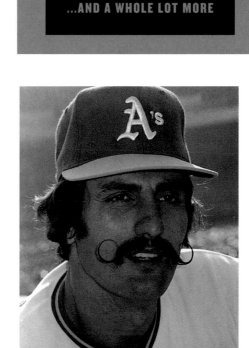

Rollie Fingers' clutch performances in the 1972-74 Series (sixteen appearances, two wins, and six saves) helped open the door to Cooperstown.

1972

OAKLAND ATHLETICS

4

CINCINNATI REDS

3

Despite losing Reggie Jackson with a leg injury, the A's took Game One, 3–2, behind Ken Holtzman's pitching and two home runs from an unlikely hero, backup catcher Gene Tenace. After the game, Pete Rose still didn't seem to get it about the A's. "I don't think they have a lot of punch," he told reporters. But Sparky Anderson was unnerved. "Gee whiz, you don't know what these A's are going to do," he lamented.

The teams then swapped the next two games, with the A's winning Game Two, 2–1, behind Catfish Hunter, and the Reds getting their first victory in a 1–0 thriller won by Jack Billingham over Blue Moon Odom. When Tenace homered again and the A's won Game Four, 3–2, Oakland had a seemingly insurmountable 3–1 Series lead.

But, as A's Manager Dick Williams put it, "If I'd known what would happen the next two games, I'd have celebrated that win more." With a run in the eighth and another in the ninth, the Reds withstood yet another Tenace home run and eked out a 5–4 win, barely holding on as pinch runner Blue Moon Odom was thrown out at the plate to end the game. Game Six, the first not to be decided by one run, also went to the Reds, 8–1.

Somehow, after all this, the Series was tied. It looked as if the National League might prevail once again. Tenace gave the A's a 1–0 lead in Game Seven with a single and a 2–1 lead with a double in the sixth—his eighth and ninth RBI of the Series, when no other A's player had more than one. Another run scored on a double by Sal Bando, giving the A's a 3–1 lead, but then the Reds trimmed the lead to 3–2 with a run in the eighth.

After that it was up to charismatic Oakland reliever Rollie Fingers. With two out in the ninth, Fingers hit Darrel Chaney with a pitch, bringing up the ever-dangerous Pete Rose. In *Champagne and Baloney: The Rise and Fall of Finley's A's*, author Tom Clark vividly tells what happened next:

> Rose furiously wipes his bat with a towel in the on-deck circle, staring out at Fingers with a steely malevolence—his jaw set, his mouth drawn tight. Then he steps up to the plate, digs in and slices the air with the hard arcs of his practice swings, his eyes never leaving the pitcher all the while. Rollie looks in at Dave Duncan for the sign, winds and fires a fastball that Rose cuts at with all his might. It has all the makings of a historic swing: there's the comic-book "crack" of the bat, and the ball soaring up heart-stoppingly toward left, sending Joe Rudi on his horse, but—ah!—now Rudi slows as he reaches the warning track and puts his glove up, and the ball nestles into it, and he's still gently clutching it as he runs in toward the dugout, and for the first time since 1930 the A's are world champs!

Even with Reggie Jackson injured, the A's overcame the powerful Reds in 1972.

Nobody was talking about "respect" when the A's overcame a tough Baltimore team in the playoffs and marched back into the World Series in 1973. Especially not when their opponents turned out to be the unlikely New York Mets, who somehow won the N.L. East with an 82–79 record and then shockingly upset the powerful Reds in a bitter playoff series. If any team was lacking in respect, it was the Mets.

1973

OAKLAND ATHLETICS 4

NEW YORK METS 3

As Williams put it in *No More Mr. Nice Guy*: "[T]hose 'Amazin' Mets' were no longer the miracle kids of 1969, although they did have three good pitchers in Tom Seaver, Jerry Koosman, and Jon Matlack, and some fairly good hitters in young John Milner, Rusty Staub, and Cleon Jones…. Their biggest advantage, though, was that we had Charlie."

The A's increasingly erratic owner, Charlie Finley, reared into view after Game Two, a wild one won by the Mets, 10–7, in twelve innings, to even the Series 1–1. The game, called "a gigantic goulash of mistakes and wonders" by Roger Angell, featured twenty-eight hits, several fly balls lost in the sun, five Oakland errors, six innings of relief work from Mets stopper Tug McGraw, and forty-two-year-old Met Willie Mays stumbling both on the basepaths and in the outfield—and then driving in the tie-breaking run with a scratch single in the twelfth, the last hit of his career.

Oakland second baseman Mike Andrews made two errors in that game, on consecutive plays in the twelfth. Manager Dick Williams never blamed Andrews for the errors, but Charlie Finley was furious. In cahoots with a team doctor, Finley forced Andrews to sign a paper admitting that he had an injured shoulder. Andrews would be replaced on the roster, Finley announced, by a young infielder named Manny Trillo.

The players had put up with a lot from Finley over the years, but this was too much. "It's the bushest thing I've ever seen," said captain Sal Bando after hearing the news. The A's considered going on strike. Dick Williams called a team meeting and announced, "I am resigning after the Series." Even after Commissioner Bowie Kuhn forced Andrews' reinstatement, the team was still in turmoil.

Jerry Koosman and the overmatched Mets took the A's to a seventh game in 1973.

In 1973 Ray Fosse (#10), Sal Bando, and Darold Knowles celebrate the A's second consecutive championship.

Any other team would have crumbled amid the distractions. But, as Tiger pitcher Denny McLain said, "I am convinced it is Finley who keeps the A's together. The players have such a common bond in their collective hatred of the man that this hatred makes the A's an even better team when they cross the white lines."

The A's proved it by winning Game Three at Shea Stadium, 3–2, a tense ten-inning affair that featured brilliant pitching from Tom Seaver and Catfish Hunter. But then Jon Matlack shut down the A's in Game Four and Koosman did the same in Game Five—and suddenly the underdog Mets had a 3–2 Series lead and the chance at their second miracle in five seasons.

But it wasn't to be. Hunter outdueled Seaver in Game Six, a 3–1 Oakland win featuring Reggie Jackson's three hits and 2 RBI. Then John Matlack, who'd pitched brilliantly his first two starts in the Series, simply didn't have it in Game Seven. He gave up home runs to Bert Campaneris and Reggie Jackson (making a bid for "Mr. October" fame) early in the game. The Mets could do little with Ken Holtzman and two relievers as the A's held on for a 5–2 win and the Series.

Dick Williams was as good as his word, walking away from the A's after the Series ended. "I couldn't enjoy it," he said of the victory. "This was Charlie's team out there now. I was finished."

But there's always someone out there willing to manage for even the most overbearing owner. In 1974, under the leadership of stern, stoical Alvin Dark, the A's went to the World Series for the third straight time, this time facing the Los Angeles Dodgers. Again Team Turmoil was boiling—as shown by the angry scuffle between pitchers Blue Moon Odom and Rollie Fingers before Game One.

On the field, though, the A's were always in control. The Dodgers had a strong pitching staff, led by starters Andy Messersmith and Don Sutton and reliever Mike Marshall. But the A's had an almost uncanny ability to play their opponents' game—and to play it just a bit better. The 1974 Series was no exception.

Reggie Jackson and Steve Garvey: Great players, worlds-apart personalities.

Four of the five games in the Series finished with the identical score of 3–2, while the other was 5–2. Time and again, as they'd done the past two years, the A's got the clutch performance when they needed it: a crucial strikeout in relief from Catfish, a big hit from Bert Campaneris, great fielding from second baseman Dick Green, a home run from Jackson or Joe Rudi.

As a result, the Dodgers were able to capture just one game, Game Two behind Sutton. The A's won the other four, one each for Rollie Fingers, Ken Holtzman, Catfish Hunter, and Blue Moon Odom, for their third Series title in a row.

But there was a sense, even as they celebrated, that their run was nearing its end. "I don't think Charlie Finley enjoyed the Series that much," commented Dark. "He seemed tense and distraught throughout."

Indeed, black clouds were gathering. The owner's past contract shenanigans, his endless battles with Bowie Kuhn, and his unwillingness to play by the rules of free agency would soon lead to the loss of Reggie Jackson, Catfish Hunter, Rollie Fingers, and other stars. By 1979, the A's would plummet to 108 losses, and the brawling, long-haired, irreverent dynasty of 1972–74 would be just a distant memory.

1974

OAKLAND ATHLETICS

4

LOS ANGELES DODGERS

1

I SHOULDA KEPT MY MOUTH SHUT

NEVER UNDERESTIMATE THE POWER OF A GOOD QUOTE...TO MOTIVATE YOUR OPPONENT.

"If I said that the American League was as good as the National League, I'd be lying."
  —Cincinnati Reds' Manager Sparky Anderson before the (American League) Oakland A's beat the Reds in the 1972 World Series.

"Bring on Ron Stupid!"
  —Frank Robinson, making the Mets' utility player Rod Gaspar a symbol of the team's inferiority before the 1969 Series—which the Mets won in five games.

"If he's all that great an outfielder, he should be able to adjust. If he can't adjust, tell him to watch the way I play right field—or buy a ticket and sit in the stands."
  —Frank Robinson again, after hearing Roberto Clemente complain about the conditions at Baltimore's Memorial Stadium. Clemente went on to field brilliantly (and hit .414) in Pittsburgh's seven-game Series win in 1971.

"A good team, not great. Lucky. Bloops, pop-ups that fell in, every umpire's decision, every break."
  —Yankee manager Billy Martin, explaining why the 1976 Cincinnati Reds swept the Yankees in one of the most one-sided World Series of all time.

"Why shouldn't we pitch to Ruth? I've said it before, and I'll say it again, we pitch to better hitters than Ruth in the National League."
  —Giants' manager John McGraw, just before Ruth slammed two home runs and led the Yankees to victory over the Giants in the 1923 Series.

Met pitchers befuddled
Frank Robinson during the
1969 Series, holding him
to a .188 batting average.

10 BEST SERIES

NO. **-2**

1975

"How can a manager of a losing team call it the greatest game ever played?" asked the Cincinnati Reds' Sparky Anderson. "Well, winning or losing, a man can't lie to himself." Sparky, of course, was talking about Game Six of the 1975 World Series between his Reds and the Boston Red Sox, a four-hour-long marathon whose twists and turns, comebacks and heartbreaks have long since entered the realm of legend. It was the crowning moment in one of the greatest Series ever played.

The American public was ready for—no, hungry for, desperate for—a transcendent Series in 1975. The nation was just emerging from one of the darkest eras in its history, a span which had seen economic misery, the uneasy end of the Vietnam War, and the Watergate scandal culminating in the resignation of President Richard Nixon.

Baseball itself hadn't come through the turbulent era unscathed. As had happened periodically throughout the game's history—and as continues to happen today—baseball was being criticized for being too slow, too old-fashioned, nowhere near as exciting as America's more violent pastime, football. It was time for some new faces, some likable heroes, and, most of all, some exciting games to bring the fans back.

And that's exactly what the Reds and Red Sox provided. The magnificent Reds were at the height of their powers, featuring perhaps the most potent line-up since the Yankees of the 1920s. Facing Joe Morgan, Johnny Bench, Pete Rose, Tony Perez, George Foster, and Ken Griffey, how could a pitcher survive?

Meanwhile, the Red Sox boasted two exceptional rookies: Fred Lynn (.331, 21 home runs, 105 RBI) and Jim Rice (.309, 22 home runs, 102 RBI), alongside such established stars as Carl Yastrzemski and Dwight Evans and the great, eccentric pitcher Luis Tiant. This matchup promised baseball nirvana.

1975

PURE JOY

It's Fred Lynn versus Johnny Bench in one of the greatest World Series of all time. (P.S.: Lynn was out at the plate.)

Game One, at Fenway Park, was breathlessly tight until it suddenly wasn't. The Reds' Don Gullett and the Red Sox' Tiant matched zeroes through six innings—and then, without warning, the Sox erupted for six runs in the bottom of the seventh. The Reds could make nothing of Tiant's remarkable array of bizarre motions and varied windups, and Boston cruised to a 6–0 win.

Game Two set the mood for the Series. The Sox scored a run in the first, saw the game tied in the fourth, and then went ahead with another run in the sixth. The score stayed 2–1 until the ninth, when Boston reliever Dick Drago took over for starter Bill "Spaceman" Lee. Just like that, the Reds' offense finally erupted, doubles by Bench and Davey Concepcion bracketing a single by Griffey to score two runs and gain the Reds the victory that evened the Series.

Game Three, at Cincinnati's Riverfront Stadium, was another classic. The Reds moved out to a 5–2 lead on homers by Bench, Concepcion, and Cesar Geronimo, only to see the Sox come back on blasts by pinch hitter Bernie Carbo and (in the ninth) Dwight Evans, tying the game 5–5. In the bottom of the ninth, Boston catcher Carlton Fisk (who claimed batter's interference) threw a ball into centerfield trying to get the runner at second on a sacrifice. Joe Morgan then singled to drive in the winning run to give the Reds a 2–1 Series lead.

1975

CINCINNATI REDS

4

BOSTON RED SOX

3

Game Four was a classic of a different kind. The Sox scored five runs in the fourth to take a 5–2 lead. Luis Tiant immediately gave back two of the runs, then hung on grimly for the last five innings (helped by a game-saving catch with two men aboard by Fred Lynn in the ninth) for the 5–4 win. All over Boston and Cincinnati, formerly dark hair was turning gray.

In Game Five, two home runs by Tony Perez and tidy pitching from Gullett gave the Reds a 6–2 win and a 3–2 Series edge. Sportswriters began planning their valedictory columns, giving credit to the Sox while acknowledging that the Reds were a better, deeper, more resilient team.

And then came Game Six, delayed for three days by rain, which gave everyone endless hours to obsess. "It's just a stay of execution for Boston," said confident Joe

Safe! Pete Rose makes it to third in the ninth inning of Game Seven on Joe Morgan's Series-winning single.

Morgan. Carl Yastrzemski didn't agree, but even he was as cautious as only a long-suffering Red Sox star could be. "It doesn't matter if it rains today, tomorrow, Monday. We've still got to beat them two straight—sometime," he said.

Ten minutes after the game started, the Sox were on their way, taking a 3–0 lead on Fred Lynn's first-inning home run. But Luis Tiant was arm weary. Three runs in the fifth (the highlight being Griffey's two-run triple that Lynn just missed as he crashed into the wall), two in the seventh, and one in the eighth gave the Reds a 6–3 lead, and, it seemed, the Series.

Not so fast. Pinch hitter Bernie Carbo, facing Reds reliever Rawly Eastwick with two men on in the bottom of the eighth, blasted a three-run home run to tie the game, sending Boston fans into transports of joy. ("[T]he chill of the lachrymose had become mad, sensuous Fenway again," was how sportswriter Peter Gammons put it the next day.)

"THESE TEAMS ARE SO CLOSE THAT THEY SHOULD CALL THE GAME OFF, DECLARE US CO-CHAMPIONS OF THE WORLD, AND STAGE A PICNIC AT OLD FENWAY."

The Sox almost won the game in the ninth, loading the bases with no outs but failing to score. Then Dwight Evans stole a probable home run from Joe Morgan in the eleventh, making a play that Sparky Anderson called "the best catch I've ever seen an outfielder make."

The exhausting, thrilling game went to the bottom of the twelfth, well past midnight. Carlton Fisk, leading off, caught hold of a pitch by Pat Darcy and sent it soaring down the left-field line. "And all of a sudden, the ball was there, like the Mystic River Bridge, suspended out in the black of the morning," wrote Gammons.

That was it, the moment that made baseball thrilling again to the millions of fans watching the game on television— the game that won back a place for baseball in America's heart. While fans in the ballpark followed the flight of the ball, a snafu by the camera crew kept viewers' eyes on Carlton Fisk "waving wildly, weaving and writhing and gyrating along the first-base line, as he wished the ball fair, *forced* it fair with his entire body," as Roger Angell put it.

The ball hit the foul pole. Fisk, engulfed by ecstatic fans, made his joyful way around the bases ("I straight-armed somebody and kicked 'em out of the way and touched every little white thing I saw," he said), and at 12:24 A.M., Game Six was over at last.

Game Seven, later that same day, was another superb contest, but fans and writers had run out of superlatives. "It was a good play that opened on the night after the opening night of *King Lear*," Angell said. Added Bill Lee: "It's a darn shame we have to play it. These teams are so close that they should call the game off, declare us co-champions of the world, and stage a picnic at old Fenway."

But they played the game. Once again, the Red Sox jumped out to a 3–0 lead, and Lee kept the Reds off the scoreboard through five. But in the top of the sixth, the Reds got a man on, bringing the dangerous Tony Perez to the plate. Perez hit a two-run homer, bringing Cincinnati to within a run.

The Reds tied the game in the seventh, and Boston fans began to realize that this might not be their year after all. Then, in the ninth, the Reds got two men on with two out, bringing Joe Morgan to the plate. If ever there was a time for the outspoken, super-confident star to come through in the clutch, it was now.

With two strikes, Sox pitcher Jim Burton almost fooled Morgan with a slider. "It was a good pitch, down and away," Morgan said. "I wanted to go to the opposite field with it—to left." It was far from the hardest ball ever hit by Morgan, but it was just hard enough to get past the infield for a single. It brought in the run that won the game and—after Will McEnaney set the Red Sox down in the bottom of the ninth—the Series for the Reds.

Typically, it was Roger Angell in *The New Yorker* who best explained why the 1975 World Series set its grappling hooks so deeply into the hearts of even casual baseball fans. The Series reminded us, he wrote, of the deep satisfaction of "*caring*—caring deeply and passionately, really caring—which is a capacity or an emotion that has almost gone out of our lives.... Naïveté—the infantile and ignoble joy that sends a grown man or woman to dancing and shouting with joy in the middle of the night over the haphazard flight of a distant ball—seems a small price to pay for such a gift."

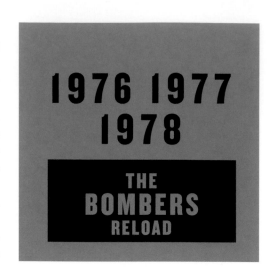

**1976 1977
1978**

THE
BOMBERS
RELOAD

Baseball seemed to take a breath in the 1976 World Series, as if it was still recovering from the nail-biting suspense of 1975. Led by George Foster (29 home runs, 121 RBI), Ken Griffey (.336), Pete Rose (.323), and league MVP Joe Morgan (.320, 113 runs, 111 RBI, 60 stolen bases), the Reds won 102 games and then swept past Philadelphia in the playoffs to make their fourth Series appearance in seven seasons. Their opponent, though, was a famous old team showing up on the big stage for the first time since 1964: the New York Yankees.

Under the hard-driving leadership of Billy Martin (a walking, snarling definition of the word "fiery"), the Yankees won the A.L. East easily. Then the Yankee pitching staff (Catfish Hunter, Doc Ellis, Ed Figueroa, and closer Sparky Lyle) and offensive stars Thurman Munson, Chris Chambliss, and Graig Nettles led the team past the Kansas City Royals in a thrilling five-game playoff series.

Despite their stars, the Yankees looked young and anonymous against the massively talented Reds—a perception not changed by the Reds' easy 5–1 victory behind Don Gullett in Game One at Cincinnati's Riverfront Stadium. Game Two, played at night under frigid conditions, was closer. Catfish Hunter fell behind 3–0 and then pitched stoically as the Yankees fought back to tie—only to see the Reds win on an error by Yankee second baseman Fred Stanley and a single by Tony Perez.

The Yankees were down two games to none and heading home—but nobody watching thought they had any chance to catch up. Not even the Yankee manager. "Billy Martin was a nervous wreck at this point," Thurman Munson recalled. "Billy wasn't exactly Mr. Optimism."

1976

**CINCINNATI
REDS**

4

**NEW YORK
YANKEES**

0

Game Three was played in near-freezing weather—again at night, by the dictate of Commissioner Bowie Kuhn. "Man, it was cold," Munson said in his autobiography. "Only the commissioner sat there without four sweaters and a topcoat…. He wasn't going to look cold for anyone."

The Reds' bats were warm enough, though. They jumped out to a quick 3–0 lead off of Doc Ellis and, despite Munson's three hits, cruised to an easy 6–2 win. Game Four was a little better, with the Yankees trailing only 3–2 into the ninth inning. Munson had four more hits (he ended the Series 9 for 17), but Johnny Bench crashed two homers—including a three-run blast in the ninth—and drove in five runs as the Reds swept with a 7–2 victory.

Joe Morgan had the last word: "I'm glad we won," he said, "but last year was a lot more fun."

The Yankees added the talkative, insecure, and vastly talented Reggie Jackson to the line-up for 1977, the final combustible piece to a team that already included irascible Thurman Munson, practical joker Graig Nettles, otherworldly Mickey Rivers, bantam rooster Sparky Lyle, and lit-TNT Billy Martin. The Bronx Zoo had been born, and no one would ever accuse the Yankees of being anonymous again.

But perhaps the most important addition was a far quieter one: Ron Guidry, pitching his first full season, went 16–7 and gave the Yankees a true ace to accompany an ailing Catfish Hunter and newly acquired Don Gullett.

The Yankees made it back to the Series by beating the Royals in the deciding fifth playoff game for the second year in a row. This time, however, their opponents weren't the Reds, but the L.A.

1977

NEW YORK YANKEES

4

LOS ANGELES DODGERS

2

Dodgers, who rode strong years from Steve Garvey, Tommy John, and others to the N.L. pennant.

Game One, at Yankee Stadium, was a barn-burner. The Dodgers took a quick 2–0 lead off Gullett, and then watched as the Yankees scored single runs in the first, sixth, and eighth innings to go up 3–2. A Dodger run in the ninth tied the game, but then Sparky Lyle shut down L.A. for three innings, allowing the Yankees to capture the game on a Paul Blair single.

Game Two was over almost as soon as it began. Billy Martin, out of arms after the tense playoff series against Kansas City, had to turn to sore-armed Catfish Hunter, who hadn't pitched in a month. "Make sure you watch the first inning, because I may be gone by the second," Hunter told his son before the game. In fact, he made it into the third, giving up five runs in the Dodgers' easy 6–2 win.

When the Yankees took Game Three, 5–3, behind Mike Torrez, and Game Four, 4–2, behind Guidry, the Yankees, up three games to one, were poised for a Series win almost as colorless as the one the Reds inflicted on them in 1977. But the Dodgers rose to the challenge for one day, pounding Don Gullett and two relievers in a 10–4 win.

That brought the teams to Game Six, back at Yankee Stadium. Never has there been a more perfect example of the single game—and the single achievement—that saves and defines a Series.

All Reggie Jackson did in that game was hit three home runs: a two-run shot in the fourth inning to give the Yankees a 4–3 lead, another two-run blast in the fifth to extend the lead to 7–3, and a wallop leading off the eighth inning deep into the center-field bleachers. Three at bats, three round-trippers, one 8–4 Yankee win, and the first Series championship for the Bombers in sixteen years.

After the game, the normally cocky Jackson sounded as stunned by his achievement as everyone else was. "There's a part of me I don't know," he said. "There's a ballplayer in me who responds to all that pressure. I'm not sure I hit three home runs but the ballplayer in me did."

And then, at the very end of a tumultuous, difficult season, he added: "Maybe now, for at least one night, I can feel like a real superstar."

Reggie Jackson and the rest of the Yankees were back in the Series in 1978. Once again, their opponents were the Dodgers.

But this Series never stood much of a chance of going down in history. Like the Chicago Cubs' 1908 triumph, or the Yankees' win in 1951, the 1978 contest was an afterthought to a season that ranks with the greatest of all time, a season that Roger Angell accurately described as "one of the most absorbing, surprising, and painful—painful, above all— baseball campaigns ever."

Painful especially if you were a fan of the Boston Red Sox. Bouncing back from their devastating seven-game defeat to the Cincinnati Reds in 1975, the Sox steamrolled to a fourteen-game A.L. East lead in midsummer behind a monster year from Jim Rice…only to see the lead crumble in the face of an almost inconceivable onslaught from Ron Guidry (25–3) and the Yankees. The season ended in a tie, of course, and then the Yankees won the agonizing playoff game at Fenway Park, 5–4, to capture the crown.

Perfection in triplicate: Reggie Jackson's trio of Game Six home runs in the 1977 Series. "It was the happiest moment of my career," Reggie said of his feat.

A quiet moment between Reggie Jackson and Catfish Hunter, who came back from arm miseries to help the Yankees win the 1978 Series.

It was no surprise that the Yankees came into the Series exhausted. The Dodgers took advantage in Game One, driving Ed Figueroa from the mound in the second inning of an 11–5 win. Game Two was closer, but again the Dodgers finished on top, 4–3, behind Burt Hooton.

Fans wondered if they were watching the third consecutive dull World Series—with little more than a faint hope that something like Reggie's 1977 heroics would come along. But this Yankee team was battle-toughened: the players had weathered Billy Martin's increasingly irrational outbursts, culminating in his replacement as manager by Bob Lemon, and they could handle being down 2–0 to the Dodgers.

Ron Guidry began to restore order in Game Three, a tidy 5–1 victory. Game Four, far closer, was made famous when Reggie Jackson stuck out his hip (purposely or not) to deflect a throw in the baseline between first and second, preventing a double play and setting up a two-run inning that tied the score, 3–3. Stoical pitching by Yankee closer Goose Gossage held the Dodgers hitless for two innings until the Yankees scored on a tenth-inning Lou Piniella single to even up the Series.

Game Five was a laugher, a 12–2 win for the Yankees' young Jim Beattie over veteran Burt Hooton. By now the Yankees had all the momentum, and even when they led Game Six by only 3–2 in the sixth inning, no one watching believed they would lose.

Catfish Hunter—pitching just a few months after he thought arm woes had ended his career—held the Dodgers to just two runs in seven innings. Reggie Jackson hit a two-run homer (his seventh in the last two Series) and the Yankee mighty mites, infielders Bucky Dent and Brian Doyle, each had three hits. (They'd end up the Series batting .438 and .417, respectively). The Bombers cruised to a 7–2 victory and their second Series championship in a row.

At the end of such a long, excruciating, exhilarating season, the Yankees took time to appreciate what they'd accomplished. "They said we couldn't come back, but we did come back and that's what makes it so sweet," said Hunter. Added Manager Bob Lemon: "The team is wonderful, the front office is wonderful, I'm just happy as hell."

Happy as hell and glad it was over.

1978

NEW YORK
YANKEES

4

LOS ANGELES
DODGERS

2

The 1979 World Series between the Pittsburgh Pirates and the Baltimore Orioles was memorable for many things. It gave N.L. MVP and future Hall of Famer Willie Stargell the chance to finally show off his great talents on a nationwide stage, just as former teammate Roberto Clemente had done eight years earlier. It matched the powerful Pirate "family" of sluggers—Stargell, Dave Parker, Eddie Murray, Bill Madlock—against a Baltimore pitching staff that featured Cy Young winner Mike Flanagan (twenty-three wins), Jim Palmer, and Scott McGregor. It was one of only four Series ever to see a team come back from a three-games-to-one deficit to win.

But what everyone was talking about as the World Series began was how darn *cold* it was. The Canadian magazine *Macleans* called the two teams "The Boys of Shiver," and several games of the Series were played in perhaps the worst conditions ever: a combination of snow, sleet, rain, and icy temperatures that made every pitch, every fielding play, an adventure. The weather turned a potentially classic Series into an endurance contest for players and fans alike.

Game One in Baltimore, postponed for a night, was played at the end of a snowy, rainy day, in temperatures that began at forty degrees and plummeted from there. "The ball felt like a big, cold marble," said Eddie Murray. As the teams combined for six errors—the ball sometimes obscured from the fielders' view by their own icy clouds of breath—the Orioles held on for a 5–4 win.

Willie Stargell hit his first Series home run in that game. It seemed only right, since the even-tempered, thirty-eight-year-old had been the soul of the young, high-spirited Pirates all season. "If I had to describe myself," he said, "it would be like a big oak tree. Good roots. A strong trunk." Dave Parker called Stargell his idol. "We'll do anything for him," Parker said.

Including win under terrible conditions. Game Two was played in ear-numbing cold and freezing rain. Manny Sanguillen drove in the tiebreaking run in the ninth, and the Pirates' storklike reliever, Kent Tekulve, came in to shut down the Orioles for a critical 3–2 Pirate win.

The Series moved to Baltimore, but nothing changed. It was still cold, still rainy—rainy enough to delay Game Three for an hour in the third inning, with the Pirates leading 3–2. When the game resumed, the Orioles promptly drove Pirate starter John Candelaria from the mound, scoring five runs en route to an 8–4 win. Game Four ("the coldest baseball I have ever sat through," said Roger Angell) was similar, with the Pirates jumping out to a 6–2 lead, only to lose 9–6 when the Orioles dismantled the usually unflappable Tekulve.

At this point, with Baltimore up 3–1, the Series looked destined to be one of the most one-sided of all time. But the Pirates, as close-knit as any team in recent memory, used the unity they'd preached all year to hang together even when facing quick dismissal from the playoffs.

Game Five began with another blow to Pirate hopes: Bruce Kison, their dependable starter, had hurt his arm in the cold during Game One, and couldn't pitch. Instead, Manager Chuck Tanner had to turn to thirty-seven-year-old journeyman Jim Rooker, who'd gone

1979

THE FAMILY

Willie Stargell stroking one of his four hits—two doubles, a single, and a two-run homer—in Game Seven of the classic 1979 Series. "Under pressure," he said, "you want to be at peace with yourself." Stargell always was.

1979

PITTSBURGH PIRATES
4
BALTIMORE ORIOLES
3

Family: The Bucs mob pitcher Kent Tekulve and celebrate their improbable championship.

just 4–7 during the regular season. In chilly but improving conditions, Rooker pitched a gem for five innings, then watched Bert Blyleven shut down the Orioles the rest of the way in the Pirates' 7–1 victory. For six innings of Game Six, John Candaleria and Jim Palmer matched zeroes. Then, in the seventh, a hit by Parker and a sacrifice fly by Stargell gave the Pirates two runs. They scored two more in the seventh, Kent Tekulve pitched three innings of overpowering relief, and suddenly the Series was tied, with all the momentum seemingly on the Pirates' side.

Of course, as the saying goes, momentum is only as good as your next day's starting pitcher, and once again the matchup seemed to favor the Orioles. They had Scott McGregor going for them against the Pirates' Jim Bibby.

The Orioles scored the first run on a Rich Dauer home run, but after that the game was like a replay of Game Six. The Orioles could do nothing with Bibby and a parade of relievers, while the Pirates clawed back to score two runs in the sixth on Stargell's two-run homer (one of Stargell's four hits that day). Tekulve got out of a jam in the eighth inning—the Orioles' final threat—and, when the Pirates added a pair of insurance runs in the ninth, the Series was over.

After the game, Stargell (who batted .400, with three home runs and 7 RBI) summed up the Pirates' wonderful season. "No words can express what we've done," he said. "We've worked hard. We've scratched and clawed. We weren't trying to be sassy or fancy. We're just a ballclub that is a family in our clubhouse."

The irrepressible Willie Stargell leaps for joy after the Pirates' Game Two win.

Mike Schmidt was the embodiment of a World Series hero: strong-browed, gimlet-eyed, with a mouth that turned down at the corners. Even his moustache looked like it wanted to beat you. And, after losing in the playoffs in 1976, 1977, and 1978, Schmidt and his Philadelphia Phillies finally gave fans the chance to see if his image matched reality.

Though Phillies fans and others with long memories still fondly recall Schmidt's monster 1980 season (forty-eight home runs, 121 RBI, the MVP award) and his superb performance in the Series, others have even more vivid memories of a far more unlikely hero—a practical-joking screwball pitcher with a devilish grin: Tug McGraw.

While Schmidt was all fierce intensity, McGraw was something else again, a cheerful man who disarmed fans and loved to talk

to the press. How could anyone dislike a pitcher who gave his fastballs names like the Peggy Lee ("Is That All There Is?"), Cutty Sark ("It sails"), and Frank Sinatra ("Fly Me to the Moon")?

In 1980, the Phillies barely edged the Houston Astros to grab their first pennant in thirty years. Their opponents were the Kansas City Royals, another team with a recent history of agonizing defeat: in 1976, '77, and '78, they fell to the Yankees in the playoffs. But 1980 was the charm for George Brett and the Royals, as they swept past the Yankees and into their first World Series.

Brett, suffering from what was undoubtedly the world's most famous case of hemorrhoids, was not at full strength as the Series started. The Phillies took advantage, taking a big lead in Game One and then surviving two home runs by the Royals' Willie Mays Aikens before McGraw held on for a 7–6 win. In Game Two, four runs in the eighth off Royals' closer Dan Quisenberry bailed out ace Steve Carlton as Philadelphia won, 6–4, to go up two games to none.

Brett had surgery for his hemorrhoids after Game Two. To calm the Royals, Manager Jim Frey called a team meeting. Frey's pep talk, according to the players, served to relax rather than inspire them. "It got us laughing," said Dan Quisenberry. "We were all amused at the quality of his four-letter words."

Fully recovered, Brett blasted a home run in Game Three and the Royals staved off disaster by scoring a run in the tenth to win, 4–3. Then Willie Aikens hit two more home runs to lead the Royals to a Series-tying 5–3 win in Game Four. "They talk about Babe Ruth!" shouted teammate Clint Hurdle after the game. "They talk about Lou Gehrig! Now they'll talk about Willie Aikens."

The Phillies' Tug McGraw, always cool, calm, and collected on the mound.

At least till the next game, when the Royals fell behind 2–0, scrambled back to take a 3–2 lead…and then saw the Phillies score two in the top of the ninth to go ahead, 4–3. McGraw, in his third inning of relief, loaded the bases on walks in the bottom of the ninth before striking out Jose Cardenal to end it.

After this stunning victory, the Phillies were all optimism. Later, McGraw recalled listening to Schmidt complain as they drove to Veterans Stadium for Game Six. "I play the whole game, drive in runs, hit homers, steal the bases, make great defensive plays for nine full innings, and you come in, pitch the last inning, and get all the glory!" Schmidt griped. To get his revenge, Schmidt added, he would jump on Tug after the last out, just to guarantee that he'd get his picture in the paper.

It happened just that way. Steve Carlton held the Royals scoreless into the eighth, while Schmidt (2 RBI) and the Phillies moved out to a 4–0 lead. Then, after the Royals scored once, it was Tug's turn again, his fourth appearance in six games.

As policemen with horses and dogs came onto the field to keep the Philadelphia fans from running amok, an exhausted McGraw loaded the bases in the ninth. After getting two strikes on dangerous Willie Wilson, McGraw wasted a Cutty Sark, and then came back with another fastball that Wilson swung at and missed.

"I threw my arms up to the sky and turned toward third base," McGraw recalled. "There was Schmitty coming toward me at the mound, just like we had joked about. He dove at me and the photographers captured it."

It seems unlikely that McGraw minded being on the bottom of the pile.

Mike Schmidt displays his long-awaited World Series championship ring—the only one he'd ever wear.

1981

NIGHTMARE'S END

What a disaster the 1981 season was. Bad enough that it was interrupted by a players' strike for seven weeks, resulting in the cancellation of a third of the season. ("[N]o line scores, no winning and losing pitchers, no homers and highlights, no records approached or streaks cut short, no 'Meanwhile, over in the National League,' no double-zip early innings from Anaheim or Chavez Ravine, no Valenzuela and no Rose, no Goose and no Tom, no Yaz, no Mazz, no nothing," lamented Roger Angell midstrike.)

But then, even as the players came back onto the field, the magnates who run baseball made a decision that just made things worse. They divided the season into two halves—pre- and post-strike—and called it a split season, with first-half and second-half champions. Then they added an entire new round of playoffs, pitting the two champions against each other.

After the two rounds of roundly ignored playoffs, the surviving Yankees and Dodgers faced off in the World Series. The Yankees were just three years removed from their back-to-back championships in 1977–78, but the Dodgers had a lot more to prove: they hadn't won a Series since 1965 and had been Yankee victims in both '77 and '78.

The Series began in ho-hum fashion, with the Yankees' Ron Guidry winning Game One, 5–3, and Tommy John pitching a four-hit shutout in Game Two. The Dodgers collected a total of nine hits in the two games while showing off the rickety state of their infield defense. (Second baseman Davey Lopes alone committed six errors in the six-game Series.)

"IT WAS A SERIES IN WHICH A TEAM WITH AN INFIELD THAT HAD ALL THE STEADINESS OF A ROWBOAT IN A TYPHOON OUTSCRAPPED A TEAM THAT LEFT MOST OF ITS FIGHT IN AN ELEVATOR SHAFT."

Despite walking seven in a long, sloppy Game Three, Fernando Valenzuela held on to give the Dodgers their first win, 5–4. Ten pitchers paraded through Game Four, which featured four doubles, a triple, three home runs (including one by Reggie Jackson), seventeen hits in toto, three errors (including a costly one by Reggie), and one Series-tying 8–7 win by the Dodgers.

A World Series tied at two should be able to build up some suspense, but instead it was in danger of being drowned out by outside distractions. The most flagrant distraction came from Yankee owner George Steinbrenner, who showed up one morning in Los Angeles with a bandaged hand and an unverified tale of a fistfight with unknown assailants in an elevator. It was past time, everyone agreed, to turn the page and look forward to next year.

1981

LOS ANGELES
DODGERS

4

NEW YORK
YANKEES

2

But there was still some baseball to play. In Game Five, the Dodgers survived three more errors as Jerry Reuss outpitched Ron Guidry for a 2–1 win. And then, finally, the Series came to an end. When soon-to-be-fired Yankee Manager Bob Lemon took starter Tommy John out after four innings of a 1–1 Game Six, the Dodgers feasted on five relievers and ran away with a 9–2 victory.

No one except a few of the players even pretended that the Series ranked anywhere other than among the worst of all time. "It was a Series in which a team with an infield that had all the steadiness of a rowboat in a typhoon outscrapped a team that left most of its fight in an elevator shaft," summed up columnist Ray Fitzgerald.

Bob Watson is out at the plate in a Series that remained tight until Game Six.

Pedro Guerrero, a fearsome hitter throughout his career, blasted two home runs, a double, and a triple among his seven hits in the 1981 World Series. Ken Landreaux and a batboy congratulate Guerrero after his Game Five homer.

Milwaukee is a no-nonsense Midwestern city, blue-collar and proud of it. And so were the Brewers of the 1980s, a team of burly, unkempt stars like Gorman Thomas, Ted Simmons, Paul Molitor, Robin Yount, and Moose Haas who played smash-mouth baseball, rampaging to the American League pennant with a league-leading 216 home runs and 891 runs scored.

Their opponents in the 1982 World Series were…well, something else again. Whitey Herzog's St. Louis Cardinals were a team of speedsters, perfectly suited to their spacious, artificial-turf field at Busch Stadium. The entire team hit a mere sixty-seven homers—less than just the Brewers' Gorman Thomas (thirty-nine) and Ben Oglivie (thirty-four) combined—but they made up for their lack of power with high batting averages, great base running, and sensational defense provided by such stars as Willie McGee, Ozzie Smith, and Keith Hernandez.

After the flat 1981 Series, here was a matchup worth looking forward to. Even the managers provided a stark contrast. The Brewers' Harvey Kuenn was a strong, silent type, making as few moves as possible. ("The Harvey Kuenn face gives no indication of the manager's inner machinations," wrote Dick Kaegel in *The Sporting News*. "The large hunk of chewing tobacco moves slightly. He spits. Slowly, he starts to the mound.")

And Whitey Herzog? Mouthy and energetic enough to earn the proudly worn nickname the White Rat, he was a master tactician, never satisfied, always fiddling with the line-up, always looking for the little edge that might lead to a win. "Whitey's wheels, it seems, spin in sixteen directions," wrote Kaegel.

The Cardinals didn't get to show off many of their skills in Game One. They were completely shut down by Mike Caldwell while the Brewers pounded out seventeen hits (including five by Paul Molitor and four for Robin Yount) in a 10–0 rout. Typically, Whitey Herzog shrugged it off: "We got a good old-fashioned butt-kicking," he said. "I'm glad we didn't have a double-header."

The Cardinals administered their own brand of butt-kicking in Game Two, stealing three bases and edging across a run in the eighth on a bases-loaded walk to win, 5–4, tying the Series.

In Game Three, in Milwaukee, speedster Willie McGee showed some uncharacteristic muscle, hitting two home runs while stealing one from the Brewers' Gorman Thomas with a stunning catch as the Cards won, 6–2. For six innings, it looked like Game Four would go the same way, as St. Louis built a 5–1 lead. But then an error by pitcher Dave LaPoint opened the floodgates to a six-run seventh inning for the Brewers and a 7–5 win. Once again, the Series was tied.

Game Five went the Brewers' way too, 6–4. It was a classic, messy, unwieldy Milwaukee victory, with Mike Caldwell gutting his way through 8 ⅓ innings while giving up fourteen hits.

1982

ST. LOUIS CARDINALS

4

MILWAUKEE BREWERS

3

Back home in St. Louis, with their backs against the wall, the Cardinals played loose in Game Six. It was Don Sutton and the Brewers who played as if they had everything to lose, committing four errors and going down meekly as the Cards swamped them, 13–1.

All of which led to the seventh game of an entertaining Series. The Brewers built a 3–1 lead, but the Cardinals were hitting on all cylinders now. Keith Hernandez had two hits and two RBI, the Cardinals scored three in the sixth and two more in the eighth, ace reliever Bruce Sutter shut down Milwaukee for the last two innings, and the Cardinals had their first championship since 1967.

Bill Veeck, who'd been in baseball for a long time, was amused by the messy events. "It was a fan's delight," he said. "But it had to be a complete horror to baseball purists. I hope our Little Leaguers were busy playing Pac-Man during the Series instead of watching the games."

Willie McGee, Ozzie Smith, and others got all the ink, but St. Louis catcher Darrell Porter was one of the Series' unsung heroes.

The 1982 Series was hard-fought from first inning to last. Here the Brewers' Robin Yount gets one of his twelve hits.

Jim Palmer on the mound, his laser blue eyes fixed on Pete Rose, Joe Morgan, and Tony Perez at the plate. You'd think the 1983 World Series pitted the Baltimore Orioles against the Cincinnati Reds. And you'd be half right. The veteran-heavy Orioles were, in fact, representing the A.L. in the World Series, but their opponents were the Philadelphia Phillies, home to a squadron of Cincinnati stars wrapping up their careers. Morgan (.230), Perez (.241), and Rose (.245) were each over forty, and only Morgan—with sixteen home runs and eighteen stolen bases—significantly helped the team to its second Series appearance in four years.

Mike Schmidt (forty home runs, 109 RBI) and John Denny (nineteen wins) were far more essential to the Phillies championship than the aging superstars. Similarly, thirty-seven-year-old Jim Palmer went only 5–4, while younger stars like Eddie Murray (thirty-three home runs) and twenty-three-year-old Cal Ripken, Jr. (.318) led the Orioles. The big names were still around, but the new era had begun.

As it turned out, the Phillies' one bright moment came in Game One. A tense pitchers' duel between John Denny and Scott McGregor, the game stayed 1–1 until the eighth, when Garry Maddox hit a home run to give the Phillies a 2–1 win. Morgan, a clutch player even at the end, had a homer to provide Philadelphia's other run. Game Two wasn't as close: old-timer John Lowenstein went 3–4 with a home run as Mike Boddicker pitched a three-hitter and the Orioles won, 4–1, to knot the Series.

"WHAT AMERICA WAS SEEING WAS AN OLD BALL CLUB COMING APART."

In Game Three, Phillies Manager Paul Owens benched Pete Rose in favor of Tony Perez. Rose refused to sit quietly, calling himself "heartbroken" and "humiliated" and providing a distraction the Phillies didn't need. Then, in the game itself, Steve Carlton couldn't hold a 2–0 lead, light-hitting Oriole catcher Rick Dempsey hit two doubles, and the Orioles won, 3–2. Jim Palmer, making his only Series appearance, got the win in relief.

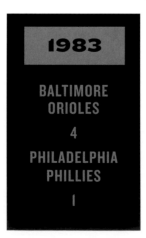

1983

BALTIMORE ORIOLES

4

PHILADELPHIA PHILLIES

1

The Series-tilting Game Four was another one-run affair, but it wasn't actually that close: When the Orioles took a 5–3 lead in the seventh, most fans could see where this Series was headed. Even a single and double by the restored Rose weren't enough to keep the Phillies from losing, 5–4.

Two straight close losses seemed to take the heart out of the Phillies. It also didn't help that Mike Schmidt was suffering through a nightmarish Series that ended with his garnering a lone single in twenty at bats, bringing down fierce boos from the unforgiving Philadelphia fans. "What America was seeing," wrote Furman Bisher, "was an old ball club coming apart."

In Game Five, Eddie Murray broke out of a slump with two home runs, Series MVP Rick Dempsey got two more hits, Scott McGregor shut down the lifeless Phillies on five hits, and the O's clinched, 5–0.

It was, most agreed, a Series that was merciful in its brevity.

In his last postseason hurrah, thirty-seven-year-old Jim Palmer pitched in relief in Game Three—and got the win.

Every once in a while, baseball produces a perfect team, an ideal combination of speed and power, of offense and defense, of starting pitching and relief. A team that seems destined for immortality—or (as opposing fans hope) for a humiliating collapse in the face of pressure.

In 1984, baseball produced just such a team: the Detroit Tigers. While none of their players led the league in any category, the Tigers had a star or near-star at virtually every position. Kirk Gibson (twenty-seven homers) in right field, Chet Lemon (twenty homers) in center, Lance Parrish (thirty-three homers) behind the plate, Jack Morris (nineteen wins) and Dan Petry (eighteen wins) starting, and A.L. Cy Young and MVP Willie Hernandez (nine wins, thirty-two saves) in the pen.

1984

I AM TIGER, HEAR ME ROAR

"I DON'T KNOW IF THE CUBS COULD HAVE DONE ANY BETTER AGAINST THE TIGERS, BUT THEY SURE COULDN'T HAVE DONE ANY WORSE."

Unflappable Jack Morris, who won two games in the Series, was "the best pitcher I ever managed," according to Sparky Anderson.

Almost too good to be true, the Tigers seemed primed for a fall. But fall is the one thing the Tigers did not do. Instead they started the season 35–5, cruised to 104 wins, captured the A.L. East by fifteen games, swept Kansas City in the playoffs, and marched into the World Series as if they owned the trophy already.

The same couldn't be said of the San Diego Padres, the surprising N.L. champion. A big year from perennial batting champion Tony Gwynn (.351) helped carry the Padres to the N.L. West flag against weak competition (no other team in the division even finished at .500), despite a mediocre pitching staff and not much power.

Everyone expected the N.L. East champion Chicago Cubs to dismantle the Padres, but it didn't happen. The Padres won in five games, disappointing all those who had hoped for a contest between the Tigers and Cubs, two of baseball's most storied franchises.

The Padres went into the Series prohibitive underdogs to the powerful Tigers, and this was one case where perception equaled reality. "I don't know if the Cubs could have done any better against the Tigers," wrote Padre Manager Dick Williams in *No More Mr. Nice Guy*, "but they sure couldn't have done any worse."

The first two games, played in San Diego, gave promise of a tight Series. In Game One, the Tigers' Jack Morris gave up two runs in the first inning, but that was all, as the Tigers came back

1984

DETROIT TIGERS
4
SAN DIEGO PADRES
1

for a 3–2 win. Then, in Game Two, Andy Hawkins and Craig Lefferts combined for 8 1/3 innings of one-run relief as the Padres tied the Series with a 5–3 victory.

But that was it for suspense. In Game Three, Padre pitchers gave up eleven walks, while San Diego batters managed ten hits but only two runs in a 5–2 Tiger win. Game Four wasn't any better. Padre starter Eric Show lasted less than three innings as the Tigers jumped out to a 4–1 lead, then cruised to an easy 4–2 win.

At this point, all the Padres could hope for was a Game Five win and a chance to play in front of the San Diego fans again. But that was a pipe dream. The Tigers scored three runs in the first, with Kirk Gibson blasting a two-run home run to lead the way. The Padres fought back to tie, but in the fifth the Tigers showed once and for all that they were a champion facing something far less.

"I CAN GET HIM OUT."

Kirk Gibson singled and moved to third after two walks. Then Rusty Kuntz hit a pop fly into short right field. "As the ball went over the stands, I lost it," said Padre right fielder Tony Gwynn. As a result, second baseman Alan Wiggins had to catch it and then make an off-balance throw as Gibson trotted home in what must have been the first "sacrifice pop-up" in Series history.

In the bottom of the eighth, with the Tigers leading 5–4 and runners on second and third, Gibson came to the plate. Padres' fireballing reliever Goose Gossage, nearing the end of his career, begged Dick Williams to be allowed to pitch to Gibson instead of giving him an intentional walk. "I can get him out," Gossage insisted.

Tiger Manager Sparky Anderson, seeing Gibson heading toward the plate, flashed four fingers, meaning, "He's gonna walk you." Gibson flashed back ten, meaning, "No, he's gonna pitch to me, and ten bucks says I'm gonna hit it out." The result seemed inevitable. Gossage challenged Gibson with a fastball, and Gibson sent it into the second deck of Tiger Stadium to give the Tigers an 8–4 lead. "It kind of cuts your heart out," Gossage said, "because now you're a piece of meat."

A few minutes later, the game and Series were over. The Tigers, 1984's perfect team, had barely broken a sweat completing their dream season.

By the mid-1970s the Kansas Royals were perennial winners. Led by superstar George Brett, who "could get good wood on an aspirin," in the words of Manager Jim Frey, the team won the A.L. West in 1976, '77, and '78, but were stymied by the Yankees every year in the playoffs. In 1980, they actually made it to the World Series, only to lose to the Philadelphia Phillies.

Then, after some down years, the Royals won their division again in 1984, only to be steamrolled by the juggernaut Detroit Tigers. When Kansas City edged out California by a single game to win the West in 1985, fans would have been forgiven for expecting the worst—especially when the Royals fell behind A.L. East champion Toronto, 3–1, in the playoffs. But then the Royals reeled off three straight victories and headed back to the Series again. Were they primed for more heartbreak, or would this finally be the Royals' year?

Kansas City's opponents in the I-70 Series were their down-the-highway neighbors, the St. Louis Cardinals. The dangerous Cards, 1982 World Champions, featured Whitey Herzog's speed-pitching-and-defense attack, headed by John Tudor, Ozzie Smith, and Willie McGee. Though Vince Coleman, the team's leading speedster, was injured in a freak accident before the Series began, many observers thought that the more experienced Cardinals would have an easy time with the young Royals.

When the Cardinals won the first two games in Kansas City, behind strong pitching by Tudor in Game One and a four-run, two-out rally in the ninth inning of Game Two, it looked like Kansas City fans' frustrations would reach new heights. Then twenty-one-year-old Bret Saberhagen gave the Royals their first win, but when John Tudor shut out the Royals in Game Four, the Cardinals were just one victory away from their second championship in four years.

They never got it. Danny Jackson pitched a five-hitter in the Royals' 6–1 Game Five win. And then came Game Six, back in Kansas City, and one of the most famous and controversial World Series brouhahas of all time.

For seven innings St. Louis' Danny Cox and K.C.'s Charlie Leibrandt matched zeros. Then the Cardinals scored a run in the eighth, and soon the Royals were down to their last three outs, facing Cardinal closer Todd Worrell.

Pinch hitter Jorge Orta led off the ninth with a grounder to first base. Jack Clark tossed the ball to Worrell, seemingly nipping Orta by a stride. But umpire Don Denkinger called Orta safe. And suddenly the Cardinals just disintegrated. Clark missed an easy foul pop by Steve Balboni (who then sin-

1985

KANSAS CITY ASCENDS

Ozzie Smith and the rest of the Cardinals flipped after a blown call went against them in Game Six.

1985

KANSAS CITY ROYALS

4

ST. LOUIS CARDINALS

3

gled), catcher Darrell Porter committed a passed ball, Hal McRae walked, and Dane Iorg singled to drive in two runs for the ballgame. Somehow, amazingly, the Series was going to Game Seven.

"We lose the game," Whitey Herzog wrote later, "and deep in my heart, I knew we'd lost the Series."

His team must have felt the same way. Cardinal ace John Tudor didn't have a thing as George Brett had four hits and Kansas City scored eleven runs in the first five innings on their way to an 11–0 win and an improbable Series victory. Worse, St. Louis' Game Seven behavior left an indelibly bad taste in the mouths of everyone watching. In the fifth inning, protesting a ball call, pitcher Joaquin Andujar threw an all-time temper tantrum, screaming and cursing and having to be escorted off the field.

"THE CARDINALS LOST THE WORLD SERIES EVEN WHILE THEY WERE WINNING IT."

Sportswriter Curry Kirkpatrick was disgusted, accusing the Cardinals of sullenness and childish behavior far beyond the call of duty. "Long before John Tudor put his gone-south paw through a dugout fan; before Joaquin Andujar put his mouth where his brain might have been; before the rest of the St. Louis Nuthouse Gang attempted to justify a preposterous, deserved, team-effort humiliation…long before all this, the Cardinals lost the World Series even while they were winning it," Kirkpatrick wrote in *Sports Illustrated*. "Surely somewhere along I-70 they misplaced the sense of fun and sportsmanship, elegance and tradition, that being a St. Louis Cardinal once meant."

No one loved to play baseball more than George Brett (hoisting Bret Saberhagen), and his infectious enthusiasm carried the Royals to their first championship in 1985.

THE FIVE STAGES OF GOATDOM

▌ THE EVENT

"Write in the pages of world's series baseball history the name of Snodgrass. Write it large and black. Not as a hero, truly not. Put it in rather with Merkle, who was in such a hurry that he gave away a National League championship. Snodgrass was in such a hurry that he gave away a world championship."

—*The New York Times*, reporting on Fred Snodgrass' "muff" of a tenth-inning fly ball which gave the Boston Red Sox an extra out, leading to the two-run inning that gave them the 1912 World Series over the New York Giants.

"In the late innings, Eddie Murphy opened an inning for the A's by reaching first safely. Eddie Collins, the next batter, hit a line drive to [second baseman Johnny] Evers' left, which Johnny knocked down but couldn't handle. Murphy, an extremely fast man on the bases, went from first to third on the hit.

"Evers, for some reason or other, failed to relay the ball back to the infield after he picked it up in short right field. Instead, he walked slowly back to the infield, tapping the ball in his glove. I looked over and yelled, 'Johnny, watch the plate.' He didn't seem to hear me.

"Just at that time, Murphy made a break for home. And by the time Evers recovered, Murphy had scored easily. The inning ended 4–2 in favor of the A's.

"Well, when Evers returned to the dugout, he was crying like a baby."

—Hall of Famer Rabbit Maranville, describing the 1914 World Series between the Boston Braves and the Philadelphia Athletics. The Braves went on to win the Series, keeping Evers from eternal goatdom. From *Sport Magazine*.

"Well, Casey went strictly with his hard-breaking curve, the one that snapped off at the plate. Now, with a 3–2 count on Henrich, I called for a curve and figured that's what he was going to give me. And that's where I blew the whole thing. He gave me an overhand curve and it broke down and got past me. I was looking for the wrong pitch."

—Mickey Owen, describing his two-out, ninth-inning, third-strike passed ball that gave the Yankees a new lease on life—and a stunning win—in the 1941 Series. From the 1991 World Series program.

2 DENIAL

"I told people I broke Honus' record. But I didn't tell them which one."
—Roger Peckinpaugh, whose eight errors in the 1925 Series eclipsed Wagner's old mark of six and helped cost the Washington Senators the Series.

"Henrich missed it by more than I did; he's the one that ought to be famous. I at least touched the ball."
—Mickey Owen on Henrich's third-strike swing in 1941.

"In my mind, I didn't lose the World Series…there were a lot of other people who had more to do with losing than I did."
—Bill Buckner, whose error on Mookie Wilson's ground ball allowed the winning run to score in Game Six of the 1986 Series.

3 ANGER

"Why do you want to know about that goddamn record? I played in three World Series. I was the most valuable player and I was a major leaguer for eighteen years when there were only sixteen major league teams in the world. And all you want to know about is that goddamn record for errors."
—Roger Peckinpaugh

"I'm tired of it. I don't want to hear about it anymore. You can tell the people in Boston to mind their own business."
—Bill Buckner

4 SELF-CRITICISM

"I should have been alert, I blame myself. Charge it up to me."
—Johnny Pesky, who held the ball while Enos Slaughter scored the winning run in Game Seven of the 1946 Series.

"If there was a dumb play to be made, I was always there."
—Mickey Owen

5 ACCEPTANCE

"I can look in the mirror and say to myself that I got everything out of myself that I possibly could."
—Bill Buckner

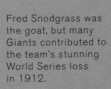

Fred Snodgrass was the goat, but many Giants contributed to the team's stunning World Series loss in 1912.

B oy, did everyone despise the New York Mets in 1986. Arrogant. Cocky. Brash. Those were just some of the (printable) adjectives pasted on the Mets as they rampaged through the National League East. Darryl Strawberry loping around the bases after smashing a home run, Gary Carter bumping chests with Ray Knight after another win, Lenny Dykstra and Wally Backman grinning and spitting tobacco juice while driving opposing pitchers crazy atop the batting order—it all added up to 108 wins and the eternal enmity of fans and sportswriters outside New York.

The World Series presented a fresh, intriguing matchup: the noisy, self-confident Mets against a quieter Boston Red Sox team that starred Wade Boggs, Bruce Hurst, Marty Barrett, and Calvin Schiraldi. The Mets were in the Series for the first time since 1973, the Red Sox since 1975.

To the joy of many, the Mets were flat in the first two games at Shea Stadium. Boston took Game One, 1–0, as lefty Bruce Hurst bested Ron Darling, and Game Two, 9–3, as the Sox blasted Dwight Gooden. But then Lenny Dykstra—a big-game player throughout his career—led off Game Three with a home run off Oil Can Boyd, and the Mets went on to score four first-inning runs and cruise to a 7–1 victory behind Bob Ojeda. Game Four was just as easy, a 6–2 win for Ron Darling featuring two homers by Gary Carter and another blast by Dykstra.

With the Series knotted, Game Five seemed pivotal. Again, Dwight Gooden had nothing, giving up four runs in the first five innings. That was enough for Bruce Hurst, who wasn't as commanding as he'd been in Game One, but strong enough to hold on for a 4–2 win. The Sox were a game away from finally winning their first World Series since 1918.

Across the country, fans and writers cheered at the prospect that the cocky Mets would be humbled. "Now the best of all October miracles is in the on-deck circle," wrote Thomas Boswell (not even a Boston fan!) in the *Washington Post* before Game Six. But neither Boswell nor the most nightmare-prone Red Sox fan could have predicted what would take place at Shea Stadium two days later.

The game was a thriller from the beginning, with the Sox scoring runs in the first and second innings off Bob Ojeda to take a 2–0 lead, only to see the Mets tie it with two in the fifth. One more run for each team sent the game into extra innings.

In the top of the tenth, the Sox scored twice off young Mets pitcher Rick Aguilera for a 5–3 lead. The big blow was a home run by Dave Henderson, hero of the Sox' thrilling playoff victory against the California Angels. It seemed almost inevitable now that Boston would finally break the Curse of the Bambino.

In the bottom of the inning, Wally Backman and Keith Hernandez flied out against closer Calvin Schiraldi, leaving the Mets down to their final out. "You could see Hernandez on the television screen, throwing his bat and helmet in disgust and resignation and ducking down the runway that leads to the Mets' clubhouse," recalled reporter Phil

1986

THE BAD GUYS
WIN

1986

NEW YORK
METS
4
BOSTON
RED SOX
3

Bob Ojeda pitched superbly twice, keeping the Mets in a Series they seemed destined to lose.

Pepe. The other Mets too had lost hope, according to outfielder Mookie Wilson. "Nobody was saying, 'We'll get 'em, we can still win this thing.'"

What happened next is burned into the brains of every Boston fan—including writer John Hough, Jr., who describes the events in his 1988 book *A Player for a Moment*. Hough picks up the action as he, his wife, Tess, and his friend Kib watch on television as the Mets, down to their last out, send Gary Carter to bat.

> "Do you realize," I said, as much to myself as to the others, "that we're about to see the Red Sox win the World Series?" The world would never be the same.
>
> Gary Carter was at the plate. Here I made a fatal mistake.
>
> "Don't make the last out, Gary," I said.
>
> "Are you crazy?" Kib said.
>
> "He's a nice guy," I said. "Let him get a single."
>
> Gary looked almost frightened up there, the edges of his mouth pulled back, forehead rumpled. He got his single, cracking Calvin Schiraldi's fastball into left field. Nice going, Gary. The hit will console you through the winter. Now let's finish them off.
>
> With two strikes, the pinch hitter [Kevin] Mitchell pushed a ground ball up the middle that crawled somehow between Barrett and Spike Owen. Suddenly, the tying runs were on base. The room got quiet.
>
> With two strikes, Ray Knight punched a floater over Barrett's head, dumping the ball out there with the handle of his bat. Carter scored, Mitchell circled to third, the tying run. We were now in deep, deep trouble. This wasn't going to be as simple as I thought. The hitter was Mookie Wilson, and John McNamara, the Sox' manager, walked out to the mound and called in the overweight righty, Bob Stanley.
>
> "Oh, Jesus!" I yelled. "Not Stanley, oh my god."
>
> "Isn't he any good?" Tess inquired innocently.

Bill Buckner at the low
point of his career.

"He's a bum!" I yelled.

The truth is, I've always considered Stanley a decent pitcher, a view
not held by most Red Sox lovers. My despairing yell was to propitiate
whatever gods were throwing this scare into us. The scare was a lesson:
don't get complacent. *All right,* my soul cried. *Now give us our victory.*

Historians have forgotten, if they ever noticed, that Stanley
pitched well that night. He threw two strikes past Mookie, and when
Mookie kept nicking foul balls, Stanley never gave him anything good
to hit. The wild pitch wasn't Stanley's fault: [catcher Rich] Gedman
should have caught the ball. Gary Carter, who likes Gedman personally, was clear about this. Mookie jackknifed out of the way, the ball
grazed Gedman's mitt and was gone. Mitchell danced home, and the
game was even.

Kib yelled, I remember, *"Oh, no, oh, Jesus!"* A *crie-de-coeur,* stricken
and angry both. Kib, too, is an artist, and I value that yell of his. It made
us kin forever.

And so the tea leaves had lied to me. My heart cooled and hard-
ened. I was sick to death of rooting for the Boston Red Sox. I sank back
in the sofa wondering bitterly how the gods would contrive to allow Ray
Knight to score from second.

Having taken the rap for Gedman, Stanley battled on. As Mookie
would point out, rolling the ball to the first baseman wasn't what he had
in mind. He didn't even pull it hard; if he had, Evans in right might have
reached it in time to hold Knight at third or gun him down at the plate.
Through Buckner's legs it went, and Knight frolicked home. The Mets
swarmed out to celebrate, and Bill Buckner limped off the field a legend.

We left quickly, saying leaden goodbyes. The autumn stars winked
across the blue-black dome of the sky. Up and down the street the houses all slept. Some were
summer houses, asleep till May or June, when this World Series would be history.

In the car my wife said, "Maybe they'll win tomorrow."

"No," I said. "They won't win tomorrow."

Game Seven was delayed a day by rain, but—as John Hough well knew—curses are patient. The Sox jumped out to
a quick 3–0 lead off Ron Darling, and a weary Bruce Hurst held the lead until the sixth. But it was clear that Hurst was
struggling, and the Sox couldn't add to their lead off Mets' reliever Sid Fernandez.

In the sixth, the Met bats finally awoke, with Keith Hernandez providing a bases-loaded single as New York scored
three to tie it. In the seventh, facing a shell-shocked Calvin Schiraldi, the Mets scored three more. Though the Sox
mounted one more desperate rally to draw within a run, Mets closer Jesse Orosco pitched two hitless innings, Darryl
Strawberry slammed a home run, and the Mets walked away with the game and the Series, 8–5.

"The dark cloud suddenly disappeared here just before noon Tuesday, right on time for the sun to shine on the New
York Mets' world championship parade. The chill drizzle crawled northeast up the coast, headed for Boston just in time,"
wrote a mourning Thomas Boswell from New York. "For sun to bathe New England on this day would be like wearing a
white tux to a wake."

t was a long way from the green-grass, wooden-grandstand fields that many fans considered the cathedrals of their youths, but it sure did work.

Minneapolis' Hubert Horatio Humphrey Metrodome (affectionately called the Homerdome), a hulking monstrosity that shook like a giant eardrum when filled with howling fans, was the Twins' secret weapon in 1987. At peak moments, the crowd noise could exceed 110 decibels—about what a jet plane makes when it takes off. If that wasn't bad enough, it was also hard for fielders to pick up the ball off the bat, both because of the odd glare cast by the lights and because of the Minnesota fans' penchant for waving their white "homer hankies" when things got exciting.

Simply put, opposing teams loathed playing at the Homerdome. In 1987 the Twins, led by Kirby Puckett (.332) and sluggers Kent Hrbek, Gary Gaetti, and Tom Brunansky, took advantage to the tune of a 56–25 home record. Their road mark was an atrocious 29–52 (with only nine of the wins coming after the All-Star break!), but their home-field advantage allowed the Twins to go 85–77 overall. This mediocre record would have placed them just fifth in the A.L. East, but it was enough to capture the West.

Then, somehow, the Twins defeated the powerful Detroit Tigers in the playoffs, becoming one of the least likely World Series participants in years.

Representing the N.L. were the St. Louis Cardinals, still smarting from their nightmare loss in the '85 Series. Whitey Herzog's Cardinals provided a stark contrast to the slugging Twins, once again hitting fewer homers than any other team in either league but making up for it with fine pitching, defense, and team speed.

In Game One, at the Metrodome (the first World Series game ever played indoors), St. Louis seemed shell-shocked by the teeth-rattling noise of the Metrodome. Minnesota outfielder Dan Gladden blasted a grand slam and Frank Viola pitched eight tidy innings in the Twins' 10–1 win. Game Two was more of the same, as a six-run fourth led Bert Blyleven and the Twins to an 8–4 victory.

Luckily for the deafened Cardinals, Games Three, Four, and Five were in St. Louis, It also helped that the Twins usually played like hairless Samsons away from home. John Tudor pitched seven dominating innings and speedy Vince Coleman stole two bases in Game Three as the Cards won, 3–1. Game Four was even easier, with the Cardinals scoring six in the fourth for an easy 7–2 win. Then, completing the home-field sweep, Danny Cox and two relievers shut down the Twins as the Cards won again, 4–2.

Improbably, St. Louis needed just one more game to capture their second World Series in six years. Back in Minnesota, though 55,000 fans did what they could to prevent it, bellowing from

1987

HOMERDOME-FIELD ADVANTAGE

Simultaneously joyful and intense, Kirby Puckett, the heart of the Twins, hit .357 in the Series.

1987

MINNESOTA TWINS

4

ST. LOUIS CARDINALS

3

the first pitch, St. Louis jumped out to a 5–2 lead in the fifth. But Samson had regrown his hair. Don Baylor keyed a four-run Minnesota fifth with a two-run homer, Kent Hrbek blasted a grand slam in the sixth, Kirby Puckett had four hits, and the Twins tied the Series, 11–5.

Game Seven, mercifully, was something else again: the closest thing to a pitchers' duel anyone had seen in the Metrodome in weeks. The Cardinals jumped out to a 2–0 lead off Frank Viola, but the phlegmatic Viola gave up no more. Single runs in the second, fifth, sixth, and eighth gave the Twins a 4–2 lead and a remarkable World Series victory.

After the Series, the ever-plainspoken Whitey Herzog put it best. "They have a very good ballclub—in their park," he said of the Twins. "But their ballpark didn't beat us. We got beat because we couldn't keep them [from hitting home runs] in their ballpark."

Twins' slugger Kent Hrbek blasts a grand slam in Game Six.

"AT PEAK MOMENTS, THE CROWD NOISE COULD EXCEED 110 DECIBELS— ABOUT WHAT A JET PLANE MAKES WHEN IT TAKES OFF."

A cauldron of pure noise: The Hubert Horatio Humphrey Metrodome fans in all their glory.

From 1988 through 1990 the Oakland A's were clearly the best team in baseball. They won 104, 99, and 103 games with a potent offense led by charismatic "Bash Brothers" Jose Canseco (96 home runs and 282 RBI in the three seasons) and Mark McGwire (104 home runs, 302 RBI), along with lead-off hitter extraordinaire Rickey Henderson.

The A's pitching was almost as impressive. Clockwork starter Dave Stewart won twenty-plus games each season, Bob Welch won twenty-seven in 1990, and closer Dennis Eckersley posted some of the best years ever by a relief pitcher, compiling 126 saves during the three years.

So why haven't the 1988–90 A's been anointed among the all-time greats? Because, like the Mets of the mid-1980s, they simply didn't win enough. Every year, even when they captured the World Series in 1989, someone or something else stole the headlines. They were a team with no weaknesses, except the ability to become immortal.

After years of mediocrity, the A's captured the A.L. West flag easily in 1988 and cruised into the World Series. Their opponents were the unlikely Los Angeles Dodgers, a so-so team carried by two stars: MVP Kirk Gibson, who fired up a club long considered too cool and unemotional, and pitcher Orel Hershiser.

Hershiser was a fine pitcher throughout his career, but in 1988 he was unearthly. He finished the year with twenty-three wins and a 2.26 ERA—including a record fifty-nine consecutive scoreless innings to close the season. No one, simply no one, could hit him.

Fittingly, it was Hershiser's five-hit shutout in Game Seven of the playoffs that sent the Dodgers to the World Series instead of the heavily favored Mets. But the Dodgers were hurting, especially Kirk Gibson, who was crippled by leg injuries and doubtful to play in the Series at all.

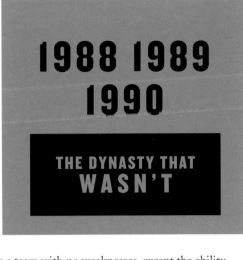

1988 1989 1990

THE DYNASTY THAT WASN'T

It's time to boogie as skipper Tommy Lasorda crows over the Dodgers' upset 1988 Series win.

Orel Hershiser finished an unprecedented string of brilliance with two victories in the 1988 Series.

1988

LOS ANGELES DODGERS

4

OAKLAND ATHLETICS

1

In the 1988 and 1990 Series, Jose Canseco endured miseries at the plate, going a combined 2 for 31. "It was not exactly the kind of performance from which legends are born," said columnist Tom Barnidge.

The relentless drumbeat touting the A's as the prohibitive Series favorite enraged Dodger Manager Tommy Lasorda. "We are just honored to be in the World Series with Oakland," he said sarcastically.

Game One began with the Dodgers' Mickey Hatcher hitting a two-run blast off Dave Stewart. But when Jose Canseco tagged Dodger pitcher Tim Belcher for a grand slam in the second to give Oakland a 4–2 lead, no one was much surprised.

The A's clung to a 4–3 lead until there were two outs in the bottom of the ninth, when baseball history was made. Kirk Gibson (who'd spent the entire game on the trainer's table, his legs packed in ice) hobbled to the plate as a pinch hitter with a runner on first base and the magnificent Dennis Eckersley on the mound.

To Dodger catcher Mike Scioscia, what followed was "the greatest World Series at bat you're ever going to see." To Oakland Manager Tony LaRussa, it was "heartbreak…the worst of memories." For Gibson, it was the culmination of a dream: "I go up there, I step on the field, the crowd goes nuts. I have already visualized hitting a home run to win the game."

Eckersley got two strikes on Gibson, who looked gimpy and overmatched at the plate. The ailing slugger managed to work the

count to 3–2. Then Eckersley threw a slider away—perhaps ball four, except that Gibson swung at it. The ball flew toward the right-field bleachers, as the great announcer Jack Buck gave what has become the most famous of all World Series calls. ("This is gonna be a home run! Unbelievable!… And the Dodgers have won the game! Five to four!… I don't believe what I just saw!")

Gibson's home run seemed to drain all the life from the A's. "What it did was not only win the game for us, but it also won the Series because they were never able to recover," said Tommy Lasorda.

Orel Hershiser was on the mound for the Dodgers in Game Two. Though he always seemed ice-cold on the mound, Hershiser confessed to suffering from postseason jitters "like little butterflies. The feeling you get when something wakes you out of a deep sleep and you wonder if somebody is in your home."

But no one was home for the A's, as Hershiser set them down easily on a three-hit, 6–0 shutout win. The A's scratched out two runs in Game Three (including Mark McGwire's sole homer and RBI for the Series), good enough for a 2–1 victory, but on the field they still seemed shaken and unsure of themselves.

Game Four was another tight one, but the Dodgers' Tim Belcher and Jay Howell outpitched Dave Stewart as L.A. won again, 4–3. After that, the end result was inevitable: Orel Hershiser pitched Game Five, an easy 5–2 win that made the Dodgers one of the most unexpected, unlikely World Champions of all time.

After their crushing loss in 1988, the young A's were unbowed. "This year in the Series, we just didn't hit," said Mark McGwire. "But we'll know how to handle things next year because we'll all be salty veterans."

McGwire, Jose Canseco, and the rest of the disappointed A's got a chance to prove their resilience in 1989, when they again captured the A.L. West and muscled their way into the World Series by beating Toronto in five games. In the Series they met their across-the-Bay Bridge counterparts, the San Francisco Giants, who were making their first Series appearance since 1962.

To put it briefly, in the 1989 Series the A's did everything they were supposed to do in 1988. Dave Stewart and Mike Moore each won two games (giving up a total of six runs in twenty-nine innings); Dennis Eckersley was unhittable; Canseco batted .357; new acquisition Rickey Henderson batted .474 with a double, two triples, a home run, and three stolen bases. The A's won the World Series in four straight, thoroughly dominating the Giants in every aspect of the game.

But it barely seemed to matter. Today, few recall the details of the 1989 Series, except for the most important detail of all: the massive earthquake that struck the Bay Area just a few minutes before Game Three was about to begin at Candlestick Park. Dozens died in the quake, which also caused billions of dollars of damage. Though the fans and players at Candlestick were spared, the Series seemed suddenly irrelevant.

While the cities tried to clean up the damage, Commissioner Fay Vincent postponed the Series for twelve days. When it resumed, with the A's leading two games to none, all the joy and life and momentum seemed to have disappeared. The A's crushed the Giants, 13–7, in Game Three, then pounded them again, 9–6, for the sweep.

"Sweep Gives Oakland 'Best in 20 Years' Label" read the headline in *The Sporting News* after Game Four. But Bob Verdi's column in the same publication gave a better sense of how unimportant the A's triumph seemed to Oakland in 1989. "They had hoped to hold a parade for their A's in this blue-collar city sometime soon," Verdi wrote, "but baseball didn't matter now, not with highways and overpasses wracked by cracks and fissures."

1989

OAKLAND ATHLETICS

4

SAN FRANCISCO GIANTS

0

10 WORST SERIES

NO. 3

1989

The A's were back at it again in 1990, riding an MVP season from Rickey Henderson and a Cy Young year from Bob Welch to the A.L. West flag. When they then destroyed the Red Sox in the playoffs, it seemed that this might be the greatest of all the great Oakland teams.

For the third year in a row, the A's faced a new N.L. opponent—this time the Cincinnati Reds, under first-year Manager Lou Piniella. Like the Giants before them, the Reds seemed destined to fall easily to the powerful A's. Cincinnati had several strong players, including Barry Larkin (.301), Eric Davis (twenty-four home runs), and Tom Browning (fifteen wins), but no true superstars. It was a shock when they defeated the powerful Pittsburgh Pirates in the playoffs, but no one gave them much of a chance against the Bash Brothers & Co.

But the A's, looking for some recognition not clouded by memories of the previous year's earthquake, just didn't have it in 1990. The Reds cruised to an easy Game One victory, 7–0, then overcame a Jose Canseco homer and scored a ninth-inning run off Dennis Eckersley to win Game Two, 5–4. Game Three was no better for the floundering A's, as the Reds' Chris Sabo homered twice and the Reds won easily, 8–3.

1990

**CINCINNATI
REDS
4**

**OAKLAND
ATHLETICS
0**

Stunningly, the Reds had a 3–0 Series lead—but at least the A's had Dave Stewart pitching for them in Game Four. Stewart had his best stuff, clinging to a 1–0 lead over Jose Rijo until the top of the eighth. Then, as had happened throughout the Series, the A's fell apart. A single, a bunt base hit, an error, a ground out, and a sacrifice fly gave the Reds two runs. No, Cincinnati's big rally didn't conjure up memories of Babe Ruth's 1932 "called shot," but it was enough for a 2–1 win and a Series sweep.

The champions, in the words of Chris Sabo, were a team with "no MVP, no Cy Young winner—just a team where everybody does his job."

And the A's? They were unquestionably the greatest team of their era…and the greatest "might have been." As a bitter Dennis Eckersley put it: "We won a division and we won a pennant. But we'll be remembered now for getting our ass kicked."

Baseball came second: A lowered flag marks the tragic earthquake that interrupted the 1989 Series.

1991

A CLASSIC
ALL THE WAY

After three years of alternately flat, tragic, and one-sided World Series, it was time for a true classic. Even the stories of the two contenders—the Minnesota Twins and Atlanta Braves—added spice to the Series. After their 1987 championship, the Twins had fallen on hard times, dropping all the way to last in 1990 with a 74–88 record. The Braves, with no comparable recent record of success, were even worse in '90, staggering home with a last-place 65–97 record.

Then, in 1991, everything came together for both teams. The Twins, led by perennial All Star Kirby Puckett (.298) and hard-nosed pitchers Scott Erickson (twenty wins) and Jack Morris (eighteen wins), vaulted to 95–67 record and marched past the Toronto Blue Jays in the playoffs. Meanwhile, the Braves rode a big year from Ron Gant (thirty-two home runs) and solid starting pitching from Tom Glavine, John Smoltz, and Steve Avery to an astonishing 94–68 mark, then edged Pittsburgh in a thrilling seven-game playoff series.

Never before had a team made it from last place to the World Series in one year. Now two teams had done it in the same year.

The Twins were favorites going in, especially with their not-so-secret weapon, the cacophonous Metrodome. Game One, one of only two games not to be decided by a single run, went pretty much according to Homerdome form. The Twins' Kent Hrbek and Greg Gagne hit home runs, Jack Morris pitched seven gutty innings, the fans screamed and waved their "homer hankies," and the Twins won, 5–2.

Game Two was tenser. The Twins scored two unearned runs in the first on a home run by Chili Davis off Tom Glavine, but the Braves came back to tie the game, 2–2. There the score remained until the bottom of the eighth, when Twins rookie Scott Leius hit a solo shot off Glavine for a 3–2 win.

The Twins, improbable Series champs for the second time in four years.

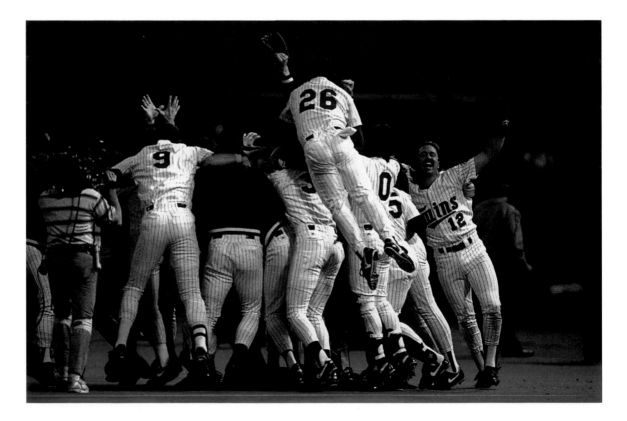

Two games in Minnesota, two Twins wins.

The Series moved to Atlanta, and immediately the Braves started playing better. By the end of five innings, Atlanta had a 4–1 lead, but home runs by Chili Davis and Kirby Puckett brought the Twins back to a 4–4 tie. It stayed that way until the twelfth, when Braves second baseman Mark Lemke singled to drive in David Justice with the winning run.

Lemke, a sudden star after playing nearly eight hundred games in the minors, was stunned by the media attention—and well aware of how fleeting his fame might be. "You play each game as if it is your last because one day you're going to be right," he said.

But Lemke's fame extended another day. In Game Four, the Braves' John Smoltz matched Jack Morris, both pitching superbly in a game that was tied, 2–2, until the bottom of the ninth. There was Lemke, slugging a triple with one out and then scoring with a nifty slide on a sacrifice fly by Jerry Willard for the win that knotted the Series.

Lemke's rampage continued in Game Five. He slammed two more triples, while David Justice drove in five runs and Lonnie Smith homered in the Braves' easy 14–5 blowout.

Game Six, back in Minnesota, was a nailbiter all the way, tied 3–3 into the tenth inning. As the Homerdome fans yelled hoarsely, Kirby Puckett stepped to the plate in the bottom of the tenth. "It might have been the first time I can remember going up there looking to hit one out," he said after the game. "But today, I did a lot of things I don't usually do."

Puckett's home run, just over the plexiglass wall in left-center field, gave the Twins a thrilling 4–3 win. The Series was headed to a seventh game. "Somebody's got the storybook," said an exhausted Twins' Manager Tom Kelly. "I wish somebody would let us in on the ending."

Game Seven, pitting Atlanta's twenty-three-year-old John Smoltz against his childhood idol, thirty-six-year-old Jack Morris, quieted even the boisterous Homerdome throngs. "[T]he crowd was spellbound with everybody else," wrote columnist Jim Klobuchar in the *Minneapolis Star Tribune.*

As he stepped into the batter's box to face Morris, lead-off hitter Lonnie Smith took a moment to shake Twins catcher Brian Harper's hand. "Let's have a good one," he said.

They didn't have a good one. They had a great one, a scoreless game through three, six, nine innings. As the innings rolled on, Game Seven became the stuff of ever-increasing dread—the realization among players and fans alike that the World Championship, the entire season, would most likely rest on a single run, a single play.

That play almost occurred in the top of the eighth, when Lonnie Smith singled, but then lost track of the ball on Terry Pendleton's double and failed to score. In the *Star Tribune*, writer Steve Aschburner predicted that Smith's baserunning blunder would someday "rank alongside the antics of Fred Snodgrass, Mickey Owen and Bill Buckner as one of the worst plays in Series history."

1991

MINNESOTA TWINS

4

ATLANTA BRAVES

3

But he was wrong: What fans remember today isn't Smith's foible, but the rugged intensity of Morris glowering on the mound, the smooth, easy motion of Smoltz as he mowed the Twins down, and the increasing awareness that this might be the finest Game Seven in Series history.

Smoltz left in the eighth, but Morris stayed on. Neither team scored in the eighth or the ninth, and Morris set the side down easily in the tenth. Leading off the bottom of the inning, Dan Gladden doubled. When Chuck Knoblauch laid down a sacrifice bunt, the Twins had the winning run just ninety feet away from home plate.

Reliever Alejandro Peña intentionally walked Puckett and Hrbek to set up the force at any base, and the Braves brought the infield and outfield in. But at last in this brilliantly played and managed game, a strategy didn't work. Pinch hitter Gene Larkin, in just his fourth at bat of the Series, hit a single over the drawn-in outfield to score Gladden with the run that gave Jack Morris a ten-inning shutout win and the Twins the World Series championship.

"What more can you want?" said winning manager Tom Kelly after the game. "What more can you ask for?"

Nothing. Sometimes baseball gives you everything.

Gritty Series MVP Jack Morris produced one of the greatest pitching performances in postseason history in Game Seven.

F eaturing superstars like Joe Carter, Roberto Alomar, Dave Winfield, Jimmy Key, 1991 World Series hero Jack Morris, and itinerant star pitcher David Cone, the 1992 Toronto Blue Jays were an outstanding team from top to bottom—and a superb candidate to finally bring a World Series Championship to Canada. And didn't Canada know it! "We're keenly aware that we don't just represent just one little burg," said Winfield, shaking his head at the intensity of Canada's focus on the Series. "We represent an entire country."

But the Blue Jays had just a big obstacle to making their homeland happy: the Atlanta Braves, back after their heartbreaking loss in the 1991 Series. The Braves threw twenty-game winner Tom Glavine in Game One in Atlanta, while the Blue Jays—hoping to give the Braves nightmare flashbacks—chose Jack Morris. For five innings, as the Blue Jays took a 1–0 lead on Joe Carter's home run, Morris was as dominant as ever. But when Atlanta catcher Damon Berryhill blasted a three-run homer in sixth, Glavine and the Braves had all they needed for a 3–1 victory.

For seven innings of Game Two, it seemed as if the seasoned Braves might have an easy time of it with the neophyte Jays. John Smoltz was overpowering and the speedy Braves, led by renegade football star Deion Sanders, stole five bases as the Braves took a 4–2 lead. But the Jays scored a run in the eighth and put a man on in the ninth against Atlanta closer Jeff Reardon. Then, like a bolt from the Blue Jays, pinch hitter Ed Sprague slugged a two-run homer to give Toronto a 5–4 win.

Game Three was played in the new Toronto Skydome, and it was a humdinger, as the Jays' Candy Maldonado stroked a bases-loaded single in the bottom of the ninth to give Toronto a 3–2 win. Game Four was more of the same, yet another pitcher's duel (this time between Tom Glavine and Jimmy Key) that ended with the Jays on top, 2–1.

The Jays were so close to fulfilling all Canada's dreams—and in front of the home crowd, too. But Game Five was a Braves blowout, as John Smoltz bested Jack Morris, 7–2.

Back to Atlanta for Game Six—yet another nail-biting contest in what must rank as one of the most consistently tense, low-scoring Series of all time. The Jays moved to a 2–1 lead in the fourth, and Braves Manager Bobby Cox pulled shaky pitcher Steve Avery from the game. But Braves relievers Pete Smith, Mike Stanton, Mark Wohlers, and Charlie Leibrandt kept the Jays off the scoreboard for the next six innings, while the Braves tied the score in the bottom of the ninth on a two-strike, two-out single by Otis Nixon.

The game stayed tied until the top of the eleventh, when Dave Winfield came to the plate with runners on first and second. Winfield had had an invisible Series

1992
1993

MAPLE LEAFS TRIUMPHANT

After his miserable 1981 World Series with the Yankees, Dave Winfield was looking for redemption—and he got it in 1992 with his Series-winning hit in the ninth inning of Game Six.

1992
TORONTO BLUE JAYS
4
ATLANTA BRAVES
2

so far (4 for 21, with just 1 RBI), following up the nightmarish, 1-for-21 performance in his only other Series, in 1981 with the Yankees. The 1981 disappearing act led owner George Steinbrenner to dub Winfield "Mr. May," and Winfield had not yet proved the mouthy owner wrong.

But redemption is always just one at bat away. Winfield expiated all past sins with a double, driving in both runs to put the Jays up, 4–2. The Braves scored a run off of Jimmy Key in the bottom of the inning, but Mike Timlin fielded Otis Nixon's bunt and threw the speedy Brave out at first to end the superb game and give Canada its first World Series championship.

After the game, Dave Winfield was both exhausted and exhilarated. "This team has heart," he said, "it has character, it has pitching, hitting, defense, it clawed back from deficits, didn't listen to negative press, pulled together on the field and off, and had a lot of fun."

"HOW COME I KEEP HAVING NIGHTMARES ABOUT THIS ONE GAME, THE LONGEST NINE-INNING NIGHT GAME IN THE HISTORY OF BASEBALL? IT WASN'T LONG ENOUGH?"

Lenny Dykstra hit .348 with four home runs in the '93 Series...but it wasn't enough.

After the tight, tense events of the '92 Series, which pitted two similarly quiet, hard-working teams, fans were ready for something a little different in 1993. And boy, did they get it.

The Jays were even stronger than they'd been in '92, with Rickey Henderson, Dave Stewart, and Paul Molitor joining returning stars Roberto Alomar and Joe Carter. Their opponents in the '93 Series, a world apart from the unflashy Braves, were the scruffy, loud, boisterous Philadelphia Phillies, personified by tobacco-spitting Lenny Dykstra, bulgy John Kruk, and closer Mitch "Wild Thing" Williams.

The two teams presented entertaining contrasts. "The Blue Jays' image is scrubbed and efficient," said James Deacon in Canada's *Maclean's Magazine*. "For the Phillies, meanwhile, the familiar phrase 'winning ugly' is a literal as well as figurative truth." The *Toronto Sun* sponsored a contest about how ugly the Phillies were, with the winning entry reading, "The Phillies are so ugly the turf spits back."

Even the Phillies knew (and gloried in) how they looked on the national stage. Said pitcher Larry Anderson, "It's the ugly stepsister being invited to the prom by the best-looking guy in class."

1993

TORONTO BLUE JAYS

4

PHILADELPHIA PHILLIES

2

In Game One in Toronto, the Jays played Phillies-style baseball, making three errors but also pounding out ten hits in a messy 8–5 victory. Game Two was more of the same, with the two teams combining for ten runs on twenty hits as the Phillies evened things, 6–4. Down at Philly's Veterans Stadium for Game Three, the pattern continued, as Paul Molitor got three hits (towards his eventual total of twelve in twenty-four at bats for the Series) and drove in three runs in the Jays' 10–3 shellacking of the shell-shocked Philly staff.

Then came Game Four. How to describe this game, perhaps the most memorable in the history of that usually dignified spectacle called the World Series? "I had nightmares all winter," cried out Bruce Buschel in *Philadelphia Magazine* the next spring. "[H]ow come I keep having nightmares about this one game, the longest nine-inning night game in the history of baseball? It wasn't long enough? It has to continue in the dark, dank Vet of my unconscious, played and replayed, extended and altered by irrational substitutions?"

It was long enough: four hours and fourteen minutes. It featured two homers and four RBI for Lenny Dykstra, five RBI for Philly's Milt Thompson, five RBI for Toronto's Tony Fernandez, five lead changes, eleven pitchers, and a final score of 15–14, Toronto, as Philadelphia closer Mitch Williams couldn't hold a 14–9 lead. "That was a war out there," said a stunned Dave Stewart after the game. "It didn't look like any of the pitchers could get *anyone* out."

The two teams were clearly still exhausted when they played Game Five the next night—a game that Philadelphia, behind 3–1 in the Series, had to have. Their starter, Curt Schilling, came up big, stopping the Blue Jays on five hits in a quick 2–0 win. The Phillies' hopes were alive for another day.

Though played at the Skydome, Game Six was another Philly special. The Blue Jays jumped out to a 5–1 lead, only to see the Phillies erupt in a five-run seventh, keyed by Dykstra's three-run homer (his fourth of the Series). The game remained 6–5, Philadelphia, until the ninth, when Mitch Williams came in to try to send the Series to a seventh game.

A walk and a one-out single by Molitor put the tying and winning runs on base. Everyone who was watching that night remembers what happens next. Pale with tension, the scruffy, unshaven Williams faced the ever-cool Joe Carter at the plate. Carter worked the count to 2–2…and then blasted Williams' next pitch over the left-field fence. The Blue Jays had won the game, 8–6, and their second consecutive Series.

Canada's joy was unrestrained—and so was Joe Carter's. "Everyone who has ever played baseball has dreamed of hitting a home run in the bottom of the ninth to win a World Series," he said after the game. "I can't tell you what it feels like to actually do it."

E very so often, the World Series presents a match-up of polar opposites. After a year off due to the player's strike, 1995 gave fans just such a contest: the Cleveland Indians, with offensive stars Albert Belle, Manny Ramirez, Kenny Lofton, and Jim Thome, versus the Atlanta Braves, home to a spectacular pitching rotation of Tom Glavine, John Smoltz, Steve Avery, and new arrival Greg Maddux.

Game One, in Atlanta, pitted future Hall of Famer Maddux against postseason star Orel Hershiser. The Braves managed only three hits and three runs—but it was enough, since Maddux held the Indians to only two hits and two runs.

Tom Glavine started Game Two against veteran Dennis Martinez, and the game was almost a repeat of the first: a tight, tense battle won, 4–3, by the Braves on catcher Javy Lopez's two-run homer. "They're aggressive swingers," the precise, crafty Glavine said of the Indians' sluggers. "They're the kind of team I feel like I can do well against."

Their backs already against the wall, the Indians pulled out Game Three in front of their hometown fans. They drove John Smoltz from the mound with four quick runs, then scored a run in the eighth and another in the eleventh to

1995

THE BRAVES WIN ONE

David Justice struggled in the Series—but then hit the home run that gave the Braves Game Six and the Series, 1–0.

Tribe slugger Albert
Belle mourns a lost
Series opportunity.

win, 7–6—their first World Series victory since 1948. But Atlanta came right back to win Game Four, as Steve Avery outpitched Ken Hill, Ryan Klesko hit a home run, and the Braves won, 5–2.

Now the Indians were down to possibly their last chance—and facing Greg Maddux to boot. But Maddux didn't have his best stuff in Game Five, while Orel Hershiser did. Home runs by Jim Thome and Albert Belle enabled the Indians to withstand a two-run Braves ninth inning and hold on for a 5–4 win.

1995

ATLANTA BRAVES

4

CLEVELAND INDIANS

2

The only thing that keeps the next outing from entering the pantheon of the best Series-deciding games of all time is that it came in Game Six, not Seven. In all other ways, it was a classic white-knuckler from first pitch to last.

Even better, it had an intriguing backstory. After Game Five, Braves slugger David Justice had criticized Atlanta fans for not cheering enthusiastically enough. Then as he stepped to the plate for his first at bat, Justice found out that the hometown crowd was certainly adept at booing. With perfect timing, Justice turned the boos to cheers with a home run in the sixth to give the Braves a 1–0 lead.

That was enough for Tom Glavine. The left-hander, a superb postseason pitcher, held the powerful Indians to just one hit in eight innings. The Indians, wrote *The Sporting News'* Michael Knisely, "knew exactly how Glavine would try to beat them, with his down-and-away, down-and-away, down-and-away changeups; and still they couldn't put bat to ball."

Holding onto the 1–0 lead, the Braves brought closer Mark Wohlers to the mound in the ninth. After Glavine's curves and sliders, Wohlers' fastballs must have looked like they were going 150 mph. The Indians went down in order, and the Braves had their first Series triumph in three tries in the 1990s.

"What this does," said Atlanta pitching coach Leo Mazzone, "is put the final stamp on one of the greatest pitching staffs of all time." The Indians, for one, couldn't disagree.

The worst World Series of all time took place in 1919, when several members of the Chicago White Sox were paid to throw the Series to the Cincinnati Reds. The second worst Series took place much more recently, in 1997, when the Florida Marlins took on the Cleveland Indians.

How could that be? Let us count the ways.

The Marlins, who won, had a team earned-run average of 5.48. None of their starters managed to post ERAs under 5.00, and Kevin Brown, their staff ace, boasted an 8.08 ERA for his two starts. (Rookie Tony Saunders, thrown into the fire in Game Four, ended his career with a 27.00 Series ERA.) Indian pitchers weren't much better, managing a less-than-stellar 4.66 ERA.

The pitchers' stats would have been even worse if not for the fact that they gave up nine unearned runs, courtesy of the thirteen errors committed by the two teams in the seven games. No one player was responsible for a large proportion of this error total: The bad fielding was spread around among eleven players.

Partly as a result of the above shenanigans, nearly every game lasted well more than three hours, and two of them easily broke the four-hour mark.

1997

A SERIES TO FORGET

Florida owner Wayne Huizenga celebrated the Marlins' Series win—even as he plotted to dismantle the team.

Just two games were decided by a single run, and only the seventh was truly a thriller. And even this spectacular eleven-inning finale was ruined for discerning fans because:

The wrong team won.

The wrong team was the Florida Marlins, a living, breathing example of most everything wrong with baseball in recent years. The fault didn't lie with the Marlin players, but with team owner Wayne Huizenga. Whether you were a Marlins' fan or not, Huizenga's words and actions during and after the Series served to drain the games of most of their enjoyment.

"With all due respect to the Atlanta Braves and their 716 wins this decade, the Florida Marlins are the Team of the '90s," Tom Verducci bitterly wrote in *Sports Illustrated*. "They reached the World Series by playing checkbook baseball and capitalizing on the three gizmos produced by major-league owners this decade: expansion, the wild card, and interleague play."

In spending $89 million to coax free agents Moises Alou, Al Leiter, Kevin Brown, Gary Sheffield, and other stars to play for his expansion team, Huizenga was only playing by the rules. But to threaten to dismantle the team while the Series was going on—"It's more important to us to get a new stadium than to win the World Series," he said—well, that was unforgivable.

Still, there was some entertainment to be gotten out of the games themselves, as long as you weren't picky. In Game One, at Miami's Pro Player Stadium, it was watching twenty-two-year-old Livan Hernandez outpitch thirty-nine-year-old veteran Orel Hershiser in the Marlins' 7–4 win. Game Two saw Cleveland's Chad Ogea pitch strongly as the Indians knotted the Series with a 6–1 victory.

1997

FLORIDA
MARLINS

4

CLEVELAND
INDIANS

3

Game Three…well, Game Three in Cleveland had all the finesse of a monster-truck rally. Eleven pitchers, twenty-six hits, six errors, seven runs in the top of the ninth for the Marlins, four runs in the bottom of the inning for Indians, and a 14–11 Marlins win in just four hours and twelve minutes.

Game Four was less messy but also less entertaining, an easy 10–3 romp for Jaret Wright and the Indians. Though Game Five appeared tighter, it took three runs in the bottom of the ninth to bring the Indians close in an 8–7 Marlins win.

Games Six and Seven were legitimately better. Chad Ogea pitched well again—and also hit a double to drive in two runs—as the Indians captured the penultimate game, 4–1. And then the Indians jumped out to a 2–0 Game Seven lead behind Wright, who gave up only a solo homer to Bobby Bonilla in the seventh. The game remained 2–1, Indians, until the bottom of the ninth, when Moises Alou and Charles Johnson singled off Indians' closer Jose Mesa, and Craig Counsell hit a sacrifice fly to tie the game.

On to the bottom of the eleventh. Bobby Bonilla singled to lead off. One out later, Craig Counsell hit a grounder to shortstop Tony Fernandez…who muffed the ball. "I believe that the Lord doesn't send you more than He thinks you can bear," Fernandez said when asked about his critical error.

With the bases loaded, Edgar Reneteria came to the plate. His single scored Counsell with the run that won the Series and sent 67,000 Marlin fans home to celebrate.

For about five minutes. Seemingly before the field was cleared, Huizenga (despairing of the new ballpark he felt he needed) announced his attention to sell off the Marlins' stars. He was as good as his word: Before the start of the next season, in the words of *Sports Illustrated*'s Rick Reilly, the Marlins were "scaled, gutted and filleted…. Wildly popular first baseman Jeff Conine? Gone. World Series hero Moises Alou? Gone. Ace right-hander Kevin Brown? Gone."

And gone with them any trace of the joy hometown fans feel when their team wins the World Series. "Maybe this is rock-bottom," wrote Dave Kindred after the Series was over.

We can only hope so.

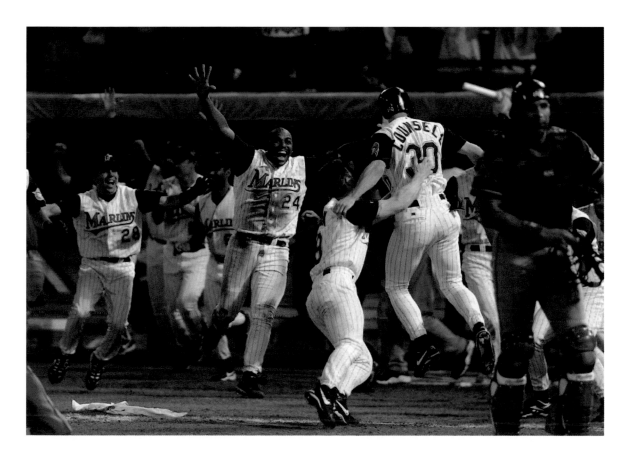

The Marlins' celebration lasted barely a nanosecond. By the beginning of the following season, nearly all their stars would be playing for other teams.

SWEET VICTORY

Nothing matches a team's first World Series championship for sheer joyful intensity—especially if you live in a town with no long history of baseball success. Washington fans in 1924, Detroit rooters in 1935, Brooklynites in 1955, Los Angelenos in 1963, and Oakland fans in 1972 all shared the same vivid understanding, at last, of what it meant to root for the best team in baseball.

In 1985 it was Kansas City's turn. After losing in the playoffs in 1976, 1977, 1978, and 1984, and in the World Series in 1980, the Royals won a thrilling, controversial Series against St. Louis, coming back to win the final two games in front of the home crowd. "It's funny, you know," wrote longtime K.C. fan and baseball historian Bill James, writing in his 1986 *Baseball Abstract* after Game Seven. "I've been as big a baseball fan as you can be all my life, but *I never knew a baseball game could make you feel so good.*"

James's description of the hours he and his wife, Susie, spent following the Royals' victory will fill fans of every first-time champion with a nostalgic glow:

> Susie and I drove to an area of Kansas City called Westport. Thousands, maybe tens of thousands of people swarmed the streets, in many places packed so tight that it was difficult to move. It was past midnight on Sunday; the bars were closed in self-defense, and people wandered around the crowd trying to buy beer or sell it. There were many more buyers than sellers, and the area was as dry as the Sahara in a half hour. Virtually the entire crowd wore blue, but absurdity is in the eye of the beholder, and there were no eyes to sense the absurdity of us as we meandered in circles, slapping high fives with passing strangers (including, when street conditions permitted, those riding by in convertibles and dune buggies), grinning and singing and yelling in the air phrases without meaning, spelling or distinguishable syllables, hugging and holding onto loved ones, catching an occasional spray of Budweiser in the face from a colleague in revelry, joining in war chants scarcely more intelligible than the random shouts, climbing fire escapes to hang hastily designed banners from the windows of cooperating samaritans, wandering around and around until the faces of others became familiar landmarks of the scene, seeing others dance and weep with joy and sharing the feeling with them and wanting for the evening not to end and for sleep not to come and divide us from what had happened that night....
>
> It was two weeks before anyone had a thought about anything else.

Q: What's the biggest problem with baseball dynasties? A: Most of their World Series aren't very interesting. It's true. The greatest teams in baseball history are usually so much better than their competition that they win so easily that non-hometown fans just yawn. Look at the Chicago Cubs of 1907–08, who lost a grand total of one game to Ty Cobb's Detroit Tigers. Or the Boston Red Sox of 1915–16 and 1918, who were extended to six games just once in the three years. Or, heaven forbid, the Lou Gehrig/Joe DiMaggio Yankees of 1936–39, who won their World Series 4–2, 4–1, 4-0, and 4-0. Ain't we got fun!

The Yankee dynasty that captured the World Series in 1996, 1998, 1999, and 2000, suffered from the same problem. They were just too good. Worse, they not only played spectacular baseball, they did it with class and grace. In contrast to the Mickey Mantle–led teams of the

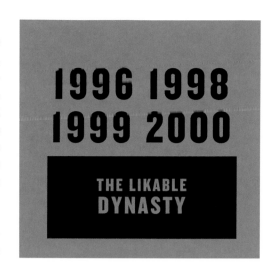

1996 1998 1999 2000

THE LIKABLE DYNASTY

1950s and the three-headed George/Reggie/Billy monster of the 1970s, the image of the late-1990s Yankees was dictated by modest superstars like Bernie Williams, Mariano Rivera, and Derek Jeter, and, most of all, calm, stoical Manager Joe Torre.

"Look at the Yankees' manager today: He is a rock," wrote oft-cynical Dave Kindred in *The Sporting News* in 1996. "Every previous Yankee manager in the twenty-five years of Steinbrenner's ascendancy has been a nervous breakdown waiting to happen. Looking at Joe Torre sitting calmly on the bench, you'd think, 'Yeah, a meteor is coming at us, and the world's about to become a cinder, but Joe's cool, we'll be cool, he'll come up with something.'"

In 1996, the Yankees were not yet an unstoppable force. In fact, they were underdogs against the defending champion Atlanta Braves, and they looked out of their league in the first two games at Yankee Stadium. In Game One, John Smoltz shut the Bombers down on four hits while his teammates used Andy Pettitte for

Remember when the Yankees were underdogs? All that changed when the Yankees stormed back for a six-game triumph over the Braves in 1996—giving the Bombers their first championship since 1978.

batting practice in a 12–1 Braves win. Game Two was little better: a six-hit, 4–0 gem for Greg Maddux and Mark Wohlers.

Describing the mood on the plane-ride home, Yankee pitcher David Cone said, "We were thoroughly embarrassed. It was like, Let's save some face."

Cone, a big-game pitcher from way back, did just that in Game Three. It was a tight, tense game throughout, which the Yankees finally put away, 5–2, on the strength of Bernie Williams' two-run homer in the eighth.

Then came Game Four. "An epic?" wrote Tom Verducci in *Sports Illustrated*. "*Ben-Hur* didn't take as long and had a smaller cast." The game lasted nearly four and a half hours, featured thirteen pitchers, virtually every position player on both teams—and one of the greatest comebacks in Series history.

The Braves scored four in the second, one in third, and one in the fifth to take a 6–0

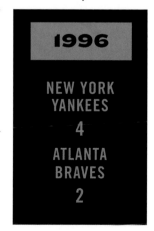

1996

NEW YORK
YANKEES
4

ATLANTA
BRAVES
2

lead. The Yankees came back with three in the sixth, but the game remained 6–3 into the eighth, when the Yankees put two men on and brought bottom-of-the-roster Jim Leyritz to the plate against the Braves' fireballing Mark Wohlers.

When Wohlers threw Leyritz a 100-mph fastball, Leyritz fouled it back. "He'd given him his best shot, and Jimmy was on it," commented David Cone. Switching tactics, Wohlers threw a slider—and Leyritz blasted it over the wall. Tie game…until the tenth, when the Yankees scored twice to win, 8–6, and knot the Series at two.

The Braves seemed shell-shocked after that. They could do nothing against Andy Pettitte in Game Five, and when Brave outfielder Marquis Grissom dropped Charlie Hayes' fourth-inning fly ball, Cecil Fielder drove Hayes in with a double to give the Yankees a 1–0 lead.

"HE'D GIVEN HIM HIS BEST SHOT, AND JIMMY WAS ON IT."

That game featured one of the greatest endings in World Series history. With two outs and a runner on third in the bottom of the ninth, Luis Polonia faced Yankee closer John Wetteland. Six times Wetteland threw a fastball, and six times Polonia fouled the pitch off. "When someone keeps fouling off pitches like that, you know he's going to hit it well," said Derek Jeter.

Jeter was right. Polonia jumped on pitch number seven, smashing it on a line toward right-center field. Right fielder Paul O'Neill, playing despite a gimpy left hamstring, seemed to take forever to catch up to the ball. ("It took off on me and I panicked," he said later.) But at the last second, just as it seemed destined to be a game-tying double, O'Neill reached out at full extension and caught it, slamming into the wall and letting out a victory yell a moment later. The Yankees had won to take a 3–2 Series lead.

The deciding game was overshadowed by the news that Joe Torre's ailing brother, Frank—after a long wait—had been the recipient of a successful heart transplant. (You can't make this stuff up.) But Torre was there in the dugout, stone-faced as always, an island of calm in hectic times.

Hits by O'Neill, Joe Girardi, Derek Jeter, and Bernie Williams gave the Yankees an early 3–0 lead over Greg Maddux. Jimmy Key gave up just a run in five innings, and then the Yankees' sterling bullpen took over. John Wetteland made it interesting by giving up a run in the ninth, but held on for his fourth save of the Series as the Yankees wrapped up their first World Series championship since 1978—and one of their most satisfying ever.

The stunned and distraught Braves squandered a two-game lead to lose four straight and the 1996 Series.

1998 was a whole lot less fun. Fans, still trying to get the bad taste of the Florida Marlins' 1997 post-Series clearance sale out of their mouths, were hoping for something better. But expectations weren't very high when the Yankees compiled an astonishing 114–48 regular-season record and then marched into the Series to face the anonymous San Diego Padres, who featured just one true star: Future Hall-of-Famer Tony Gwynn.

Hopes flared briefly as the Padres jumped to a 5–2 lead in Game One on two homers by Greg Vaughn and one by Gwynn off David Wells. But Joe Torre's Yankees were nothing if not patient, and in the seventh inning they struck against Padre ace Kevin Brown and two relievers. Seven runs scored on a three-run homer by Chuck Knoblauch and a grand slam by Tino Martinez, and the Yankees were on their way to a 9–6 win. Somehow, everyone watching knew the Series was over right then.

Game Two, a 9–3 win for Orlando "El Duque" Hernandez featuring homers by Bernie Williams and Jorge Posada, did nothing to dispel these feelings. And, though the Yankees fell behind 3–0 in Game Three, no one was surprised when a homer by Scott Brosius helped draw the Yankees within one—or when Brosius' eighth-inning blast off ace closer Trevor Hoffman wrapped up another Yankee win.

The Padres were flopping around like fish in the bottom of the boat by now, and the Yankees took full advantage in Game Four. Andy Pettitte, Jeff Nelson, and Mariano Rivera held the Padres to seven hits and no runs, Derek Jeter had two hits, and the Yankees cruised to a 3–0 win and a Series sweep that put a cap on their magnificent season.

1998

NEW YORK YANKEES

4

SAN DIEGO PADRES

0

1999's World Series was no better. This time the Yankees' shooting-gallery ducks were the Atlanta Braves, a team that dominated the National League in the 1990s but (with the single exception of 1995) seemed unable to win the Series. The Yankees, on the other hand, never had that problem. When they got to the Series, they almost always won it.

The Braves' Greg Maddux held a 1–0 lead until the eighth inning of Game One, when—to no one's surprise—two errors and a wild pitch led to four Yankee runs and a seemingly inevitable 4–1 win. Just as inevitable was Game Two, a 7–2 Yankee rout for David Cone that wasn't even as close as the final score.

Game Three was more fun, with the Braves staking Tom Glavine to a 5–1 lead against Andy Pettitte. But Glavine, usually a sure thing in big games, couldn't hold the lead, and Chuck Knoblauch's two-run homer in the eighth tied it. Then it was a battle of the bullpens, and the Yankee bullpen never loses such a battle. Three relievers, including Mariano Rivera, combined for 6 $^1/_3$ scoreless innings, while Chad Curtis hit his second home run of the game to give the Yankees a 6–5, ten-inning win.

Game Four was a foregone conclusion. The Yankees scored three off John Smoltz in the third, Jim Leyritz hit a home run, new Yankee Roger Clemens pitched strongly, and the Yankees went home with a 4–1 win and a Series sweep.

1999

NEW YORK YANKEES

4

ATLANTA BRAVES

0

To no one's surprise, the Yanks were back in 2000. This year, though, the Series featured an interesting twist: For the first time ever, the Yankees and Mets were playing in the World Series.

If ever there were a year to dethrone the Yankees, 2000 seemed to be the one. The team had an indifferent year, culminating in losing a stunning fifteen of eighteen games to end the season with a total of only eighty-seven wins. They struggled throughout the playoffs even to make it to the Series.

But these were the Yankees, battle-tested and ever-dangerous in the postseason. And, just as had happened in 1998 and 1999, events in Game One would provide the deciding moments of the Series.

Behind the gutty pitching of Al Leiter, the Mets took a 3–2 lead into the ninth inning at Yankee Stadium. Paul O'Neill led off against Mets closer Armando Benitez. It was a crucial at bat for the aging O'Neill, who at first seemed over-matched against the flame-throwing Benitez. But somehow O'Neill stayed alive, fouling off pitch after pitch as he worked the count.

"That at bat right there shows you what Paul O'Neill means to this club," an admiring Derek Jeter told Richard Lally in *Bombers*. "Look at how he battled Benitez on every pitch." Added O'Neill, "The big thing with two strikes is not to panic…. The key for me is to stick with what I do and not try to get into the pitcher's head."

"IT SEEMED, TO STUNNED FANS, THAT THE YANKEES MIGHT NEVER LOSE A WORLD SERIES AGAIN."

Benitez walked O'Neill on a full count, and all across the country non-Yankee fans understood what the words *impending doom* meant. The doom impended swiftly: Two singles and a sacrifice fly tied the game, Yankee relievers shut down the Mets in extra innings, and the Yankees won in the twelfth on a single by Jose Vizcaino. The Yankees were up, one game to none.

After that, the ultimate result seemed inevitable. The Yankees' offense exploded for six unanswered runs in Game Two—which featured the Roger Clemens–Mike Piazza fiasco. (Clemens, who had beaned Piazza in a previous meeting, fired the barrel of Piazza's broken bat toward the Mets' catcher after a foul ball.) The game ended 6–5 because the Mets scored five in the ninth, only to fall agonizingly short.

The bizarre fracas between the Mets' Mike Piazza and the Yanks' Roger Clemens provided most of the fireworks in the 2000 Series.

2000

NEW YORK YANKEES

4

NEW YORK METS

1

Unlike the Padres or Braves, the Mets actually won Game Three, scoring two in the eighth to beat El Duque, 4–2, in front of their fans at Shea Stadium. That made Game Four pivotal, and after Mike Piazza hit a two-run homer to pull the Mets within 3–2 in the third, hope stirred. But after Piazza's blast the Mets showed all the comeback ability of a ground sloth trapped in a tar pit, and the game ended with the same 3–2 score. To no one's surprise, the Yankees held a commanding 3–1 Series lead.

Game Five followed a similarly painful pattern. The Mets took a 2–1 lead in the second, but then could do no more. Al Leiter pitched valiantly once again, giving up only a game-tying home run to Derek Jeter in the sixth. There the game remained until the ninth, when an arm-weary Leiter loaded the bases and then gave up a two-run single to likable scrub Luis Sojo. Mariano Rivera shut down the Mets in the bottom of the ninth, and the Yankees had their third consecutive World Series title.

It seemed, to stunned fans, that the Yankees might never lose a World Series again.

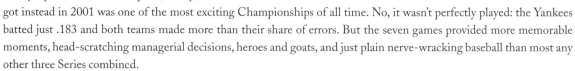

2001

TIMELESS

I n 2001, baseball fans got lucky. They got a classic Series—and, more importantly, they also got an event to rally around, to focus on, to take their minds off of the devastating events of September 11, just six weeks in the past. With a cloud of dread still hanging over the country—fear reflected in every bag searched, every long security line at Yankee Stadium and Bank One Ballpark—people grabbed hold of the Series as if it was a lifeline back to some sense of normality.

As Joe Torre put it as the Series began: "It makes us feel good that we are finally able to provide some satisfaction to people, because during the time right after the tragedy, it was a helpless feeling sitting at home and being of no use whatsoever."

Given the circumstances, one could have forgiven the two teams if they'd provided us with a quick, messy, distracted Series. What we got instead in 2001 was one of the most exciting Championships of all time. No, it wasn't perfectly played: the Yankees batted just .183 and both teams made more than their share of errors. But the seven games provided more memorable moments, head-scratching managerial decisions, heroes and goats, and just plain nerve-wracking baseball than most any other three Series combined.

And towering over the seven games were three of the greatest pitchers of their generation: The Yankees' ageless Roger Clemens and the Diamondbacks' brilliant Curt Schilling and incomparable Randy Johnson.

The Series didn't start out so well. In Game One, Schilling shut down the Yankee offense, while New York fielders displayed uncharacteristic butterfingers, in the D'backs' easy 9–1 win. ("The Yankees are the greatest team of our era," said Arizona's Mark Grace, "but even great players make mistakes.") The next day, Matt Williams' three-run home run was all Randy Johnson needed in a three-hit 4–0 Arizona win.

The most terrifying figure ever to stand on the pitcher's mound: Randy Johnson.

For the first time since 1996, the Yankees were down 2–0 in a World Series. But they were headed home to Yankee Stadium, the ballpark where other teams go to lose. So no one was much surprised when Clemens combined with Mariano Rivera to stifle the Arizona offense and win Game Three, 2–1.

And then the Series began to gain stature. Curt Schilling came back to start Game Four, and again he stopped the Yankee bats cold as the D'backs moved out to a 3–1 lead. But Arizona Manager Bob Brenly (undoubtedly thinking ahead to a possible Game Seven) decided that Schilling had had enough after just eighty-eight pitches. Brenly went with twenty-two-year-old closer Byung-Hyun Kim, who struck out the side in the eighth. But with two outs in the ninth and Paul O'Neill on first, Kim faced Tino Martinez—who promptly whacked the first pitch he saw over the fence for a game-tying homer.

Giving more fuel to the second-guessers, Brenly then left the obviously shaken Kim in the game. One inning later, Derek Jeter ended it with a home run on the sixty-second pitch that the young reliever had thrown.

Just one day later, almost unbelievably, the same scenario played out again. Ninth inning, Arizona holding a two-run lead, a man on base, the arm-weary Byung-Hyun Kim pitching…and another veteran hitter, Scott Brosius, up at bat. "Isn't the safest place in a storm the scorched spot where lightning has already struck?" asked *SI*'s Tom Verducci. It must have been a rhetorical question: Brosius blasted a Kim slider to tie the game.

Only once before in World Series history had a hitter tied a game with a two-out, two-run homer. Now the Yankees had done it two nights in a row. Three innings later, Yankee phenom Alfonso Soriano singled in the winning run of the Yankees' stunning 3–2 victory. Somehow, the Yankees had a 3–2 Series lead.

But the Diamondbacks had the overwhelming Randy Johnson on the hill in Game Six. Give him a run, and chances were he'd make it stand up—without requiring Kim to enter the game.

The Diamondbacks gave Johnson a run…and then another, and another, and…. The game was 15–0 after four innings. For some reason, Brenly chose to leave his ace on the mound through seven innings and 104 pitches, leaving the second-guessers baying again.

Curt Schilling started the final game against Roger Clemens. When some doubted the wisdom of going back to Schilling for the third time in nine days, at least one expert observer snorted. "If you can't pitch on three days' rest in the World Series, go home," said Bob Gibson, who made a Series career out of pitching—and winning—on short rest. "You've got plenty of time to rest in December and January."

In a classic pitchers' duel, Schilling and Clemens were locked in a 1–1 battle through seven innings. Then, in the eighth, Soriano hit a home run to give the Yankees a 2–1 lead—with automatic closer Mariano Rivera waiting in the bullpen. For the first time, even stunned Arizona fans began to believe this might be the Yankees' year…*again*.

In a moment of highest drama, Brenly called on Johnson to get out of an eighth-inning jam. Just a day after throwing more than 100 pitches, the left-hander

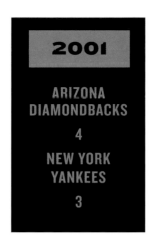

2001

ARIZONA DIAMONDBACKS

4

NEW YORK YANKEES

3

A common sight: a Yankee strikes out against the Diamondbacks' flamethrowers. This victim was Scott Brosius.

"IF YOU CAN'T PITCH ON THREE DAYS' REST IN THE WORLD SERIES, GO HOME."

got out of the inning—and then retired the Yankees quickly in the ninth. Still, the Diamondbacks were trailing by a run, and facing Rivera, as the last half-inning of the year began.

Mark Grace, first up, muscled an inside cut fastball into center for a single. "If I hadn't, it probably would have hit me in the chest," he said later.

As everyone expected, catcher Damian Miller followed with a bunt back to Rivera. But the normally cool reliever made a terrible throw to second, the ball going into centerfield. Suddenly the D'backs had the tying run on second, the winning run on first.

Another bunt attempt was turned into a force at third for the first out. But that was the last out Rivera would get, as Tony Womack followed with a solid hit to score the tying run. A hit batsman loaded the bases, bringing up the Diamondbacks' leading slugger, Luis Gonzalez.

Gonzalez didn't even attempt to slug Rivera's cut fastball. Instead, he choked up on the bat for the first time all year. With a one-strike count, he swung at a nasty pitch, broke his bat…and watched, along with joyful Arizona fans and disbelieving Yankee ones, as the ball floated over the drawn-in infield, just out of the reach of Derek Jeter, and landed a few inches into the outfield for one of the softest Series-winning hits of all time.

"I made the pitches I wanted to make," said Rivera after the game, his first loss in fifty-two postseason appearances. "They can say they beat me."

Said Grace about the comeback against the Yankees and their peerless closer: "It was like winning in the bottom of the ninth against God."

Solidarity with a wounded city went a long way in 2001—but only so far.

Glass slippers for everyone! After a season in which a strike loomed like a buzzard over roadkill—only to be narrowly averted and then instantly forgotten—the postseason provided a telling blow to arguments that major-league baseball suffers from a disastrous lack of competitive balance. Some familiar faces made the playoffs, of course: The previous year's champion, the Arizona Diamondbacks; the dynastic New York Yankees; the perennial Atlanta Braves; and regular contenders the Oakland A's.

But none of them won even a single playoff series. Before the eyes of amazed and grateful fans, the 2002 postseason became a veritable Cinderella Festival. When the Angels defeated the Twins in five games in the League Championship Series, and the Giants did the same to the Cardinals, the resulting Series matchup brought together two teams equally deserving of underdog status: the Angels, who in forty-one years of existence had never made the Series, and the Giants, whose last championship came in 1954, when they still played in New York.

And there were other similarities: this single-state World Series pitted two teams that featured largely no-name pitching but unquestionably spectacular offense. Who would have guessed that California, and not Motown, would turn out to be the real Hitsville, USA?

Barry Bonds, whose 2001 (seventy-three homers) and 2002 (.370 batting average) seasons were the finest back-to-back years since Babe Ruth, was the Giants' colossus. But he wasn't alone: Jeff Kent, J. T. Snow, Rich Aurilia, Benito Santiago, Reggie Sanders, and David Bell all had the ability to give opposing pitchers fits. No easy outs in that line-up.

The Angels were even more relentless. Troy Glaus, Tim Salmon, Darin Erstad, Brad Fullmer, Garret Anderson, Scott Spiezio, and others showed in the playoffs they could whack the ball all night and well into the morning. Twice in the earlier rounds Angel hitters strung together ten hits in a single inning—and it seemed entirely possible that, against the Giants' mediocre pitching, they might up that to twenty.

Game One in Anaheim, by the standards of this Series, was a pitchers' duel, a tense game featuring 3 $^{1}/_{3}$ innings of hitless relief by Giant pitchers Felix Rodriguez, Tim Worrell, and Rob Nen. Barry Bonds, continuing to put to rest his reputation as a poor postseason player, slugged a mammoth home run in the second inning (Giant hitting coach Gene Clines, watching the blast, exclaimed "Oh, my god!" in tones suggesting he'd just been struck by a thunderbolt from above). Reggie Sanders and J. T. Snow added less prodigious home runs, and the Giants held on for the 4–3 win.

2002

ANAHEIM ANGELS

4

SAN FRANCISCO GIANTS

3

Game Two was a classic, a holiday piñata (in the shape of a rally monkey?) stuffed full of treats. The unstoppable Angels roared to a 5–0 first-inning lead, but the Giants, riding second-inning homers by Reggie Sanders and David Bell, cut the lead to 5–4. The Angels then extended their lead to 7–4, only to see the Giants tie it up—and then pull ahead 9–7 in the fifth inning. The Angels rallied to take an 11–9 lead in the eighth on Salmon's second home run.

Angel closer Troy Percival got the first two outs in the ninth and then faced Barry Bonds. Percival threw a fastball, Bonds swung, and the ball rocketed into the upper deck, 485 feet away. ("I think I provided

Troy Glaus legs out the double that gave the Angels their stunning Game Six win.

all the power," the Angels' pitcher said later.) But that was all the Giants got, falling one run short in the Angels' wildly entertaining 11–10 win.

Game Three provided a bit of a break from the intensity of the first two—but no better pitching. Amassing sixteen hits (and batting around in both the third and fourth innings), the Angels cruised to an easy 10–4 victory. Bonds hit yet another magnificent homer, but this was the Angels' game all the way.

Backs against the wall, the Giants eked out a 4–3 win in Game Four, coming back from a 3–0 deficit and beating the Angels' twenty-year old phenom, Francisco Rodriguez, with a run in the eighth on David Bell's single. "He's had a clean playoff slate," said Jeff Kent of Rodriguez, who'd been 5–0 in the playoffs, "and we were hoping to dirty it a little bit."

Given a new life, the Giants pounded the Angels 16–4 in Game Five to take a 3–2 Series lead as Kent, who'd been quiet, broke out with two home runs. Now, heading back to Anaheim, the Giants needed only one more win to capture their first championship since 1954—and their first ever in San Francisco.

GENE CLINES, WATCHING THE BLAST, EXCLAIMED "OH, MY GOD!" IN TONES SUGGESTING HE'D JUST BEEN STRUCK BY A THUNDERBOLT FROM ABOVE.

When Bonds homered yet again and the Giants held a 5–0 lead in the seventh inning of Game Six, the Series seemed over. But the Angels' Scott Spiezio, a classic anonymous Series hero, led the way. In the seventh, with two on, he hit a long fly to right off Felix Rodriguez. The ball carried and carried and eventually slipped over the wall for a three-run homer that suddenly made it a game again.

In the eighth, the Angels came all the rest of the way back, scoring three runs to pull out a stunning 6–5 win.

When the Giants took a 1–0 lead in Game Seven, it looked as though they might have recovered from the shock of losing Game Six. But (need we remind you?) these were the Angels. Their starter, rookie John Lackey, pitched a steadfast five innings, and Garret Anderson's three-run double off Livan Hernandez in the third inning gave the Angels a 4–1 lead. "He made a mistake out over the plate, and he paid for it," said Anderson.

With ace work from relievers Brendan Donnelly, Francisco Rodriguez, and Troy Percival, the Angels never relinquished the lead. The Giants got two men on against Percival in the ninth, but Kenny Lofton's long fly ball came down short of the fence, and the game and the Series were over. The Angels had captured their first championship, and a joyful, messy, improbable affair it was from start to finish.

"We deserve it," Percival said after the game. And who would argue?

Barry Bonds was far from a choker in the Series but all his heroics couldn't carry the Giants to victory.

Wave of victory: The Angels, jubilant over their first-ever championship.

Rookie phenom Francisco Rodriguez, all of twenty years old, pitched like a seasoned veteran through-out the playoffs.

PERFECT GAMES, SHARED MEMORIES

STEPHEN KING

When all the World Series numbers have been crunched, all the controversies discussed, all the heroes and goats anointed, what does baseball mean to us? In the following essay, first published in the 1991 World Series program, Stephen King tells us what it means to him—and comes up with an answer that is at once deeply personal and universal.

This is a story about two boys, both nine years old, and two baseball games—World Series games. There's no deep meaning or moral to this story, but to me it illustrates one of baseball's most pleasing aspects: the almost ceremonial way in which the joy of the game is handed down from generation to generation. It is that ceremonial handing-down more than anything intrinsic in the game, that makes baseball one of the landmarks of American culture.

One of these boys, Stevie, was nine in 1956. He and his brother were raised by a working mother who never had the benefit of a support group, a day care center, or an Equal Rights law, yet managed to raise Stevie and his older brother pretty well.

In the mid-1950s Stevie was a Dodger fan because his mother was. She became a Brooklyn booster because her co-workers at the Stratford, CT, Laundry were Dodgers fans. Stevie's Mom was the only white lady on the eight-woman crew which ran the speed ironer—a machine better known by its gruesome nickname, the mangler. The other ladies were black, and rooted for Da Bums because the Dodgers had given Jackie Robinson a chance to play in the previously all-white Major Leagues.

Did I say these ladies *rooted* for the Dodgers? They *damn near worshipped* the Dodgers. Stevie's Mom began rooting simply to please her friends, but after a hilarious trip with them to Ebbets Field, she became converted.

Children inherit their parents' sports and political affiliations, so Stevie rooted for the Dodgers and the Republicans, and hated the Yankees and the Democrats. Then, on one magic day in the fall of 1956, all that changed.

"DID I SAY THESE LADIES ROOTED FOR THE DODGERS? THEY DAMN NEAR WORSHIPPED THE DODGERS."

The pin that allowed sportswriters to witness the Boston Braves' shellacking of the powerful Philadelphia Athletics in 1914.

Stevie came home from school that afternoon, tuned the tiny black-and-white Video King TV to the World Series, and quickly realized that something very odd and exciting was going on. He didn't know what it was—he had come in during the third inning—and, most mysterious and infuriating and tantalizing of all, the announcers kept talking around it. All he knew for sure was that it had something to do with the Yankee hurler, a man named Don Larsen, and as Larsen relentlessly set down one Dodger batter after the other, the boy had a hazy idea of what that something was.

A game in which his beloved Dodgers generated no offense at all—a World Series game, at that!—should have been boring, but this one wasn't. It was, in fact, so exciting that it was a form of torture. The boy grew up to be a passionate Red Sox fan, and an eternal, implacable foe of all things Yankee…but for two hours on that October afternoon, he rooted for the Yankees and Larsen with all his heart and mind and soul.

The final Brooklyn batter, a pinch-hitter named Dale Mitchell, struck out. Stevie leaped to his feet along with the whole crowd at the ballpark. From the TV, the tinny voice of Mel Allen was screaming: *"Larsen's pitched a no-hitter…holy cow, LARSEN'S PITCHED A PERFECT GAME!"*

Stevie pogo'd wildly around the living room of the tiny third-floor apartment which he shared with his mother and brother, but he never turned from the small, bulging eye of the Video King as he jumped for joy, and he saw something he never forgot: Yogi Berra expressing all of the boy's own happiness by leaping into Larsen's arms like a large, deliriously happy frog.

And if there was anything to mar the perfect happiness the boy felt at seeing the perfect game brought safely home it was this: he was alone. There was no one there with whom he could share this marvelous, this well-nigh-unbelievable thing. His mother was at the laundry and his brother, no baseball fan, was out with his buddies. Later, he discussed what he had seen with his mother, at the supper table. There is no Dad in this picture, although it's the Dads who are the keepers of this particular tradition; Dad stepped out when Stevie was two. Even big brother, David, two years older, didn't remember him.

On this occasion, however, Mom did just fine. Moms almost always do.

Now let 30 years pass in a flash. It is 1986, and this time the nine-year-old's name is Owen. He has come to Fenway Park to see his first-ever World Series game and his eyes are everywhere, trying to take in everything at once. There *is* a Dad in this picture, and although Owen's no little kid anymore, he holds his father's hand very tightly. As pointed out, kids get their baseball and political allegiances from their parents. This makes Owen a passionate Democrat and an even more passionate Red Sox fan.

The game is a long way from Larsen's economical classic, and there is no happy ending for Owen or the Red Sox fans who have crowded into Fenway on this night. The Red Sox send Dennis "Oil Can" Boyd to the mound, and The Can Man, as Owen calls him, does not fare well. The Mets step off to a 4–0 lead and beat the Old Towne Team, 7–1.

Worse things are waiting, as all Red Sox fans know (the names of Stanley, Schiraldi, and Buckner are forever engraved on their hearts), but for Owen, this is bad enough. It has been a long night ending in a dry hole. As he and his father walk, hand-in-hand, out into the chilly October night, he begins to cry.

The father puts an arm around him and thinks: *That's all right. If you're going to be a Red Sox fan, they won't be the last tears you'll cry…and there are worse things to cry over than baseball heroes who are toppled for only an evening. Caring enough to cry…that's not such a bad thing, even if it's just a baseball game you're crying over.*

That thought leads the father to another, happier one: a World Series game he saw when he was the nine-year-old, and as addicted to Davy Crockett cards as his youngest son is to Topps and Fleer

Hidden message: Inside this 2001 World Series ring, minted just weeks after September 11, are the words "Never forget."

"IT'S THAT GIVING—THAT PASSING ON—THAT I LOVE MOST ABOUT BASEBALL IN GENERAL AND THE WORLD SERIES IN PARTICULAR. I REALLY BELIEVE THAT ANY WORLD SERIES GAME A MAN OR WOMAN CAN WATCH WITH THEIR NINE-YEAR-OLD SONS OR DAUGHTERS IS A PERFECT GAME."

baseball cards. He says: "Did I ever tell you I saw Don Larsen pitch his perfect game in the '56 World Series?"

Owen looks up at him. The expression on his face is a mixture of interest, amusement, and a surprisingly adult cynicism.

"How did you do that?" Owen asks.

"TV," the father replies promptly.

"You really saw it on TV, dad? I thought you said you didn't have one when you were a kid."

"This was the first one," Owen's dad says. The Video King, salvaged from a second-hand appliance store, had made its debut in the King apartment the month before.

"And you really *saw* it?"

He sees his father is not just trying to cheer him up, and an expression of fascination steals over the kid's face.

"Uh-huh. I was in the apartment all by myself."

"Oh," his son says. He thinks it over, then adds: "That must have been a bummer."

His father smiles and nods. Not a bummer, but it was better tonight. Tonight he and his son had watched the game with about 35,000 close friends and fellow New Englanders. The Red Sox lost, but being there was still pretty fine. And it occurs to him that maybe he can change the past; just because he was alone in the apartment when Larsen pitched the perfect game in 1956 doesn't mean he has to *stay* alone.

"Want me to tell you about it?" I asked.

"Sure," Owen agreed, and by the time we got back to our hotel, we had both forgotten that night's bitter defeat. We had lost a new one, but won one of the great old ones all over again.

It's that giving—that passing on—that I love most about baseball in general and the World Series in particular. I really believe that *any* World Series game a man or woman can watch with their nine-year-old sons or daughters is a perfect game. I like to think and hope that someday—maybe in 2016—there'll be three of us—me, Owen, and Owen's nine-year-old—leaving the park, perhaps to celebrate a Red Sox World Championship.

That would be pretty great, all right, and the only thing greater than being there would be passing it on.

What time is it? Time for another Yankee dynasty.

I am everlastingly grateful to the sportswriters who have employed their canny, perceptive, and above all passionate prose to describe the World Series during the last century. Francis Richter, Henry Chadwick, Grantland Rice, John Buckingham Foster, Ring Lardner, Heywood Broun, W. A. Phelon, John Kieran, F. C. Lane, Frank Graham, Fred Lieb, Joe Williams, Richards Vidmer, Red Smith, Jack Sher, Arthur Daley, Dave Anderson, Bob Broeg, Ira Berkow, George Vecsey, Joe Falls, Tom Verducci, Mike Lupica, Furman Bisher, and many others deserve enormous credit for keeping past Series from becoming mummified.

In writing this book, I also relied on dozens of baseball books published since the World Series became a reality in 1903, including the unbeatable old *Reach* and *Spalding Guides,* which provided some of the freshest World Series descriptions during the first thirty years of the twentieth century. Some other marvelous sources:

Aaron, Hank, with Lonnie Wheeler. *I Had a Hammer.* New York: HarperCollins, 1991

Alexander, Charles C. *Rogers Hornsby.* New York: Henry Holt, 1995

Allen, Lee. *The Cincinnati Reds: An Informal History.* New York: G. P. Putnam's, 1948

____. *The Giants and the Dodgers.* New York: G. P. Putnam's, 1964

Allen, Maury. *The Incredible Mets.* New York: Paperback Library, 1969

Alston, Walt. *A Year at a Time.* Waco, Texas: Word Books, 1976

Anderson, Dave. *Sports of Our Times.* New York: Random House, 1979

Anderson, Sparky and Si Burick. *The Main Spark.* Garden City, New York: Doubleday, 1978

Angell, Roger. *Five Seasons.* New York: Simon and Schuster, 1977

____. *Late Innings.* New York: Simon and Schuster, 1982

____. *Season Ticket.* Boston: Houghton Mifflin, 1988

____. *The Summer Game.* New York: Viking, 1972

Bak, Richard. *Cobb Would Have Caught It.* Detroit: Wayne State University, 1991

Barrow, Edward Grant, with James M. Kahn. *My Fifty Years in Baseball.* New York: Coward-McCann, 1951

Berkow, Ira, and Jim Kaplan. *The Gospel According to Casey.* New York: St. Martin's, 1992

Boswell, Thomas. *How Life Imitates the World Series.* Garden City, New York: 1982

Brown, Warren. *The Chicago White Sox.* New York: G. P. Putnam's, 1952

Bryson, Bill. *The Babe Didn't Point.* Ames, Iowa: Iowa University Press, 1989

Clark, Tom. *Champagne and Baloney.* New York: Harper & Row, 1976

Cleveland, Charles B. *The Great Baseball Managers.* New York: Thomas Y. Crowell, 1950

Cohen, Eliot, ed. *My Greatest Day in Baseball.* New York: Little Simon, 1991

Connor, Anthony J. *Voices from Cooperstown: Baseball's Hall of Famers Tell It Like It Was.* New York: Collier, 1982

Creamer, Bob. *Babe.* New York: Simon and Schuster, 1974

Dark, Alvin, and John Underwood. *When in Doubt, Fire the Manager.* New York: E. P. Dutton, 1980

Dickson, Paul. *Baseball's Greatest Quotations.* New York: HarperCollins, 1991

Durant, John. *Highlights of the World Series.* New York: Hastings House, 1963

Durocher, Leo, with Ed Linn. *Nice Guys Finish Last.* New York: Simon and Schuster, 1975

Durso, Joseph. *Amazing.* Boston: Houghton Mifflin, 1970

____. *Casey.* Englewood Cliffs, New Jersey: Prentice-Hall, 1967

____. *The Days of Mr. McGraw.* Englewood Cliffs, New Jersey: Prentice-Hall, 1969

Falls, Joe. *Detroit Tigers.* New York: Rutledge, 1975

Farrell, James T. *My Baseball Diary.* New York: A. S. Barnes, 1957

Fleming, G. H. *Murderers' Row.* New York: William Morrow, 1985

Fox, Larry. *Last to First.* New York: Harper & Row, 1970

Frick, Ford C. *Games, Asterisks, and People.* New York: Crown, 1973

Frisch, Frank, as told to J. Roy Stockton. *Frank Frisch.* Garden City, New York: Doubleday, 1962

Gammons, Peter. *Beyond the Sixth Game.* Boston: Houghton Mifflin, 1985

Gibson, Bob, with Phil Pepe. *From Ghetto to Glory.* Englewood Cliffs, New Jersey: Prentice-Hall, 1968

Golenbock, Peter. *The Spirit of St. Louis.* New York: Avon, 2000

Graham, Frank. *Baseball Extra.* New York: A. S. Barnes, 1954

____. *McGraw of the Giants.* New York: G. P. Putnam's, 1944

____. *The Brooklyn Dodgers.* New York: G. P. Putnam's, 1945

____. *The New York Yankees.* New York: G. P. Putnam's, revised edition 1958

Green, Jerry. *Year of the Tiger.* New York: Coward-McCann, 1969

Hano, Arnold. *A Day in the Bleachers.* New York: Thomas Y. Crowell, 1955

Herzog, Whitey and Kevin Horrigan. *White Rat.* New York: Harper & Row, 1987

Heyn, Ernest V., ed. *Twelve More Sport Immortals.* New York: Bartholomew House, 1951

Hodges, Gil, with Frank Slocum. *The Game of Baseball.* New York: Crown, 1970

Holmes, Tommy. *Dodger Daze and Nights.* New York: David McKay, 1953

Honig, Donald. *Baseball Between the Lines.* New York: Coward, McCann & Geoghan, 1976

____. *The Man in the Dugout.* Chicago: Follett, 1977

Hornsby, Rogers, with J. Roy Stockton. *My Kind of Baseball.* New York: David McKay, 1953

Hough, John Jr. *A Player for a Moment.* San Diego: Harcourt Brace Jovanovich, 1988

Houk, Ralph and Robert W. Creamer. *Season of Glory.* New York: G. P. Putnam's, 1988

____, with Charles Dexter. *Ballplayers Are Human, Too.* New York: G. P. Putnam's, 1962

Jackson, Reggie, with Mike Lupica. *Reggie.* New York: Villard, 1984.

James, Bill. *The Bill James Baseball Abstract, 1982–88.* New York: Ballantine, 1982–88

____. *The Bill James Historical Baseball Abstract.* New York: Villard, 1986

____. *The New Bill James Historical Baseball Abstract.* New York: The Free Press, 2001

Kahn, Roger. *The Era.* New York: Ticknor & Fields, 1993

Kashatus, William C. *Connie Mack's '29 Triumph.* Jefferson, North Carolina: McFarland, 1999

Koppett, Leonard. *The New York Mets.* New York: Macmillan, 1970

Kuenster, John. *From Cobb to "Catfish."* Chicago: Rand McNally, 1975

Lally, Richard. *Bombers.* New York: Crown, 2002

Langford, Walter. *Legends of Baseball.* South Bend, Indiana: Diamond Communications, 1987

Lewis, Franklin. *The Cleveland Indians.* New York: G. P. Putnam's, 1949

Lieb, Fred. *Baseball As I Have Known It.* New York: Coward, McCann & Geoghan, 1977

____. *Connie Mack.* New York: G. P. Putnam's, 1945

____. *The Detroit Tigers.* New York: G. P. Putnam's, 1946

____. *The St. Louis Cardinals.* New York: G. P. Putnam's, 1944

Mantle, Mickey, with Mickey Herskowitz. *All My Octobers.* New York: HarperCollins, 1994

Markusen, Bruce. *Baseball's Last Dynasty.* Indianapolis: Masters Press, 1998

_____. *Roberto Clemente: The Great One.* Champaign, Illinois: Sports Publishing, 1998

Marsh, Irving T. and Edward Ehre, eds. *Best of the Best Sports Stories.* New York: Dutton, 1964

Mathewson, Christy. *Pitching in a Pinch.* New York: Putnam, 1912

Meany, Tom. *Mostly Baseball.* New York: A. S. Barnes, 1958

_____. *Babe Ruth.* New York: A. S. Barnes, 1947

_____ and Tommy Holmes. *Baseball's Best.* New York: Franklin Watts, 1964

Morgan, Joe, and David Falkner. *A Life in Baseball.* New York: W. W. Norton, 1993

Munson, Thurman with Martin Appel. *Thurman Munson.* New York: Coward, McCann & Geoghan, 1978

Peary, Danny. *We Played the Game.* New York: Hyperion, 1994

Povich, Shirley. *The Washington Senators.* New York: G. P. Putnam's, 1954

Reichler, Joseph, ed. *The World Series.* New York: Simon & Schuster, 1979

Ritter, Lawrence. *The Glory of Their Times.* Revised edition. New York: William Morrow, 1984

Sahadi, Lou. *The Pirates.* New York: Times Books, 1980

Seaver, Tom, with Dick Schaap. *The Perfect Game.* New York: E. P. Dutton, 1970

Schecter, Leonard. *Once Upon the Polo Grounds.* New York: Dial, 1970

Smith, Red. *Out of the Red.* New York: Knopf, 1950

____. *Red Smith on Baseball.* Chicago: Ivan R. Dee, 2000

____. *Red Smith's Sports Annual 1961.* New York: Crown, 1961

____. *Views of Sport.* New York: Knopf, 1954

Sullivan, Dean A., ed. *Middle Innings.* Lincoln & London, Nebraska: University of Nebraska, 1998

Tunis, John R. *This Writing Game.* New York: A. S. Barnes, 1941

Vecsey, George. *Joy in Mudville.* New York: McCall, 1970

____. *The Way It Was.* New York: McGraw-Hill, 1974

Wallop, Douglass. *Baseball: An Informal History.* New York: W. W. Norton, 1969

Weaver, Earl, with John Sammis. *Winning!* New York: William Morrow, 1972

Will, George. *Men at Work.* New York: Macmillan, 1990

Williams, Dick and Bill Plaschke. *No More Mr. Nice Guy.* San Diego: Harcourt Brace Jovanovich, 1990

Williams, Peter, ed. *The Joe Williams Baseball Reader.* Chapel Hill, North Carolina: Algonquin Books, 1989